WRITING HISTORY IN INTERNATIONAL CRIMINAL TRIALS

Why do international criminal tribunals write histories of the origins and causes of armed conflicts? Richard Ashby Wilson conducted empirical research with judges, prosecutors, defense attorneys, and expert witnesses in three international criminal tribunals to understand how law and history are combined in the courtroom. Historical testimony is now an integral part of international trials, with prosecutors and defense teams using background testimony to pursue decidedly legal objectives. Both use historical narratives to frame the alleged crimes and to articulate their side's theory of the case. In the trial of Slobodan Milošević, the prosecution sought to demonstrate special intent to commit genocide by reference to a long-standing animus nurtured in a nationalist mind-set. For their part, the defense calls historical witnesses to undermine charges of superior responsibility and to mitigate the sentence by representing crimes as reprisals. Although legal ways of knowing are distinct from those of history, the two are frequently combined in international trials in a way that challenges us to rethink the relationship between law and history.

Richard Ashby Wilson is Gladstein Distinguished Chair of Human Rights, Professor of Anthropology and Law, and Director of the Human Rights Institute at the University of Connecticut. He has been a Visiting Professor at the University of Oslo, the New School for Social Research, and the University of the Witwatersrand. Presently, he serves as Chair of the Connecticut State Advisory Committee for the U.S. Commission on Civil Rights. Professor Wilson is the author of *Maya Resurgence in Guatemala* (1995) and *The Politics of Truth and Reconciliation in South Africa* (2001) and is the editor or coeditor of numerous books, including *Culture and Rights, Human Rights and the "War on Terror,"* and *Humanitarianism and Suffering.* This book was completed during a fellowship from the National Endowment for the Humanities (2009–2010).

D1596685

Writing History in International Criminal Trials

RICHARD ASHBY WILSON
Human Rights Institute and School of Law
University of Connecticut

CAMBRIDGE
UNIVERSITY PRESS

672300105

CAMBRIDGE UNIVERSITY PRESS
Cambridge, New York, Melbourne, Madrid, Cape Town,
Singapore, São Paulo, Delhi, Tokyo, Mexico City

Cambridge University Press
32 Avenue of the Americas, New York, NY 10013-2473, USA

www.cambridge.org
Information on this title: www.cambridge.org/9780521138314

First published 2011

Printed in the United States of America

A catalog record for this publication is available from the British Library.

Library of Congress Cataloging in Publication data

Wilson, Richard Ashby, 1964–
Writing history in international criminal trials / Richard Ashby Wilson.
   p.   cm
Includes bibliographical references and index.
ISBN 978-0-521-19885-1 (hardback) – ISBN 978-0-521-13831-4 (paperback)
1. Crimes against humanity.   2. War crimes.   3. Prosecution.   4. Evidence, Documentary.
5. Political violence – History.   6. Civil war – History.   7. War – History.   I. Title.
K5301W553   2011
341.6′9–dc22   2010044856

ISBN 978-0-521-19885-1 Hardback
ISBN 978-0-521-13831-4 Paperback

Contents

Athena to Orestes and the Furies:

I will appoint the judges of manslaughter,
Swear them in and found a tribunal here
For all time to come.
                 My contestants
Summon your trusted witnesses and proofs,
Your defenders under oath to help your cause
And I will pick the finest men of Athens,
Return and decide the issue fairly, truly-
Bound to our oaths, our spirits bent on justice.
                 – Aeschylus, *The Eumenides*

Preface and Acknowledgments

A sense of shared history is one of the main ways a people come to constitute themselves as a group or nation and to forge a collective identity and a sense of shared destiny. In times of peace and prosperity, this common past may enhance a sense of mutual purpose, instill a pride in public institutions, and fortify a civic patriotism. However, during economic and political crises, some political leaders stir up nationalist sentiments to bolster their increasingly shaky hold on power and legitimacy. Unable to effectively address deepening social and economic problems, they instead vilify an historic enemy, recall past wrongs, and seek to take advantage of the atmosphere of threat and insecurity. If armed conflict breaks out, then historical injuries may be recalled when atrocities are committed against enemy civilians, which are usually justified as reprisals necessary to ensuring the very existence of the group. Although this scenario is neither modern nor new, ethno-nationalist conflicts characterized by extensive civilian casualties became especially frequent after the end of the Cold War.

The politically instrumental use of history during an armed conflict is highly complex and selective. It is not simply a matter of fabricating outright lies, for many of the events that continue to generate a sense of grievance did really happen. As noted in this book, widespread atrocities were indeed committed against Serbs during World War II, and Hutus were cruelly subjugated by Tutsis during the colonial period in Rwanda. Although distortion of the past is widespread, the most common travesty is one of omission, wherein populist leaders neglect to mention the crimes committed by their own side or recollect them in such a way that evades accepting full responsibility. That politicians are so able to evoke historical arguments in these ways results from a prior failure of the society to engage in a full and frank encounter with past wrongdoing. In Tito's Yugoslavia, for instance, there was a deep-seated avoidance on the part of party officials to engage with the legacy of World War II, to openly admit the crimes committed by each side, and to accept responsibility. Where a pervasive regime of denial exists, the past can serve as rich pickings for political demagogues seeking to manipulate popular sentiments.

These arguments are widely accepted by many donor governments and UN agencies, which now perceive accurate historical documentation of an armed conflict as a key dimension of creating accountability and the rule of law and as an essential part of any postconflict reconstruction program. Beyond official statements and projects, however, the process of postconflict historical reflection is long-term and occurs along many tracks and in many different venues. It may occur in photographic exhibits or avant-garde art installations, or in the performing arts, such as film or theater. Talented writers of fiction such as Guatemala's Victor Montejo or South Africa's Zakes Mda offer subjective insights into the experience of an epoch of violence and insecurity that might not otherwise be imaginable. Museums and places of remembrance can ensure that mass crimes do not slip into obscurity. Teaching critical thinking about history in schools and universities is one of the principal ways in which students come to challenge the generational transmission of past animosities. Official government apologies and programs of reparations for victims have also become increasingly familiar, if uneven, ways of addressing the past. And there are more.

Although political propaganda and nationalist mythologizing is nothing new, what was novel in the post–Cold War era was the array of institutions, from national truth commissions to international criminal tribunals, set up to investigate mass violations of international humanitarian law. In the narrow window of opportunity that existed in the 1990s, an international consensus emerged regarding the need to try war crimes, crimes against humanity, and the crime of genocide in new international criminal tribunals. The first of these was the International Criminal Tribunal for the Former Yugoslavia (ICTY) established in 1993, and the International Criminal Tribunal for Rwanda (ICTR) was created shortly thereafter in 1994. These two *ad hoc* tribunals indicted more than two hundred individuals for violations of international humanitarian law and have processed a majority of their cases, though their prosecution work is now coming to an end. The permanent International Criminal Court, with jurisdiction over war crimes, crimes against humanity, genocide, and aggression was inaugurated in 2003, and its first trials are now under way.

International criminal trials are now prime venues at which a postconflict version of history is investigated, discussed, argued over, and eventually stamped with the imprimatur of a legal judgment. Yet at least since the trials of Nazi war criminals in Nuremberg during 1945–6, commentators have been asking whether courts ought to write an historical narrative of an armed conflict at all. This debate was reignited during the 1961 Eichmann trial in Israel and intensified during the Holocaust trials in France in the 1970s and 1980s. It took on new relevance during the wave of democratizations in Africa, Latin America, and Eastern Europe in the 1980s and 1990s. Now it is time to critically evaluate the historical accounts produced by modern international justice institutions and ask, Have international tribunals actually provided significant insights into the origins and causes of armed conflict? How have international justice institutions come to comprehend the wider social and historical context surrounding individual violations of international humanitarian law? Do the judgments produced by international criminal courts challenge self-serving lies about the past?

The research for this book was supported by fellowships from the National Endowment for the Humanities (2009–2010) and the Provost's Office of the University of Connecticut (2009) as well as by the Human Rights Institute of the University of Connecticut. My sincere thanks go to Gary S. Gladstein for his support of the Human Rights Institute and his sustained engagement with the empirical research on global human rights issues conducted by University of Connecticut faculty.

The initial impetus for this book began in 2000 with a conversation over lunch with my University of Sussex colleague, the Czech-born political scientist Zdenek Kavan. I had just completed a study of the South African Truth and Reconciliation Commission and was rehearsing the argument that, because criminal trials produced impoverished histories of conflicts, it was better for truth commissions to take over the task of writing history. Zdenek informed me, in his civil and urbane manner, that, although this argument might well apply to national criminal courts, it did not accurately describe the experience of international criminal tribunals. He suggested that I read some recent judgments of the International Criminal Tribunal for the former Yugoslavia, and after doing so, I could see his point. I then began to ponder the different approaches to historical evidence of national and international criminal trials and to speak to international prosecutors, defense attorneys, and expert witnesses, and this research project was born.

Over the past ten years, friends, colleagues, and students have continued to set me straight, and I am grateful to all of them. Being neither a lawyer nor a historian, I am either uniquely lacking in the expertise required to conduct this project or reasonably well placed to view the relationship between law and history with an independent eye. Whichever of the two, I have benefited from a great deal of counsel and assistance from generous friends and colleagues. I especially appreciate the commentaries of those who read sections of the book: Paul Betts, Eleni Coundouriotis, Robert Donia, Dan Saxon, and Ekkehard Withopf. As usual, Saul Dubow went beyond the call, even when hard pressed for time.

At the three international criminal justice institutions included in this study, a number of staff, former staff, or defense attorneys shared their experiences of international criminal trials and offered invaluable advice on thinking through the issues, including Predrag Dojcinović, Matthew Gillett, Richard Goldstone, Michael Karnavas, Beth Lyons, Daryl Mundis, Navanethem Pillay, Nicole Samson, Paul Seils, Paul Shoup, Sue Somers, David Tolbert, Bill Tomljanovich, Pat Treanor, and Nena Tromp-Vrkić. Andrew Corin was such a rich a source of insights into the research topic that we became coresearchers, and together we developed, implemented, and analyzed the survey on questions of law and history. All staff from the ICTY, ICTR, and ICC quoted in this book have made their comments in their personal capacity, and their remarks do not necessarily represent the views of the ICTY, the ICTR, the ICC, or the United Nations.

While writing this book, I benefited immensely from discussions with University of Connecticut colleagues Jill Anderson, Kerry Bystrom, Emma Gilligan, Shareen Hertel, Rich Hiskes, Peter Kingstone, Alexandra Lahav, and Serena Parekh. I thank Dean Jeremy Paul, Anne Dailey, Michael Fischl, and Mark Janis for welcoming me into the University of Connecticut Law School community. I am grateful to the participants at talks and seminars over the years for their perceptive comments on the ideas contained in this book: the City University of New York, Law and Society Association annual conferences, New York University and New York Law School's Law and Society seminar, the New School for Social Research, Yale University, University of Connecticut Law School, University College London, and the University of Michigan human rights seminar. Colleagues outside my own institution who helped me think through the issues include Nina Bang-Jensen, Thomas Brudholm, Kamari Clarke, Jane Cowan, Thomas Cushman, Laura Dickinson, Ilana Feldman, John Hagan, Robert Hayden, Toby Kelly, Diana Tietjens Meyers, Wiktor Osiatynski, and Miriam Ticktin. I would like to make special mention of Michael Marrus and Sally Engle Merry – both senior scholars of the law whom one can aspire to emulate.

I acknowledge the diligent research of research assistants Emma Amador, Matt Dickhoff, Lauren Donnelly, Kate Hawkins, Joshua Jackson, and Thomas Wilson. Amanda Fortner did sterling work on the tables and figures under significant time constraints. Ahmad Wais Wardak deserves praise for his involvement in both the technical aspects of the survey and the analysis of the quantitative data it produced. In adherence to the principle of individual responsibility, all errors of fact or interpretation are my own.

Finally, and most of all, I thank my wife, Helene, and our sons, Kai and Thomas, for their sympathetic encouragement of my seemingly obscure projects.

Earlier versions of two chapters of this book were published previously: portions of Chapter 1 appeared in "Judging History: the Historical Record of the International Criminal Tribunal for the Former Yugoslavia," *Human Rights Quarterly* (August 2005, Vol. 27, No. 3, pp. 908–942), reprinted with permission of Johns Hopkins University Press. Portions of Chapter 7 appeared in "When Humanity Sits in Judgment: The Conundrum of Race and Ethnicity at the International Criminal Tribunal for Rwanda," in *In the Name of Humanity*, edited by Miriam Ticktin and Ilana Feldman (2010), reprinted with permission of Duke University Press.

Figures and Tables

FIGURES

Glossary

Actus reus (Law Latin, "guilty act"): the material element of a crime

Amicus curiae (Law Latin, "friend of the court"): volunteer or appointed by the court to advise on legal issues. *Amici* have appeared in international tribunals generally when the accused has opted to defend himself or herself.

ARK: Autonomous Region of the Krajina

AU: African Union

Bosniak: Bosnian Muslim

Chetniks: Serb nationalist and royalist paramilitary organization in the Balkans before and during World War II

Dolus specialis (Law Latin, "special intent"): special or specific intent

DRC: Democratic Republic of the Congo (formerly Zaire)

FPLC: Forces Patriotiques pour la Libération du Congo, or Patriotic Force for the Liberation of the Congo

FRY: Federal Republic of Yugoslavia (1992–2003)

HDZ: Hrvatska Demokratska Zajednica Bosne i Hercegovine, or Croatian Democratic Union of Bosnia and Herzegovina

HVO: Hrvatsko Vijeće Obrane, or Croatian Defense Council of Bosnia and Herzegovina

ICC: International Criminal Court

ICJ: International Court of Justice

ICTR: International Criminal Tribunal for Rwanda

ICTY: International Criminal Tribunal for the Former Yugoslavia

JNA: Jugoslovenska Narodna Armija, or Yugoslav People's Army

LRT: Leadership Research Team of the ICTY

Mens rea (Law Latin, "guilty mind"): the state of mind the prosecution must prove that a defendant held when committing a crime

MONUC: Mission des Nations Unies en République Démocratique du Congo, or UN Mission in the Democratic Republic of the Congo

OTP: Office of the Prosecutor at the ICC, ICTR, or ICTY

Republika Srpska: Serbian Republic of Bosnia and Herzegovina

RPE: Rules of Procedure and Evidence (ICC, ICTR, ICTY)

RPF: Rwandan Patriotic Front

SDA: Stranka Demokratske Akcije, or Party of Democratic Action in Bosnia and Herzegovina

SDS: Srpska Demokratska Stranka, or Serbian Democratic Party in Bosnia and Herzegovina

SFRY: Socialist Federal Republic of Yugoslavia (1943–1992)

STA: Senior Trial Attorney in the Office of the Prosecutor at the ICC, ICTR, or ICTY

Tu quoque (Law Latin, literally "you too" defense): a defense based on the allegation that the opposing party to the conflict committed similar atrocities, often accompanied by the allegation that that party was responsible for the commencement of the said conflict.

UNICRI: UN Interregional Crime and Justice Research Institute

UNSC: UN Security Council

UPC: Union des Patriotes Congolais, or Union of Congolese Patriots

Ustashe: Pro-German state in Croatia during World War II

VJ: Vojska Jugoslavije, or Yugoslav Army (replacing JNA in 1992)

VRS: Vojska Republike Srpske, or Bosnian Serb Army

1

Assessing Court Histories of Mass Crimes

1.1. NOTHING BUT THE LAW?

Now, in a country of laws, the whole law and nothing but the law must prevail.

— Tzvetan Todorov (1996:114–5)

In the literature on legal responses to crimes against humanity, a consensus has emerged that courts of law produce mediocre historical accounts of the origins and causes of mass crimes. This book reviews recent international criminal trials, and it finds much evidence to support a critical view of law's ability to write history. At the same time, historical debates in international trials have provided important insights into the underlying factors of an armed conflict. By examining closely the concrete strategies pursued by prosecutors and defense lawyers, this study seeks to understand their motivations for venturing into the past in the first place and to discern the legal relevance of historical evidence.

A cursory review of recent international criminal trials would lend support to a skeptical stance toward the place of history in the courtroom, and at no point has the incompatibility of these two activities been more evident than during the four-and-a-half-year trial of Slobodan Milošević at the International Criminal Tribunal for the Former Yugoslavia (ICTY). With the death of Milošević in March 2006, only months before the court could pass judgment, a British *Financial Times* article diagnosed the Tribunal's central mistake: "the court confused the need to bring one man to account with the need to produce a clear narrative of war crimes and atrocities for the history books."[1] Observers condemned the prosecutor's excessive concern with history and the judges' failure to curtail Milošević's "interminable forays into Ottoman history, Balkans

---

[1] Quentin Peel, "Lessons for Prosecutors of War Crimes Trials," *Financial Times*, 13 March 2006.

ethnology, [and] World War Two Croatian fascism."[2] Prosecutor Geoffrey Nice's strategy of leading extensive historical material played into the hands of the accused, it was argued. With the international courtroom as his podium, the deposed president relished "the opportunity to present his version of history, which is his main goal in this trial. It is not about proving real facts, but – as it has always been – about reinterpreting history," as one Balkans commentator noted.[3]

Many at the Tribunal were discouraged after the *Milošević* trial ended so inconclusively, which led some to reflect on the prosecution's decision to foreground historical arguments. One member of the Milošević prosecution team, Senior Trial Attorney Dan Saxon, asked,

> Are we furthering the purposes of the Tribunal when we allow him [Milošević] to go on long historical tirades? The purpose of a criminal trial is to get at the truth about the crimes and produce a fair and reasoned judgment about the guilt or innocence of the accused and get some finality . . . so the victims can get closure. Historians can keep reinterpreting, but we only get one chance.[4]

Beyond the pragmatic need to expedite trials, there are some fundamental legal principles at stake in this discussion. Drawing inspiration from an omnipresent idea of the rule of law, the minimalist "law, and nothing but the law" conception of criminal trials is one of the few legal axioms that garners support across the political and legal spectrum.[5] Yet beneath the apparent unanimity of opinion can be found a variety of outlooks and justifications, only some of which are compatible. If we look more closely, there seem to be two broad schools of thought maintaining that courts are inappropriate venues to delineate the origins and causes of mass crimes. First, the doctrine of liberal legalism asserts that the justice system should not attempt to write history at all, lest it sacrifice high standards of judicial procedure. Second, law-and-society scholars have claimed that, even when courts attempt historical inquiry, they are bound to fail as a result of the inherent limitations of the legal process. The latter group of commentators are less inspired by liberal-democratic thinking than

---

2   Helen Warrell and Janet Anderson, "Hague Court's Record under Scrutiny," Institute for War and Peace Reporting Tribunal Update No. 444, Part 2, 17 March 2006, http://www.iwpr.net/?p=tri&s=f&o=260408&apc_state=henitriod79598b179f1bec4e34352b5115c0a7.
3   Slavenka Drakulić, cited in Tošić (2007:89).
4   Author interview, May 2006.
5   Brian Tamanaha (2004:1) writes that in the maelstrom of uncertainty after the end of the Cold War, a consensus emerged, "traversing all fault lines . . . that the 'rule of law' is good for everyone."

by critical legal studies, legal realism, and literary criticism. I deal with each of these intellectual traditions in turn.

Liberal legalism claims that the sole function of a criminal trial is to determine whether the alleged crimes occurred and, if so, whether the defendant can be held criminally responsible for them.[6] One of the most influential modern figures to argue this position is Hannah Arendt (1965:5), who insisted in her book *Eichmann in Jerusalem: A Report on the Banality of Evil* that the main function of a criminal court is to administer justice, understood as determining the guilt or innocence of an individual.[7] A court should not attempt to answer the broader questions of why a conflict occurred between certain peoples in a particular place and time, nor should it pass judgment on competing historical interpretations. Doing so undermines fair procedure and due process, and with them the credibility of the legal system. Arendt's austere legalism arose as a reaction to what she perceived as the Israeli government's undisguised efforts to harness the 1961 trial of high-level Nazi bureaucrat Adolf Eichmann to its nation-building program. Arendt observed that "it was history that, as far as the prosecution was concerned, stood in the center of the trial." She quotes Prime Minister David Ben-Gurion, stating, "It is not an individual that is in the dock at this historic trial, and not the Nazi regime alone, but Anti-Semitism through history" (Arendt 1965:19). Ben-Gurion's declarations were echoed in the opening address of prosecuting attorney Gideon Hausner, who situated Eichmann's acts in a sweeping historical narrative of anti-Semitism throughout the ages, from the pharaohs of Egypt to modern Germany.[8]

Arendt objected to the prosecution's flights of oratory, calling them "bad history and cheap rhetoric" (ibid.). For Arendt, the fact that Hausner construed Eichmann's crimes as crimes against the Jewish people detracted from seeing them as crimes against humanity at large. By portraying the Holocaust as the latest manifestation of a long history of anti-Semitism, the prosecutor neglected the distinctiveness of the Holocaust and its unprecedented industrial annihilation of Jews in Western Europe. Moreover, it overlooked the new kind of criminal that had emerged – a bureaucratic administrator who commits genocide with the stroke of a pen (276–7). Arendt applauded the efforts of Presiding Judge Moshe Landau to steer the trial away from moments of spectacle and back to normal criminal court proceedings, reasoning that the extent of the atrocities obviated the need to dramatize the events further

---

[6] Gary Bass (2000:7–8) uses the term *legalism* to characterize liberal approaches to international law. Mark Drumbl (2007:5) also uses "liberal legalist" to describe the dominant model of determining responsibility and punishment in international criminal tribunals.

[7] For a helpful discussion of Arendt's thinking on human rights, see Serena Parekh (2004).

[8] Arendt (1965:19).

(4, 230). Questions of history, conscience, and morality, she insisted, were not "legally relevant" (91). Furthermore, the requirement to do justice foreclosed any efforts to answer wider historical questions by reference to Eichmann's actions:

> Justice demands that the accused be prosecuted, defended and judged, and that all other questions of seemingly greater import – of "How could it happen?" and "Why did it happen?", of "Why the Jews?" and "Why the Germans?", of "What was the role of other nations?" . . . – be left in abeyance. (5)

For Arendt, the point of the trial was none other than to weigh the guilt or innocence of one man, Adolf Eichmann. With his receding hair, nervous tic, poor eyesight, and bad teeth, Eichmann was not a towering figure of evil, a Hitler or a Stalin. Instead he was a diligent, unreflective functionary driven by the motive of self-advancement within the Nazi bureaucracy. Despite the banality of Eichmann, "[j]ustice insists on the importance of Adolf Eichmann" (5). The court must dispense justice for one individual and not attempt to write a definitive history of the Holocaust, however tempting that might be:

> The purpose of the trial is to render justice and nothing else; even the noblest of ulterior purposes – "the making of a record of the Hitler regime which would withstand the test of history"[9] . . . can only detract from law's main business: to weigh the charges brought against the accused, to render judgment, and to mete out punishment. (253)

At the end of her account, Arendt concluded that nationalist pedagogy had detracted from the pursuit of justice and led to breaches of due process (221). Eichmann's defense was obstructed from calling witnesses and could not cross-examine certain prosecution witnesses. There was a marked inequality of arms, for no provision was made for the defense to receive trained research assistants. The disparities between the resources of the defense and prosecution were even more pronounced than at the Nuremberg trials fifteen years earlier.

Since the Eichmann trial, the justice-and-nothing-more doctrine has resurfaced repeatedly in Holocaust trials, with some commentators urging courts to adopt a minimalist approach and to eschew moral commentary and historical interpretation.[10] For example, Tzvetan Todorov (1996) has criticized the way in which Holocaust trials in France were overwhelmed by deliberations on World War II history, the Resistance, collaboration, and French national

---

[9] Here Arendt is quoting the words of Robert Storey, executive trial counsel at Nuremberg.

[10] On Holocaust trials in France, see Douglas (2001:185–96, 207–10); Evans (2002); Golsan (2000a, 2000b); Wieviorka (2002); Wood (1999:113–42).

identity. Todorov argued that the trials of Paul Touvier in the 1980s and 1990s sacrificed justice for political concerns, and he balked at the judges' opinion in the Klaus Barbie trial thus: "what is especially worth criticizing... is not that they wrote bad history, it's that they wrote history at all, instead of being content to apply the law equitably and universally" (ibid.:120).

As might be expected, many staff at international criminal tribunals adhere to some version of the doctrine of liberal legalism. Even if they qualify their views, they generally endorse a fairly restricted crime-based evidentiary approach to determining individual criminal responsibility. In my interviews, this view was more pronounced among lawyers from the Anglo-American common law tradition than those from civil law systems. Australian Gideon Boas (2007:276), former senior legal officer to the ICTY Chamber in the trial of Slobodan Milošević, writes, "A criminal trial should be a forensic process involving determination of the criminal responsibility of an individual or individuals, and not a truth commission." In our interview, Daryl Mundis, a former ICTY Senior Trial Attorney from the United States, remarked, "Historical evidence is not a significant part of the case proving that individual X committed crime Y. I may lead it in a trial, but only as background to give the judges a bearing on the context."[11] Another ICTY prosecuting attorney offered a stark assessment of the prejudicial nature of historical evidence: "History largely gives legitimacy to the Prosecutor and condemns the accused. A criminal trial must be a forensic process. Those shadows which history seeks to illuminate should not play any part in a serious criminal trial."[12]

Despite their rival position in the trial, quite a few defense attorneys appearing before international criminal tribunals also share these sentiments. After his client Momčilo Krajišnik was acquitted of genocide at the ICTY, defense counsel Nicholas Stewart commented, "It's not a truth commission, it's a criminal trial. The prosecution has to prove the case... beyond reasonable doubt."[13] Beth Lyons, defense counsel at the International Criminal Tribunal for Rwanda (ICTR), also defended a strict form of legalism: "The court can only do a limited job – to judge, based on the evidence, whether the prosecution has proved, beyond a reasonable doubt, that the accused person is guilty of the charges in the indictment. If a court goes beyond that, it treads dangerously and leaves the door open for the prosecution to politicize the proceedings."[14]

---

[11] Author interview, June 2006.
[12] Written comment, ICTY survey, 2009.
[13] Caroline Tosh, "Does Krajisnik Sentence Set Dangerous Precedent?" Institute for War and Peace Reporting, Tribunal Update No. 479, 1 December 2006.
[14] Author interview, July 2009.

1.2. THE POVERTY OF LEGAL ACCOUNTS OF MASS CRIMES

Law is likely to discredit itself when it presumes to impose any answer to an interpretive question over which reasonable historians differ.

– Mark Osiel (2000:119)

Whereas liberal legalism maintains that it is inappropriate for a court to write a historical account of a conflict, more recent approaches in law-and-society research go a step further to declare that courts will inevitably fail in this task, even when they try. A number of intertwined elements constitute this critique of legal knowledge, and I present four categories herein: incompatibility theory, the Dickensian "law is a ass" view, the partiality thesis, and the view that law is monumentally boring. Although most of these approaches are compatible and overlapping, others are mutually exclusive:[15]

1.2.1. *Incompatibility Theory*

For the historian, it can be disconcerting to see carefully researched historical material ripped out of its context by clever lawyers and used as a bludgeon to beat the other side.

– Richard Evans (2002:330)

The first approach, which I term *incompatibility theory*, lays emphasis on the distinctive methods and principles of history and law.[16] Historian Richard Evans (2002:330) identifies profound incompatibilities between legal and historical approaches to evidence. Although criminal law demands a threshold of proof that is "beyond reasonable doubt," historians deal in "the broader frame of probabilities."[17] Further, law and history test the evidence in dissimilar ways, and historians, for instance, are seldom in a position to demand to cross-examine a document's author to test its veracity.

One could add that Anglo-American law is adversarial and that expert witnesses are often subjected to a hostile cross-examination, whereas historical analysis proceeds through academic discussion and, at least in principle,

---

[15] Although the partiality thesis declares that law oversimplifies, this contradicts the "just plain boring" critique that courts are excessively embedded in detail and technical minutiae. More often than not, however, these positions reinforce one another. For instance, the partiality thesis and the "law is a ass" stance both emphasize how law's unique methods of inquiry can lead to a distorted and myopic picture of events.

[16] See Osiel (2000) and Minow (1998). See Borneman (1997:103) on the conflicting aims of historians and the justice system.

[17] Evans is Regius Professor of Modern History at Cambridge University. He served as expert witness for Deborah Lipstadt's defense in the 2000 British libel trial brought by Holocaust denier David Irving.

through ongoing peer review. Law's epistemology is positivist and realist, demanding definite and verifiable evidence typically produced through scientific forensic methods. History, however, is more pluralistic and interpretative in both its methods and conclusions. Courts often endorse one version above all others, whereas historians may integrate the elements of competing accounts. Historians often recognize that historical truths are provisional and that their evidence and conclusions are not always verifiable or free of ambiguity. Historians situate individual acts in the societal and cultural contexts as a matter of course, whereas courts are concerned with context only insofar as it impinges on questions of guilt or innocence. Establishing criminal responsibility – the main purpose of criminal trials – is "entirely alien" to what historians do, according to Richard Evans (ibid.:330). Courts demand the kind of unimpeachable facts that will allow them to prove the charges in the indictment, and if the requisite threshold of proof is not met, then a court must acquit. Historians, in contrast, are released from such imperatives and can afford to be more open to indeterminacy and a more systemic approach to causality and responsibility.

As a result of the distinctiveness of the court setting, many historians have been wary of becoming embroiled in criminal trials that involve mass violations. Henry Rousso, then director of the Institute for Contemporary History in Paris, pleaded with the president of the Bordeaux Assizes Court to exempt him from testifying when he was called as an expert witness in the 1997 trial of Maurice Papon: "In my soul and conscience, I believe that an historian cannot serve as a 'witness,' and that his expertise is poorly suited to the rules and objectives of a judicial proceedings. . . . The discourse and argumentation of the trial . . . are certainly not of the same nature as those of the university."[18] James Sadkovich (2002:40) claims that on entering the ICTY Trial Chamber in The Hague, scholars cease to be historians or social scientists and become peddlers of "false history" and "advocates, coached and questioned by the prosecution and defense."

This critique of criminal law is valuable for comprehending why history is often misunderstood and misused in the international criminal courtroom. Yet it is also worth considering how law and history can at times share similar methods and aims. In the broadest terms, both explore the details of the particular while keeping an eye on the general implications of the case in question. Both weigh evidence and finely grade its value. Both carefully weigh their sources, distinguish between primary and secondary documents, and often grant greater weight to the former. Both use eyewitness testimony and search

[18] See Letter to the President of the Bordeaux Assizes Court in Golsan (2000a:194).

for corroborating documentary evidence. Ideally, both show sensitivity to the context of individual actions and the individual's immediate social environment and historical context. Finally, both rely on overarching narratives to organize individual facts, visual images, and other forms of evidence into a coherent whole.

1.2.2. *Legal Exceptionalism, or "The Law Is a Ass"*

While historians have often highlighted the uniqueness of historical methods, a complementary view draws attention to the distinctively legal ways of knowing that arise from specialized legal precepts. As Sarat et al. (2007:2) write, "[I]nside the courtroom, law's ways of knowing seem strange, out of touch, disconnected from the usual ways in which people acquire information or make decisions." The gulf between everyday experience and legal conventions of knowledge has been a source of comment for centuries. Charles Dickens (1970:489) sharply satirized law's rejection of common sense in a scene in *Oliver Twist*, where the character Mr. Bumble, on being told that English law presumes that a wife acts under her husband's direction, explodes in frustration, saying, "If the law supposes that . . . [then] the law is a ass, a idiot."

Law's unique conventions, special categories, and exceptional rules impel courts to perceive historical events through a counterintuitive prism, which leads to all manner of unintended consequences and absurd outcomes. Richard Golsan (2000b:28), for example, derides the *"reducto ad absurdum* of the law itself"* in his analysis of the trials of Vichy intelligence agent Paul Touvier. Because of the statute of limitations on homicide in French law, the prosecution had to prove that Touvier's crimes constituted crimes against humanity, not just murder. However, to be considered crimes against humanity, they had to fulfill one rather unusual criterion. In the earlier Klaus Barbie trial, the Cour de Cassation had ruled that a conviction for war crimes, crimes against humanity, or both, could be upheld only against an individual acting on behalf of a state apparatus exercising "ideological hegemony."[19] In 1992, the Paris Court of Appeals concluded that Touvier was an agent of the wartime Vichy regime but that Vichy did not exercise an autonomous "politics of ideological hegemony" because it was dependent on the National Socialist government in Germany.[20] Vichy was held to be an inchoate puppet regime of "political animosities" and "good intentions." And yet many historians of France have argued that the Vichy regime pursued a coherent anti-Semitic

[19] Golsan (2000b:29).
[20] Golsan (ibid.:31).

ideological project of its own and that Vichy officials participated energetically in the systematic extermination of Jews.[21]

Because Touvier's crimes were not considered crimes against humanity, falling as they did outside the statute of limitations, the Court of Appeals dismissed the case, and Touvier was released. In the subsequent 1994 trial, the prosecution misrepresented the historical record to make the claim that Touvier was a German agent rather than a Vichy operative, linking his crimes to a regime wielding "ideological hegemony," as required by the Barbie precedent. Golsan (2000b:32) remarks caustically, "Now the duty to memory where Vichy's crimes were concerned resulted in encouraging the court to do violence to the very historical realities that the duty to memory was intended to preserve and foreground in the first place." Because courts follow law's own exceptional principles rather than those of historical inquiry, they can reduce complex histories to a defective legal template, and thereby distort history.

1.2.3. *The Partiality Thesis*

Trial "truths" can be partial and can get lost in the morass of juridical and evidentiary detail.
  – Alexandra Barahona de Brito, Carmen Gonzaléz-Enríquez,
    Palomar Aguilar (2001:26)

The partiality thesis extends the critique of legal exceptionalism further to point out how courts can be overly selective and limited in scope, echoing anthropologist Clifford Geertz's (1983:173) famous dictum, "Whatever it is the law is after, it's not the whole story." Whereas in the doctrine of liberal legalism, law's minimal regard for history and sociopolitical context is a cardinal virtue, for these writers, it is a cardinal error, leading courts to overlook the main characteristics of a conflict. Elements of the partiality thesis can be identified in studies of the Nuremberg trials by historians such as Donald Bloxham (2001), Saul Friedlander (1992), and Michael Marrus (1997), who all maintain that the International Military Tribunal did not adequately address the most important Nazi crime of all – the mass extermination of European Jews.[22] The trials left an incomplete and impoverished historical record because crimes against humanity were subordinated to crimes against peace and conspiracy to wage an aggressive war.

[21] Todorov (1996:32) insists that Vichy leader Marshal Pétain was independently anti-Semitic and "signed some of the harshest racial laws of the time," and he interprets the Court's exoneration of Vichy as an attempt to rescue a bruised French national identity. See also Marrus and Paxton (1995).
[22] See Douglas (2001:4) for a discussion of Michael Marrus's work on this theme.

The strategy adopted by Nuremberg prosecutors was motivated by a specifically legal rationale. Because there existed no precedent for convicting criminal defendants from other states for "crimes against humanity" against their own civilian population, Nuremberg prosecutors adopted a cautious strategy in which crimes against humanity drew legal sustenance from war crimes and the crime against peace. Kittichaisaree (2001:19) explains, "Crimes against humanity were novel.... The Nuremberg Charter linked the prosecution of this genus of crimes to the 'execution of or in connection with any crime within the jurisdiction of the Tribunal.' In effect, the crimes [against humanity] had to be committed in execution of or in connection with war crimes or the crime against peace." Consequently, the Nuremberg Tribunal paid more attention to the German war of aggression than to the systematic program to eradicate European Jews.

Many historians have concluded that the Nuremberg trials did not present an authoritative historical account of the Holocaust and that the trials may even have distorted the record for future generations.[23] In place of an explanation built on German nationalism and anti-Semitism, the court identified war and "renegade militarism" as the primary motivating factors for the anti-Jewish policies of Nazi Germany.[24] Justice Robert H. Jackson considered the extermination of the Jews not a principal Nazi objective in and of itself but a function of other war aims of the German High Command. Lawrence Douglas asserts that because the prosecution treated crimes against humanity as secondary to crimes against peace, it implicitly accepted the Nazi's portrayal of Jews as potential fifth columnists and saboteurs who had to be eliminated in pursuit of a war of conquest.[25]

Many of the preceding arguments were marshaled in the 1990s by the proponents of "transitional justice" to justify a move away from classic retributive justice and towards novel institutions such as truth and reconciliation commissions.[26] These quasi-legal commissions, it was held, ought to replace courts as the main institutions that document past political conflict because they could utilize a wider array of investigative techniques. Since truth commissions are not courts of law, they are freed from the task of determining individual guilt or innocence and therefore can conduct more contextual and open-ended inquiry and garner deeper insights into the origins and causes of

---

[23] See, for example, Marrus (1987:4). Donald Bloxham (2001) argues that the Holocaust was largely absent in the Nuremberg trials. For a defense of the Nuremberg trials' historical contribution, see Douglas (2001:65–94).

[24] See Douglas (1995:449).

[25] Douglas (1995:449). Here, the partiality thesis overlaps with the "law is a ass" critique.

[26] See Boraine (2001), Mertus (2000:157–9), and Minow (1998).

political violence. However, several studies have argued that truth commission reports are variable in quality and often based on limited investigations and poor handling of evidence.[27] In a number of cases, they have offered little improvement on standard criminal trials.

1.2.4. *"Boredom on a Huge, Historic Scale"*

Criminal trials can seem overly complex, excessively technical, and obsessed with minor procedural details. After the first flush of press interest, trials for mass crimes soon lose their appeal and are ignored by the public, who feel alienated by the morass of courtroom rules and regulations. Legal scholar Mark Osiel (2000:84–94) sets out how meticulous procedure, however necessary for ensuring a fair trial, often produces mind-numbingly monotonous stories. Although the Nuremberg trials now tower over all later discussions of international accountability, at the time, they were seen as dreary and "failed to mesmerize a distracted world."[28] For some observers, this was not any common garden-variety boredom, but "water torture of boredom" and "boredom on a huge historic scale."[29] Some modern international criminal trials have lasted more than twice as long as those at Nuremberg, and victims have "bemoaned the slow and disjointed progress" of trials.[30]

Law's tiresome proceduralism is unfortunate not only in terms of its impact on the historical value of a trial; it also can expose criminal courts to unscrupulous defense lawyers who mount a "rupture defense"[31] that undercuts the legitimacy of the court in the eyes of the media and public. In French law, the accused does not have to swear an oath to speak the truth, and this creates a situation in which "'[o]nly the accused has the right to lie,'" as the Presiding Judge in the Touvier trial sardonically observed.[32] In the Klaus Barbie trial, the prosecution proceeded methodically and soberly to the point of monotony. Into this vacuum burst Jacques Vergès, Barbie's flamboyant defense counsel, who engaged in scurrilous tactics and lurid rhetoric, including comparing Barbie's

---

[27] See Buur (2001), Ross (2002), and Wilson (2001:51–5).
[28] Alex Ross, "Watching for a Judgment of Real Evil," *New York Times*, 12 November 1995, 37.
[29] Douglas (2001:11), citing Rebecca West in her 1955 account of Nuremberg, *A Train of Powder*.
[30] Claire Duffet, "Khmer Rouge Genocide Tribunal Stumbles as French Defense Lawyer Demands New Translation," *Law.com*, International News Section, 10 December 2008, http://www.law.com/jsp/law/international/LawArticleFriendlyIntl.jsp?id=1202426601165.
[31] A rupture defense is a legal strategy that seeks to undermine the prosecution case by repetition of nonsensical, irrelevant, and spurious arguments with the aim of sowing confusion, uncertainty, and doubt. Jacques Vergès recently termed his brand of chaotic defense "defense de rupture." Duffet, "Khmer Rouge Genocide Tribunal Stumbles."
[32] Rousso (1996:163, 165).

criminal acts favorably with those of the French military in the Algerian War of Independence.[33] Similarly, international tribunals are not immune from moments of near-unbearable tedium brought on by the glacial progress of legal procedure. Nor are they free of disruptive showmanship on the part of defense lawyers. In the trial of Radoslav Brđanin at the ICTY, defense counsel John Ackerman inquired of a prosecution witness if the Serbs' detention of suspects "was any worse than the United States' incarceration of al-Qaeda suspects in [Guantanamo Bay,] Cuba," a statement he immediately retracted.[34] Senior Trial Attorney at the ICTY Dan Saxon (2005:563) writes:

> [A]s anyone who has watched some of the ICTY proceedings can tell you, trials are often long, boring, complex, and highly technical processes – so it is easy for politicians and other interested parties to distort the facts as they are presented. And because these trials, in the interest of fairness, are often so complex and technical, they are the opposite of "Show Trials."

This dismal portrayal of the courtroom needs some qualifying, and Lawrence Douglas (2001:19–21, 91–3) identifies moments of undeniable drama at the Nuremberg trials that served the ends of historical pedagogy. Douglas makes a persuasive case for both the theatrical and educational value of the Nuremberg trials, pointing to prosecutor Robert Jackson's opening statement, Jackson's cross-examination of Hermann Göring, testimonies from witnesses of the "Final Solution," the screening of the film *Nazi Concentration Camps*, and the haunting closing summation by British chief prosecutor Hartley Shawcross. There have also been moments of undeniable drama in international criminal trials; for instance, on 1 June 2005 in the trial of Slobodan Milošević, the prosecution presented a videotape showing six young, unarmed Bosnian Muslim men being taken out of a truck and murdered in cold blood by members of the Bosnian Serb "Scorpions" paramilitary group. Showing the video in the Trial Chamber had profound repercussions in the former Yugoslavia, representing as it did the awfulness of war crimes with a rawness and immediacy that could not be denied.

1.3. LAW AND HISTORY IN THE INTERNATIONAL CRIMINAL COURTROOM

The [ICTY] judges looked to history to make more sense of the crimes [in the trial of General Krstić] . . . that is perfectly appropriate in the context of

---

[33] See Wood (1999:117).
[34] See Vjera Bogati, *Brđanin* Trial, Tribunal Update No. 298, Institute for War and Peace Reporting, London, 27–31 January 2003.

international law. It is an appropriate backdrop, since you just don't kill that
many people without a context.

– ICTY prosecutor[35]

To what degree are the critiques of criminal law reviewed here applicable to
the international criminal trials established in the past decade? Have these
tribunals provided new and meaningful insights into the origins and causes of
armed conflict? Have their historical inquiries undermined due process and
violated the rights of the accused? This book seeks to answer these questions by
analyzing trials in three international criminal court settings. It starts with the
two *ad hoc* international criminal tribunals established by the United Nations
in the 1990s – one for the former Yugoslavia (ICTY) and one for Rwanda
(ICTR).[36] These experiments in international justice have incorporated
historical and background evidence in a distinctive manner when compared
with conventional practices in Anglo-American domestic courts. At times,
their trials have contained extensive deliberations on Balkan and Rwandan
history and society, and expert-witness testimony has had a significant bearing
on the main legal issues at stake in certain trials. At the end of the book, we look
to the future of international criminal justice and examine the first trial at the
permanent International Criminal Court (ICC), which was launched in 2002.

Judging international crimes and writing a history of an armed conflict are
both complex endeavors, and one of the central claims of this book is that
their relationship to one another cannot be characterized by either harmonious accord or inherent contradiction. Greater clarity might be achieved
by separating out the various elements of historical inquiry at international
tribunals and scrutinizing each in turn. This involves asking who introduces
historical evidence, for what reasons, and with what consequences for the trial
judgment. Then we can proceed to identify any patterns that may exist. What
tends to emerge is a picture that is more complex than can be found in the
discussions reviewed thus far.

The book begins by addressing structural concerns and analyzing the relationship between international tribunals and states. International tribunals
occupy a distinctive structural position outside of the nation-state system,
which can have positive implications for their ability to engage in independent
historical investigations. The categories of international crimes are quite unlike

---

35 Author interview, May 2006.
36 The ICTY was established in 1993 pursuant to UN Security Council Resolutions 808 and
827 (S.C. Res. 808, U.N. SCOR, 3175th mtg., U.N. Doc. S/RES/808 (1993)); S.C. Res.
827, U.N. SCOR, 3217th mtg., U.N. Doc. S/RES/827 (1993)). The ICTR was established on
8 November 1994 by UN Security Council Resolution 955 (U.N. SCOR, 3453rd mtg., U.N.
Doc. S/RES/955).

those found in a domestic criminal courtroom, and the rules of admissibility of evidence allow for greater leeway for the parties to introduce historical and background evidence. The main body of empirical research contained in this study, however, documents the cut and thrust of the legal process, specifically the strategies, understandings, and intentions of legal actors in international criminal trials. Jens Meierhenrich (2008:702) observes that while we have a solid grasp of the jurisprudential dimensions of international courts and tribunals, we know "close to nothing" about them as complex social institutions made up of actors with a variety of goals and assumptions. In a similar vein, Marie-Bénédicte Dembour and Tobias Kelly (2007:8) entreat social scientists to study international justice institutions "not merely as abstract entities, but as complex social processes." This book responds to such calls to pay more attention to the living law by, *inter alia*, documenting why prosecutors, defense counsel, and their respective expert witnesses argue about the past; what their motivations are; and what they hope to achieve. It ascertains whether historical evidence is merely rhetorical window dressing or whether it is integral to the prosecution or defense's theory of the case and, if so, then how.

The methods used in this empirical research project are varied and, with a bit of luck, appropriate to the topic of inquiry. Because of the emphasis on the subjective intentions of legal actors, and combined with my training as a social anthropologist, the methodology has been largely qualitative and centered around interviewing key figures at three international tribunals. Between 2003 and 2010, I conducted more than sixty in-depth interviews with judges, senior legal officers, chief prosecutors, deputy prosecutors, senior prosecuting trial attorneys, trial attorneys, investigators, defense attorneys, research analysts, and external expert witnesses at the three international tribunals included in the study – the ICTR, ICTY and ICC. I read numerous trial judgments and courtroom transcripts of the three international justice institutions, concentrating on cases where historical debates occurred.[37] To gauge the broader applicability and representativeness of the interviews, I also conducted a quantitative research exercise in association with former ICTY research officer Andrew Corin. Our survey questionnaire was administered online to sixty-nine former staff of the ICTY, defense lawyers, and expert witnesses for both defense and prosecution who have appeared before the ICTY. The survey asked participants to evaluate the versions of history emerging from ICTY trials and judgments, to rate prosecution and defense narratives of history, to assess the

---

[37] The main cases reviewed were the following: for the ICTY, *Blaskić, Brđanin, Galić, Gotovina, Hadzihasanović, Jelisić, Kordić and Čerkez, Krajišnik, Krstić, Milošević, Perisić, Prlić, Simić, Šešelj, Stakić,* and *Tadić*; for the ICTR, *Akayesu, Barayagwisa and Ngeze, Bikindi, Kambanda, Kayishema and Ruzindana, Nahimana,* and *Musema*; for the ICC, *Lubanga*.

quality and preparedness of their expert witnesses, and to identify various underlying reasons the Tribunal might have heard historical evidence. The appendix contains further details about the survey methods, and the results and analysis are interspersed throughout the book.

The combination of qualitative and quantitative methods and the attention given to the subjective motivations and mental models of the legal actors situate this study in a body of interdisciplinary law-and-society scholarship of international legal institutions. More specifically, I use the methods and theories of legal anthropology to try to make sense of what legal actors do and what they say they do.[38] Legal anthropology has, since its beginnings in the early twentieth century, been more concerned with experience than with logic, to use Oliver Wendell Holmes's famous distinction, and with process and daily practice rather than with outcome. Legal anthropology usually takes as its subject the assumptions, attitudes, and internal debates in courts in an effort to show how they shape and respond to judicial decision making. A number of insights have emerged from fine-grained empirical studies of legal practice, especially regarding the frequent divergence between the formal rules and procedure and the subjective understandings and strategizing of legal actors.[39]

The scope of the inquiry extends beyond historians and historical evidence at international criminal trials to take in other forms of background or con-textual evidence presented by expert witnesses.[40] Background witnesses testi-fying before the ICTY, ICTR, and ICC are persons with specialized training and knowledge who do not appear as eyewitnesses or material fact experts but instead offer expertise on historical, social, and political context, includ-ing the broader patterns of ethnic, religious, racial, or national identity, or specific factors in the conflict, such as economic collapse or the role of the media.[41] Political scientists, sociologists, anthropologists, art and architecture experts, and demographers have all presented evidence in international trials,

---

[38] See Clarke (2009), Drumbl (2007), Eltringham (2004), Goodale and Merry (2007), Merry (1997, 2006), Nuijten and Anders (2009), and Wilson (2001).

[39] This approach is not unique to anthropology, and one excellent account of the internal workings of an international criminal tribunal comes from John Hagan (2003), a criminologist and sociologist.

[40] "Background evidence" refers to the surrounding historical, social, or political context of a crime and can be distinguished from crime-scene evidence, including documentary evidence, forensic evidence, and eyewitness testimony of a more immediate variety.

[41] This is to a certain degree an arbitrary distinction, and lines of overlap do exist. Some eye-witnesses can also serve as experts on the wider context. For instance, Professor Fahrudin Rizanbegović, of the University of Mostar, testified in the trial of Bosnian Croat leader Jadranko Prlić on 22 May 2006 regarding the harsh conditions he experienced at the Dretelj concentra-tion camp.

and they have shaped the histories that are written by judges. By evaluating the court appearances of expert witnesses, we might comprehend more fully how international criminal justice handles nonlegal approaches to knowledge. A concern with the relationship between legal and nonlegal ways of knowing is somewhat of a departure from existing scholarship of mass atrocities, as those legal scholars who endorse a history-writing role for criminal courts tend to emphasize their educational and dramatic aspects. Mark Osiel (2000:65–7) has advocated "liberal show trials," and Lawrence Douglas (2001:4) focused on the moments of high drama at Nuremberg.[42] This study is less concerned with spectacle or legal didacticism than it is with how law as a system of knowledge filters evidence and establishes an official version of the past. Understanding why courts succeed or fail at the task of writing history requires in part an understanding of how international courts receive, embrace, or reject the various types of nonlegal evidence brought before them.

1.4. RETHINKING THE TERMS OF THE DEBATE

To be clear at the outset, this study does not advocate a greater role than presently exists for history or historians in international criminal trials. One prosecution expert witness explained persuasively: "The court cannot be expected to do the work of historians. Lawyers and judges have their own purposes and methods, which are often not the same as those of the professional historian." In previous writings (Wilson 2001), I have argued that postconflict institutions should not be overloaded with too many dissimilar and potentially contradictory functions, and the same applies to international criminal tribunals.[43] There exists no mandate to narrate the history of an armed conflict in the UN Resolutions establishing the ICTY and ICTR, nor in the 1998 Rome Statute of the ICC. Even though these statutes sometimes make imprecise references (usually in a flowery preamble) to how prosecutions might one day reconcile parties to a conflict, deter future conflict and restore peace, these are largely diplomatic embellishments with little bearing on the daily work of international tribunals. The UN Security Council Resolutions are also inconsistent on this matter. Resolution 808 (23 February 1993) declared that an international tribunal "would contribute to the restoration and maintenance of peace," but UN Resolution 827 (25 May 1993) established "an international tribunal *for the sole purpose* of prosecuting persons responsible for serious

---

[42] See also Simpson (1997) on didactic histories in war crimes trials.
[43] Nettelfield (2010) eloquently makes a similar point about unrealistic expectations with regard to the ICTY's impact in Bosnia and Herzegovina.

violations of international humanitarian law committed in the territory of the former Yugoslavia" (Article 2, my emphasis) and made no mention of a peace-building function.

Existing international courts are simply not designed in my view to fulfill other important tasks such as conflict-resolution, reconciliation, and deterrence. True, both the ICTR and ICTY belatedly created outreach programs providing briefings, lectures, workshops, and films for the public, media, and local judiciary at regional offices in Rwanda and the former Yugoslavia. These educational and information programs seldom went beyond explaining the work of the tribunals to the local populace and have received mixed reviews.[44] It is also true, as ICTY prosecutor Dan Saxon (2005:559–72) points out, that expressions of reconciliation by defendants are soundly applauded by international criminal tribunal judges in their judgments. The ICC has probably gone the furthest of any international justice institution by allowing the participation of legal representatives of survivor groups in the Trial Chamber.[45] Although noteworthy and necessary, these initiatives do not detract from the fact that the principal function of international courts is determining individual criminal responsibility for violations of international humanitarian law. The writing of a far-reaching history is more adequately achieved elsewhere, and chiefly by historians, social scientists, and others who may, of course, draw on the extensive information and documentation revealed in international trials.

Moreover, the introduction of historical and social context is not invariably a "good thing" in a trial; this depends on the quality and credibility of the evidence and whether it has any meaningful bearing on the charges. As we will see later, international tribunals can get the history of a country badly wrong when trying genocide cases as a result of their quest for certainty and fixity in defining ethnic groups. There always exists the possibility, and even the likelihood, that history is being oversimplified and misused in an international trial; that the prosecution's conception of nationalist history is overly deterministic, or that the defense's contextualization of the crimes bolsters a *tu quoque* defense in an effort to mitigate punishment.[46] When high-ranking leaders such as Slobodan Milošević, Radovan Karadžić, and Vojislav Šešelj represent themselves in a trial, historical discussions often degenerate into an undesirable spectacle that can undermine the integrity of the court.

---

[44] See Peskin (2005) on the ICTR Outreach Program, and Hazan (2004:190–1) and Klarin (2009) on the ICTY.

[45] See Blattman and Bowman (2008) and Schiff (2008:130, 133–4, 157).

[46] The *tu quoque* defense is examined extensively in Chapter 6. Briefly, the principle of *tu quoque* involves the claim that the opposing party also committed crimes and therefore any criminal acts on the part of the accused were retaliatory.

Having said all this, however, I have come to doubt the widespread view that international courts are inherently predestined to leave an impoverished historical record of mass violations of international humanitarian law. According to the critics, international tribunals should be a failure in terms of the historical version they leave behind, but the record of international trials is not that straightforward. It is not that the critiques outlined earlier are somehow misguided or inappropriate. In subsequent chapters, we will see numerous instances in which they are borne out in part or in full. However, they do not represent the whole story, and they neglect the high-quality historical accounts of the armed conflicts that have emerged. They also overlook what actually goes on behind the scenes, as researchers and prosecutors develop their cases, and in the Trial Chamber when historian expert witnesses give testimony. Critical accounts may fail to acknowledge how the liberal rules of evidence of international criminal tribunals allow broader discussions of the past, and how novel legal concepts such as genocide create specifically legal imperatives to write history and include social and political context. Even if courts produce an unsatisfying history, they may provide a body of evidence that is invaluable for historians, and so in that sense, their impact as producers of history lasts long after the trials are completed.

International criminal trials, though not without their faults, have produced historical narratives that have been much farther reaching than national courts.[47] Both the prosecution and defense have submitted historical expert-witness reports that, when viewed together as a totality, constitute a valuable compendium on the origins and causes of massive violations of international law. The adversarial process has tested the evidence time and time again, even if it has at times adopted a more narrow approach than one would wish. Perhaps most importantly, international tribunals have successfully obtained extensive documentary archives from governments that may be reviewed by future generations interested in the histories of the conflicts in the Balkans and Rwanda in the 1990s. A number of legal judgments contain extensive deliberations on the underlying causes of an armed conflict, and they exhibit a heightened concern with the intentions of perpetrators of crimes against humanity and the place of discrete acts in a systematic policy of persecution or extermination. As we will see, many international tribunal judgments steer a careful course between legal minimalism on the one hand and nationalist dramaturgy on the other hand.

[47] One clearly identified flaw is their treatment of fact witnesses and especially female testimonial witnesses in the Trial Chamber. I do not claim that international or domestic courts are preferable to truth commissions in this regard. See Dembour and Haslam (2004), Dixon (2002:697, 705), Minow (1998), Stover (2005), and Stover and Weinstein (2004).

Viewed together, there is a compelling case for rethinking the long-standing view that the pursuit of justice and the writing of history are inherently irreconcilable. There is, for instance, no evidence to support Arendt's contention that historical discussions undermine due process and fairness. Both the prosecution and defense have taken advantage of the opportunity to present their own historical experts, and they have vigorously cross-examined the other parties' witnesses. Without a doubt, there have been times when historical testimony is irrelevant, defective, and even positively scurrilous, but such evidence has not in itself caused a legal travesty, the main reason being that it has been secondary to other forms of material evidence. The guilt or innocence of the accused has not to my knowledge hinged entirely on a matter of historical import, in the absence of other incriminating or exculpatory evidence, although historical and contextual evidence has played a supporting role.

Understanding the unique quality of international criminal tribunals requires a grasp of how global politics influences their day-to-day work. International courts are not part of any nation-state's criminal justice system, and this imparts a distinctive enough character to criminal trials that we need to revisit some of the critiques developed in national settings and for the earlier Nuremberg trials. International law is a hybrid system that amalgamates Anglo-American adversarial law and the civil law system found in much of Continental Europe, Latin America, Francophone Africa, and Asia. International criminal law borrows from these preexisting systems and generates its own rules, procedures, and legal precedents, thus bringing into being a unique legal system that must be taken seriously in its own right. In addition, international tribunals regularly deal with crimes of a different order and magnitude than those conventionally brought before a domestic criminal court. One of the ICTY's most experienced Senior Trial Attorneys, Hildegaard Retzlaff-Uertz, makes a compelling case for historical inquiry on the basis of the unique nature of international crimes:

> People criticize us for doing too much history but our task is different from a domestic jurisdiction.... [W]e have to prove a widespread and systematic attack upon a civilian population, so we have to explain the whole context of a crime, what was happening around it and how the crime was part of a plan. This cannot be avoided. As long as a crime against humanity is the crime we are prosecuting at the Tribunal, you have to know the background of the crime. That's why history discussions occur in cases. Even in the Foca case which was a crime-based case, you had to show the goals of the Bosnian Serb leadership. How is it possible not to talk about history?[48]

---

[48] Author interview, May 2006.

Historical debate has become an inescapable feature of many international criminal trials, for better or worse. This is not to say that historical evidence will be led in every trial but only that contextual discussions surface at particular moments, for instance in trials of political leaders who espoused a radical ethno-nationalist ideology. Judges at international tribunals are routinely asked by both defense and prosecution to pronounce on questions of historical import, and to choose between competing historical explanations. Judges may at times deny that their judgments demarcate the underlying causes of an armed conflict, as they did in the 2001 *Krstić* Trial Judgment: "The Trial Chamber leaves it to historians and social psychologists to plumb the depths of this episode of the Balkan conflict and to probe for deep-seated causes. The task at hand is a more modest one: to find, from the evidence presented during the trial, what happened during that period of about nine days."[49] Other international judges, in contrast, openly accept that historical inquiry is a fundamental part of adjudicating a case. Navanethem Pillay, a former judge at the International Criminal Tribunal for Rwanda, affirmed the need for evidence on Rwandan history and culture in propaganda trials such as that of Ferdinand Nahimana, owner of the RTLM radio station that incited Hutus to kill their Tutsi neighbors:[50]

> We were trying words, and it was more important to understand how people made sense of those words, so we required a cultural understanding of political speeches. We equated hate speech with a violent instrument. We had to look at the context to make sense of the impact of their words and not only culture, but history and tradition.[51]

Why is historical discussion inevitable, leaving aside the question of whether it is desirable? Judge Pillay gives us a clue in her response, and Chapters 4–6 develop the idea further: because it is legally relevant. Challenging Arendt's declaration of the legal irrelevance of history in the trial of Adolf Eichmann, historical discussions are embedded in the adversarial process of the international courtroom and can shape the outcome of the trial. History does not feature because the parties are committed to the pursuit of historical commentary as an end in itself. Instead, they include contextual evidence because they believe it helps them succeed in making their legal case. Thus, it is not a matter of whether the parties produce a historical narrative, but how, to what

---

[49] *Prosecutor v. Radislav Krstić* (Case No. IT-98–33), Trial Chamber Judgment, IT-98–33-T, 2 August 2001, §2. For a detailed account of the Krstić trial, see Hagan (2003:156–74).
[50] *Prosecutor v. Ferdinand Nahimana, Jean-Bosco Barayagwisa, Hassan Ngeze* (Case No. ICTR-99–52), Trial Chamber Judgment, ICTR-99–52-T, 3 December 2003.
[51] Author interview, June 2007.

extent, and using which methods – with what motivations, guiding principles, and assumptions – and with what consequences for the international judges' determination of guilt or innocence.

Historical contextualization has assumed prominence in international trials in part because it responds to the requirements of a new class of legal concepts such as genocide and persecution that demand proof of discriminatory intent to harm a group. These crimes include a collective dimension wherein the crimes committed against individuals are a direct result of their membership in the specific protected groups that are listed in national laws and international conventions. Demonstrating the collective aspect of crimes such as genocide requires an account of intergroup relations over time. In addition, international criminal law requires that crimes against humanity be "widespread and systematic," which implies a close examination of both the historical and social context. For instance, in the Balkans, individual Croats committed extensive crimes against Serbs in the parts of Croatia that bordered Bosnia and against Serbs and Muslims in Bosnia itself. To fully grasp the events, the court requires reliable information on the ethnic, national, and religious composition of municipalities in Croatia and Bosnia; a historical account of how Croatian nationalists viewed minorities in Croatia; and an account of how some radical nationalists claimed sections of Bosnia as part of Greater Croatia. The prosecution took this view when charging Bosnian Croat leader Jadranko Prlić with participating in "a joint criminal enterprise to politically and militarily subjugate, permanently remove and ethnically cleanse Bosnian Muslims and other non-Croats in areas . . . which were claimed to be part of the Croatian Community [and later Republic] of Herceg-Bosna."[52] According to the indictment, the crimes were motivated at least in part by long-standing nationalist aspirations, insofar as "[t]he territorial ambition of the joint criminal enterprise was to establish a Croatian territory with the borders of the Croatian Banovina, a territorial entity that existed from 1939–1941."[53]

Furthermore, the crime of genocide requires proof of special intent on the part of the accused, known in legal parlance as *dolus specialis*. The accused must have been aware of, and consciously acting in pursuance of, a sustained policy of extermination of a protected group, in whole or in part. Although genocide is not always premeditated, the emphasis placed by international judges on the element of special intent means that the prosecution case may be assisted if the prosecution can connect violent methods with long-standing

---

[52] *Prosecutor v. Jadranko Prlić et al.* (Case No. IT-04-74-T), Second Amended Indictment, 11 June 2008, §15.

[53] Ibid.

political objectives. The *mens rea* (or criminal intent) requirements of genocide and other crimes against humanity impose legal imperatives on prosecutors, and some of those imperatives make recourse to history very likely, if not unavoidable. As Chapter 4 elucidates, prosecutors at international tribunals have turned to historical evidence especially in senior leadership cases, where the distance between the individual and the crimes is greatest. In so doing, they have used history to portray nationalist projects as centralized, enduring over time and prone to violence. Defense attorneys have responded in divergent ways; on the one hand, some have argued that the nationalist project in question has always been peaceful, but others have embraced an ancient-hatreds view to bolster a "chaos defense," which maintains that the accused cannot be held responsible for a spontaneous and violent popular uprising.

Historical inquiry in international trials is therefore an extension of the requirements of new categories of international criminal law. History and context are part and parcel of the process of legal reckoning in cases involving war crimes, crimes against humanity, and genocide. To my knowledge, this argument has not been applied to the international criminal tribunals established over the past two decades. Nevertheless, my approach is influenced by the work of scholars such as Lawrence Douglas (2001:4–7, 260–1), who has made the case that legal imperatives drive forward collective historical inquiry into mass crimes. Douglas has reservations regarding conventional critiques of Nuremberg, and although he accepts that crimes against Jews did not constitute the central edifice of the Nuremberg trials, "[s]till, the extermination of the Jews was importantly explored and condemned at Nuremberg, especially as it was filtered through the freshly minted legal category of crimes against humanity" (6). The idea of filtering history through the categories of crimes against humanity and genocide is fundamental to my understanding of the place of history at international tribunals, and it owes a clear intellectual debt to prior scholarship.

Since historical discussions are here to stay in the international courtroom, it is worth identifying the problems that have arisen and making suggestions for reforming the existing framework. The book concludes with a set of recommendations, some of which are easily implemented and others less so. A clearer definition of the role of historical and contextual expert-witness testimony could reduce ambiguity and confusion on all sides – the prosecuting and defense attorneys who call experts and commission expert witness testimony, the judges who hear expert evidence and weigh its value, and the experts who choose to appear before an international tribunal and may have little prior experience of courtroom convention. International courts and tribunals might establish a proper training program to attune expert witnesses to the specific conventions and requirements of international trials. There is also a definite need for a program that enhances international judges' capacity to comprehend and evaluate historical and social science research. Other proposals are farther reaching and imply a major reorganization of the way historical evidence is formulated and introduced in international criminal tribunals. These might involve innovative and independent structures for historical research that detach experts from the parties to the trial, with the aim of insulating historical testimony from the more detrimental aspects of the adversarial process of the courtroom.

2

What Does *International* Actually Mean for International Criminal Trials?

International criminal tribunals share many attributes of their antecedents, domestic courts. Trials at the ICTR and ICTY, like their common law counterparts, are propelled by the adversarial process wherein the prosecution musters its best case against the accused on the basis of the available evidence, and defense counsel contests the prosecution's claims wherever possible. Although many conventional, domestic courtroom procedures can also be identified in international tribunals, the latter institutions possess a variety of unique structural and procedural attributes as well. Institutions such as the ICC, ICTR, and ICTY are sited outside the institutional framework of the nation-state, and they are not subjected to the usual supervision and regulation of a state justice ministry. Even though they are heavily dependent on nation-states for their daily operations, each international court proudly declares its independence from national legal traditions, with the ICTY, for instance, claiming that it constitutes "a *sui generis* institution with its own rules of procedure[,] which do not merely constitute a transposition of legal systems."[1] The ICTY's rules of procedure and evidence are not entirely drawn from either the Anglo-American system or the Continental civil law system, and tribunal statements appropriately define the ICTY and ICTR as a "hybrid system."[2] The combination of international courts' distinctive institutional position and their singular rules and procedures means that stock critiques of domestic courts are not directly applicable and may require rethinking.

---

[1] ICTY press release, "Blaskic Case: Defense Objection to the Admission of Hearsay Is Rejected," The Hague, 23 January 1998.
[2] Ibid.

The ICTY and ICTR were established in the early 1990s, at a unique geopolitical juncture. As the Soviet Union disintegrated and authoritarian client regimes in Eastern Europe were replaced with popularly elected governments, many politicians and commentators lauded the triumph of liberal democracy and foretold a new era of peace and prosperity. The exuberance ebbed away quickly with Saddam Hussein's invasion and annexation of Kuwait, the Persian Gulf War in 1991, and the onset of ethno-nationalist conflicts in Yugoslavia in 1991 and Rwanda in 1994. The end of the Cold War did not augur international peace, but for a time, the UN Security Council was less characterized than previously by stalemate and deadlock, which permitted an international consensus to coalesce around creating new institutions of international criminal justice. Despite the many violations of international humanitarian law during the Cold War,[3] it was not until after 1989 that the UN Security Council could muster the political will to invoke Chapter VII of the UN Charter[4] and establish international courts to hold senior officials accountable for crimes committed within their sovereign territories. The ICTY and ICTR were both founded as temporary, *ad hoc* international tribunals to prosecute violations of international humanitarian law committed over a defined period in one country or set of countries. They were originally envisaged as short-lived courts that would prosecute a small number of strategic cases, but they have endured well beyond the three to five years initially expected.

The ICTY was established by the UN Security Council in May 1993, two years after the Balkans conflagration began, after Croatia had fought a war of succession from the Socialist Federal Republic of Yugoslavia, and at the height of the armed conflict in Bosnia.[5] Initially, the three European countries with the greatest military capacity in Europe – Britain, France, and Germany – declined to intervene to end the bloodshed.[6] The Tribunal, established on a shoestring budget, was viewed by many observers as an attempt by the United States and European countries to assuage their guilt for standing by

---

[3] On genocides during the Cold War, see Power (2002:87–245), Shaw (2003), Staub (1989: 188–231).

[4] UN Charter, arts. 39–51, signed 26 June 1945, 59 Stat. 1031, T.S. No. 993, 3 Bevans 1153 (entered into force 24 October 1945).

[5] See Statute of the International Tribunal for the Prosecution of Persons Responsible for Serious Violations of International Humanitarian Law Committed in the Territory of the Former Yugoslavia since 1991, U.N. Doc. S/25704 at 36, annex (1993) and S/25704/Add.1 (1993), adopted by Security Council on 25 May 1993, U.N. Doc. S/RES/8271993. On the ICTY, see generally Akhavan (1998); Bass (2000); Boas (2001, 2007); Hagan (2003), Hazan (2004), Moghalu (2008), Scharf and Schabas (2002).

[6] For accounts of the origins of the war in the former Yugoslavia, see Banać (1992); Bringa (2002:194); Glenny (1992, 2001).

while the slaughter of civilians occurred on European soil.[7] At the outset, the ICTY was considered a token effort that would bring only a small measure of accountability to the war-torn Balkans.[8] North Atlantic Treaty Organization (NATO) officials in the former Yugoslavia made little effort to arrest those indicted, and European foreign ministries worried the Tribunal would obstruct peace negotiations.[9]

The Tribunal's critics appeared to be vindicated during the early years, as the Tribunal proceeded at a sluggish pace, with few indictments, arrests, or trials. The first convictions were four years in coming, and these concerned low- or middle-ranking persons. By early 2000, only three senior indictees were in custody in The Hague, and both the ICTY and the ICTR were coming under growing pressure from the UN Security Council. The arrest and trial of high-level figures, such as former president Slobodan Milošević, seemed as far away as ever, and some commentators, understandably at the time, predicted that they would never be tried.[10] However, once the indictments issued by the Tribunal (161 in total) started accumulating, the ICTY became more effective than first signs had suggested. A number of high-level perpetrators were arrested and tried, and a major breakthrough came with the conviction of General Radislav Krstić for committing genocide at Srebrenica in 1995. Although the Appeals Chamber reduced the conviction to aiding and abetting, it upheld the finding that genocide had been committed at Srebrenica. The highest-profile trial to date, that of former president Slobodan Milošević, dragged on for more than four years because of the accused's ill health and the prosecution's strategy of combining the Bosnia, Croatia, and Kosovo indictments into one massive and unwieldy case. Milošević's decision to represent himself destabilized the court proceedings, and he engaged in obstructionist and vainglorious behavior that would have likely led to the disbarring of a professional legal counsel. His death in March 2006 before sentence could be passed was the ICTY's nadir, and during my research trip to The Hague weeks later, staff morale was undeniably at rock bottom.

Overemphasizing the dysfunctionalism of the Milošević trial can obscure the Tribunal's other accomplishments, notably in issuing indictments against senior leaders from all sides in the conflict.[11] Convictions for crimes against

---

7   On U.S. foreign policy toward Bosnia, see Power (2002:247–327).

8   Robertson (2002:303–5).

9   One NATO official was widely quoted as saying, "Arresting Karadžić was not worth the blood of one NATO soldier." Robertson (2002:304).

10   Scharf (1999:507, 510–11).

11   Hoare (2008:7) undertakes a breakdown of the indictments along ethnic-national lines and concludes that their distribution is more or less in proportion to the responsibility for crimes.

humanity were sustained against the president of the Bosnian Serb National Assembly, Momčilo Krajišnik; president of the Serb Autonomous Region of the Krajina, Radoslav Brđanin, and the Bosnian Croat politician Dario Kordić. Bosnian Serb army leaders Vujadin Popović and Ljubiša Beara were convicted of committing genocide at Srebrenica and Žepa in eastern Bosnia.[12] Some of the accused were found not guilty, and this, too, is an achievement of the Tribunal, as its task is not simply to convict but to ascertain whether the evidence presented supports the indictment.[13] Nearly all those convicted were also acquitted of other charges, including more serious charges such as genocide. Presently, trials are under way for the prime minister of the Bosnian Croatian Republic (Hrvatska Republika Herceg-Bosna, or HR H-B) Jadranko Prlić; the Bosnian Serb leader Vojislav Šešelj; and Radovan Karadžić, who is generally considered the undisputed Bosnian Serb wartime political leader. Commander of the Bosnian Serb army (Vojska Republike Srpske, or VRS) General Ratko Mladić, indicted for genocide in Bosnia, remains at large. An overall assessment of the ICTY's accomplishments must wait until after this final round of trials is concluded.

Rwanda's conflict can be best characterized as a war of insurgency with ethnic and racial overtones instead of a loose national federation rupturing into separate nation-states, as in the Yugoslav case.[14] From 1 October 1990 onward, the Ugandan-supported Rwandese Patriotic Army (later renamed the Rwandan Patriotic Front, or RPF) rebels mounted a number of successful incursions inside Rwanda itself, and their military campaign threatened the government in Kigali. Peace talks between the Rwandan government and the RPF resulted in the 1993 Arusha Peace Agreement, described by then Rwandan President Juvénal Habyarimana as the basis of an "ethnic reconciliation between Hutus and Tutsis."[15] Power sharing was opposed by the extremist Hutu Power faction that operated inside and outside the government. Hutu Power advocates rejected accommodation with the RPF and denounced the agreement as a return to colonial-era Tutsi domination. They clung to an extreme racial ideology that portrayed Tutsis as an alien race that invaded from the north and conspired with Belgian colonialists to oppress Hutus.[16]

---

[12] These convictions were delivered in *Prosecutor v. Vujadin Popović et al.* (Case IT-05-88), Trial Chamber Judgment, IT-05-88-T, 10 June 2010. At the time of writing, they have yet to be heard on appeal.

[13] For instance, Bosnian Croat soldiers in the *Lašva Valley* case and Bosniak military commander Naser Orić (acquitted on appeal).

[14] On the history of the armed conflict in Rwanda, see generally DesForges (1999).

[15] Mamdani (2001:189).

[16] These issues are discussed more fully in Chapter 7. Specifically on the Hamitic thesis that claims Tutsis are an alien race, see Eltringham (2006:427–31).

The Arusha Peace Agreement was never implemented, because on 6 April 1994 the Rwandan president's plane was shot down with surface-to-air missiles near Kigali airport, killing President Habyarimana and President Cyprien Ntaryamira of Burundi. Great uncertainty surrounds this event, and there has yet to be any conclusive determination of who was responsible. There has been as yet no investigation by the ICTR into who shot down the president's plane, and for a long time the Tribunal assiduously avoided investigating this issue, even though it falls within its jurisdiction and has been raised repeatedly by defense counsel. A French investigative judge, Jean-Louis Bruguière, acting on behalf of relatives of the plane's French crew, issued an international arrest in 2006 for a number of high-ranking RPF leaders for shooting down the Rwandan president's plane.[17] The warrant named Rwandan President Paul Kagame as responsible for ordering the assassination, but he could not be indicted under French law because he is a sitting head of state. Bruguière referred his dossier to the ICTR. The government of Rwanda promptly expelled the French ambassador in retaliation. Bruguière's evidence has still not been tested in a court of law. At the ICTR, defense counsel filed a motion in 2006 requesting disclosure to the Tribunal of the Bruguière Report, but judges demurred on the grounds that "evidence as to who is responsible for the crash of the President's plane would not assist the Chamber in determining the guilt or innocence of the Accused."[18] For their part, the Rwandan government issued its own report in January 2010, alleging that Hutu extremists in the government plotted to kill President Habyarimana to ignite ethnic violence, a hypothesis that one commentator observed "remains a cornerstone of the current government's legitimacy and historical narrative."[19]

Within hours of the downing of the president's plane, roadblocks were set up around the capital and throughout the country, and a hundred-day campaign of mass murder was carried out by Hutu extremists and their supporters, commonly known as the *génocidaires*. Mahmood Mamdani (2001:5–8) draws attention to the "large-scale civilian involvement in the genocide," although he notes that the *génocidaires* were armed, coordinated, and guided by Rwandan government officials. Although statistics concerning mass political killings are invariably provisional and created in conditions of great uncertainty, the

[17] Bruguière issued an international arrest warrant ("Ordonnance de Soit-Communiqué") in Paris on 17 November 2006.
[18] "Decision on Casimir Bizimungu's Requests for Disclosure of the Bruguière Report and the Cooperation of France," ICTR Trial Chamber II, Case No. ICTR-99-45-T, 25 September 2006.
[19] Josh Kron, "Extremist Officials Blamed in '94 Rwanda Assassination," *New York Times*, 12 January 2010, A6.

generally accepted figures are that some eight hundred thousand Rwandans were killed. The main victims were moderate Hutu political activists and those designated as Tutsi in the national census.[20] About 10 percent of the total Rwandan population and 85 percent of the Tutsi population were murdered.[21]

On 18 July 1994, the RPF entered Kigali and a new government took power. Although the genocide of Tutsis was halted, the killing of Rwandans did not end. The new RPF government pursued its adversaries into eastern Zaire (now the Democratic Republic of the Congo). According to various reports, up to two hundred thousand Rwandans, most of them identified as Hutus, were killed by RPF government forces.[22] More than fifteen years later, President Paul Kagame's government remains in power, and it is acting in ever more authoritarian ways. Even criticizing President Kagame or mentioning RPF crimes can carry a jail term.[23]

As the genocide in Rwanda unfolded, the international community refrained from intervention or, worse, actually exacerbated the spiral into violence. The French government supported and armed the Habyarimana regime, participated in counterinsurgency efforts against the RPF, and then shielded those responsible for the genocide in refugee camps under the guise of humanitarianism.[24] The United Nations was notoriously ineffective, making sharp troop reductions (from 2,500 to 503) at a critical juncture in April 1994, leaving an undersized contingent of UN troops who were powerless to prevent Rwandans from being executed in front of them. Ten Belgian UN soldiers protecting the moderate Hutu prime minister were themselves tortured and murdered. According to General Romeo Dallaire, the military commander of the UN Assistance Mission for Rwanda, five thousand well-trained troops could have stopped the killing.[25] On the international stage, both the UN Security Council and the Clinton State Department studiously avoided using the word "genocide," and instead coined a lesser category of "acts of genocide."[26] Refraining from using the label "genocide" released them from the responsibility of preventing genocide, which is contained in the 1948 UN Convention on the Prevention and Punishment of the Crime

[20] Power (2002:334).
[21] Verwimp (2004:233).
[22] *Economist*, "The Road out of Hell," 27 March 2004, 25–7.
[23] Josh Kron, "For Rwandan Students Ethnic Tensions Lurk," *New York Times*, 17 May 2010, A9. The article gives the example of a college professor recently imprisoned for criticizing the president during a class.
[24] According to Mamdani (2001:186), French troops assisted the Rwandan government in repelling the RPF invasion in 1990.
[25] Power (2002:376).
[26] This wording can be found in the 8 June 1994 Resolution of UNSC; U.N. Doc. S/RES/925.

of Genocide. Rwanda in 1994 was not the international community's finest hour.

In the aftermath of the mass killing, the UN Security Council passed Resolution 955 of 8 November 1994, invoking Chapter VII of the UN Charter and establishing the International Criminal Tribunal for Rwanda in Arusha, Tanzania.[27] The ICTR Statute mandates the Tribunal to prosecute those persons responsible for genocide and other serious violations of international humanitarian law committed in the territory of Rwanda and neighboring states between 1 January and 31 December 1994. This is not a mandate the ICTR has come even close to fulfilling, as we will see. The ICTR functioned at a slower pace than its counterpart in The Hague, having issued ninety-one indictments against Hutu suspects and concluded fifty-two proceedings at the time of writing.[28] Yet unlike the ICTY, genocide convictions of political and military leaders came early and were upheld on appeal. They encompassed Hutu extremists at many levels, such as Prime Minister Jean Kambanda, former minister of defense Théoneste Bagosora, Mayor Jean-Paul Akayesu, and media owner Ferdinand Nahimana.

On 16 June 2006, in one of the most momentous rulings of the ICTR, the Appeals Chamber in the *Karemera* case ruled that ICTR Trial Chambers must take judicial notice of genocide in Rwanda between 6 April and 17 July 1994.[29] The decision made genocide in Rwanda a "fact of common knowledge," placing the existence of genocide beyond all dispute at the Tribunal.[30] As a result, ICTR prosecutors were relieved of the time-consuming task of proving that genocide took place in Rwanda, something they had had to do in each and every case up to that point. The ICTY judges have not to date issued any comparable ruling on genocide in the former Yugoslavia, even though they have determined that genocide occurred in the localized area of Srebrenica and Žepa in eastern Bosnia.[31]

Although the ICTR has effectively prosecuted Hutu extremists for genocide, there have not been any corresponding prosecutions of high-ranking RPF figures, despite the fact that compelling evidence of war crimes has been

---

[27] Statute of International Tribunal for Rwanda, S.C. Res. 955, U.N. SCOR, 3453rd mtg., U.N. Doc. S/RES/955 at 3, annex (1994).

[28] At the time of writing, the ICTY had concluded 126 proceedings against indicted persons.

[29] *Prosecutor v. Édouard Karemera, Mathieu Ngirumpatse, Joseph Nzirorera*, "Decision on Prosecutor's Interlocutory Appeal of Decision on Judicial Notice," ICTR-98-44-AR73(C), 16 June 2006.

[30] Ibid., §35. The ruling defines a fact of common knowledge at §22: "The term 'common knowledge' encompasses facts that are not reasonably subject to dispute: in other words, commonly accepted or universally known facts, such as general facts of history or geography, or the laws of nature. Such facts are not only widely known but also beyond reasonable dispute."

[31] Notably in the *Krstić* Appeals Judgment and the *Popović et al.* Trial Judgment.

presented by international human rights organizations.[32] One 1994 investigation authorized by the UN High Commissioner for Refugees and led by Robert Gersony found evidence that RPF forces had killed thirty thousand civilians in reprisals between May and December 1994, during the time when the ICTR possesses the jurisdiction to prosecute crimes.[33] All international courts are accused of being partial, as victor's justice wielded against one party in the conflict, and the ICTR's lack of prosecutions against the ruling RPF make accusations of bias very hard to dispute. The ICTY cannot be seen as victor's justice in the same way, as it has prosecuted all sides in the conflict. As Boas (2007:38) points out, the ICTY was not created in a process of defeat and occupation, and no national group can reasonably be seen as "vanquished."

The third international justice institution included in this study, the International Criminal Court, is also situated in The Hague, and it is a permanent court, not a temporary, *ad hoc* tribunal. Established by the 1998 Rome Statute, the ICC's jurisdiction came into effect on 1 July 2002, and it can prosecute only crimes committed after that date and in countries that have ratified the Rome Statute, or when the accused is a member of such a state party, or when a case is referred by the UN Security Council.[34] The Rome Statute grants the ICC jurisdiction over four crimes: genocide, crimes against humanity, war crimes, and aggression. Because at the time of this writing the ICC had not completed any trials, I concentrate on the ICTY and ICTR in this and subsequent chapters and address the ICC separately in Chapter 8.

Outside the scope of this book are several UN-sponsored experiments in postconflict justice, known as "hybrid courts," many of them located in the countries where the crimes occurred. They are harder to characterize, as each adopts its own idiosyncratic amalgam of the national and international law, procedure, and personnel.[35] In the Extraordinary Chambers of the Courts of Cambodia, national judges represent a majority in each trial chamber,

---

[32] Amnesty International, "Rwanda: Reports of Killings and Abductions by the Rwandese Patriotic Army, April–August 1994," 19 October 1994, http://www.amnesty.org/en/library/info/AFR47/016/1994. For a more recent summary of nongovernmental organization accounts of RPF crimes, see Katherine Iliopoulous, "ICTR Accused of One-Sided Justice," Global Policy Forum, 31 August 2009, http://www.globalpolicy.org/component/content/article/163-general/48103-ictr-accused-of-one-sided-justice.html.

[33] In 1994, the UN High Commissioner for Refugees contracted the freelance consultant Robert Gersony to conduct an investigation into claims of RPF massacres of Hutu civilians during its insurgency. The Gersony team conducted more than two hundred interviews at nearly a hundred sites between 1 August and 5 September 1994. A draft report containing extensive evidence of a pattern of persecution of Hutu civilians by the RPF was submitted to the UN Secretary-General Boutros Boutros-Ghali but was suppressed, according to Des Forges (1999:556), with the approval of U.S. officials.

[34] U.N. Doc. A/CONF. 183/9; 37 ILM 1002 (1998); 2187 UNTS 90.

[35] On hybrid courts, see Dickinson (2003), Moghalu (2008), Shaw (2007), January (2009).

there are national and international coprosecutors, and trials are conducted according to criminal procedure in force in Cambodia but with guidance from international criminal procedure. The statutes of the Special Court for Sierra Leone and the Special Court for Lebanon ensure a majority of international judges in each trial, but the former court applies international criminal law and the latter Lebanese law, although it uses international procedure. In 2005, the ICTY began transferring cases to the region under Rule 11 *bis* of the ICTY Rules of Procedure and Evidence,[36] and one of the local courts, the War Crimes Chamber of the Court of Bosnia and Herzegovina in Sarajevo, included mixed panels of local and international judges.[37] Given these myriad variations, and taking account of the need for a relatively stable baseline of comparison, this study excludes special courts situated in the countries where the alleged crimes took place, or whose international character is heavily diluted, or both.

The following sections compare international tribunals with domestic courts, with special reference to their institutional position relative to the state. They argue that international courts have a reduced dependency on nation-states in some areas of their work and are just as dependent on states, if not more so, than domestic courts in other areas. However, returning to our theme, even though international tribunals are subjected to considerable political pressure from states, this duress does not always translate directly into distortions of the historical record.

2.2. THE POLITICS OF NATIONAL IDENTITY IN DOMESTIC COURTS

PHILINTE: Then who will plead your case before the court?
ALCESTE: Reason and right and justice will plead for me.
PHILINTE: Oh, Lord. What judges do you plan to see?
ALCESTE: Why, none. The justice of my cause is clear.
PHILINTE: Of course, man; but there's politics to fear.
       – Molière, *The Misanthrope* (1666), Act 1, Scene 1

---

[36] Rules of Procedure and Evidence, International Tribunal for the Prosecution of Persons Responsible for Serious Violations of International Humanitarian Law Committed in the Territory of the Former Yugoslavia since 1991, U.N. Doc. IT/32, adopted 11 February 1994 (hereafter ICTY Rules of Procedure and Evidence, or RPE).

[37] Since late 2009, the renewal of the contracts of the international judges has become a matter of some dispute. Bosnian Serb deputies opposed renewal in the parliament, prompting Valentin Inzko, high representative for Bosnia and Herzegovina, to extend their mandate through an executive ruling.

Why do domestic courts, as we saw in the previous chapter, so often portray the history of a conflict inaccurately and reproduce many of the national myths associated with a conflict? The previous discussion focused on reasons internal to the legal process – law's rules and courtroom procedures that seemed destined to defeat a comprehensive reckoning with the past. This section delves deeper into the political framework surrounding courts that are trying cases of mass atrocities and explores how national and international courts face similar and distinctive kinds of political pressures.

At the end of *Eichmann in Jerusalem*, Hannah Arendt (1965:270–2) remarked on the substantial political pressure on the Jerusalem court to succumb to nation-building rhetoric, and she concluded that Israel was not the ideal venue to try the Nazi war criminal. Instead, Arendt suggested, Israel could have detained Eichmann and lobbied for an international criminal court that could adhere to due process and dispense justice neutrally. This is a prescient conclusion, given that it took another four decades to set up the first truly "international" courts to try individuals for crimes against humanity and genocide. It is worth building on Arendt's observations further by scrutinizing the inordinate pressure that national governments can place on domestic courts. Domestic trials often become a battlefield over the past and future identity of the country.[38] In the model of political authority to which most national politicians subscribe, the state is an expression of the collective popular will. Exposing a postconflict state's misdeeds and moral failings too openly risks undermining its already-shaky legitimacy and authority. Openly challenging the ethnic and nationalist mythology underlying a conflict is anathema to many successor regimes. As the former ICTY deputy prosecutor David Tolbert (2009:284) writes: "successor governments . . . may have little interest in seeing the crimes adjudicated, as such trials would undermine the national myths that have developed regarding the underlying conflict and potentially put the successor's own power at risk."

In postconflict settings, a regime of denial often prevails in the speeches of leaders extolling reconciliation, in amnesty and indemnity legislation, and in lack of a proper judicial response to past crimes. Where prosecutions do occur, courts often suffer from the interference of the governments and elites who direct, supervise, administer, and fund them.[39] Successor regimes tend to be fragile and precarious, and too much legal scrutiny of past crimes may imperil the uneasy coalitions in the ruling elite, especially given that some

---

[38] Further to this argument, see the special edition of the *Journal of Modern Italian Studies* (2004).

[39] Nor are truth commissions exempt from such pressures and influences. See Wilson (2001:13–17) on the nation-building function of the South African Truth and Reconciliation Commission.

members have a personal stake in avoiding justice. The image of the nation as valiant and noble, though beleaguered and misunderstood by its internal and external enemies, is the preferred ideological justification for suppressing investigations into politically motivated crimes. Focardi and Klinkhammer (2004:330) reinforce this point when they claim that the national mythology of the "good Italian" (*Italiani brava gente*) was used to proscribe meaningful trials against Italians who committed crimes against humanity in Benito Mussolini's army and during the Holocaust.

In trials for conflict-era crimes, history becomes politicized as governments pressure courts to selectively filter the past and construct a new official account that corresponds with a heroic vision of the nation. Governments, especially those emerging from a recent civil war or authoritarian rule, have a clear interest in controlling representations of the past so as to manufacture legitimacy in the present. They may seek to portray themselves as liberators of the nation, construct a new, shared "collective memory" (as in Israel in the 1960s), or wish to rehabilitate the reputation of state institutions and officials tarnished by their authoritarian past (as in France in the 1980s).[40] Historical mythmaking appeals to governments because it can be used simultaneously to defuse domestic political dissent and display the regime's human rights credentials to the international community ("look at how bad things were then and how much better they are now").

The quest for legitimacy often subordinates justice and history to nation building. This not only applies to trials in "new" nations but also is relevant to understanding trials held in the context of long-established democratic regimes, such as France. According to Golsan (2000b:36–7), the French government manipulated its courts in an effort to shore up its authority in a context of diminishing state power; globalization; and, one might add, the political and economic consolidation of the European Union. For example, government pressures led the Court of Appeal in the 1985 trial of Klaus Barbie to retroactively redefine the category of "crimes against humanity" to fit the crime – and the criminal.[41] At other times, the explanation is more straightforward; many personnel from the prior criminal regime still occupy positions of power and authority. One need think only of the French Holocaust trials taking place during the tenure of President François Mitterrand, with his controversial record as a Vichy bureaucrat. In the Holocaust trials of Barbie, Papon, and Touvier, French courts blew with the political wind

---

[40] On nationalist history and transitional justice trials in Latin America, see Barahona de Brito et al. (2001:119–60) and Panizza (1995). On South Africa, see Buur (2001) and Wilson (2001).
[41] Golsan (2000b:29–30).

rather than holding fast to legal procedure and principle. It was not until the landmark judgment of 16 February 2009 that France's supreme judicial body, the Conseil d'État, formally recognized the country's role in deporting Jews to Nazi extermination camps while ruling out any more reparations from the French state for deportees and their families.[42]

Another explanation for the poverty of domestic legal histories relates to the way in which courts are often placed in a structural conflict with the legislative and executive branches of government. When cases are brought, the state is being asked to judge itself and make itself vulnerable to successive lawsuits and demands for reparations from victims of government-sponsored crimes. This is something that postauthoritarian states, often facing massive social pressures and constraints on state resources, are loath to do. In postapartheid South Africa, to consider one example, different state agencies pursued highly contradictory objectives. On 5 August 1996, Nelson Mandela's government's Truth and Reconciliation Commission (TRC) held public hearings in the African township of Sebokeng to the south of Johannesburg. The TRC head, Archbishop Desmond Tutu, listened sympathetically to the voices of the victims of the South African Police or South African Defense Force. At the end of its work, the TRC formulated recommendations for reparations for tens of thousands of apartheid-era victims.[43]

Meanwhile, just a few miles down the road at Vanderbijlpark Murder and Robbery Unit, police officers continued to assault and torture criminal suspects. In the estimation of Colin Bundy (1999:8), beating confessions out of criminal suspects was a "professionalized" feature of apartheid police investigation work, and this practice remained widespread even after the 1994 democratic transition. Two Johannesburg attorneys, Tony Evans and Peter Jordi, made tort claims for police criminality the center of their legal practice. They successfully sued the minister of safety and security numerous times in 1996 and in subsequent years on behalf of clients who had been tortured and beaten in police custody at Vanderbijlpark.[44] So, while one agency of the South African state was creating a forum to hear the accounts of victims

---

[42] France: Conseil d'État. Assemblée. No. 315499. 16 February 2009. http://www.conseil-etat.fr.

[43] Truth and Reconciliation Commission South Africa, Report (1998).

[44] *Themba and Pharamela v. Minister of Safety and Security* (Unreported, High Court of South Africa Witwatersrand Local Division), 97/14698, Marais, J., 8 March 2000, involving the torture by electric shock and smothering of two women by the South African Police Service on 3 June 1996. Most cases involving alleged police brutality are unreported, as they settle out of court: personal communications with Peter Jordi, July 2006 and October 2009. See Peter Jordi, "Compensation for Victims of Crime in a Civil Context," paper presented at conference "Criminal Justice: A New Decade of Consolidating Transformation," 7–8 February 2005, http://www.csvr.org.za/wits/confpaps/jordi.htm.

of assault and torture by police, another was creating more victims of assault and torture by police, which led to sizable payouts for damages.[45] Conflicts of interest of this kind mean that successor regimes seldom act as a neutral arbiter, because they are too ensnared in, and financially liable for, a criminal scenario of the state's own making. To expect domestic courts to be immune and sheltered from such political considerations, especially in countries lacking a durable tradition of rule of law and an independent judiciary, is to expect a great deal. Ardent critics of international tribunals seldom pause to consider the degree to which national criminal justice systems, in both postconflict settings and established democracies, are susceptible to meddling and malign influence from the political establishment.

2.3. NATIONALIST MYTHMAKING AND INTERNATIONAL JUSTICE

Are international criminal trials free enough of political subterfuge to warrant former ICTY President Antonio Cassese's statement: "We intend therefore to dispense justice *free from any political or ideological fetter . . .* so we might set the stage for future and broader resort to international criminal institutions to fend off terrorism."[46] Unfortunately, the reality is not quite so ideal. The two *ad hoc* tribunals are susceptible to political interference by nation-states, as they rely on the goodwill of the UN Security Council and its willingness to insist that recalcitrant states cooperate with investigations. As the ICTY deputy prosecutor David Tolbert starkly conceded, "without state cooperation you can't conduct a proper trial; you can't conduct any trial at all."[47] There were occasions when an international tribunal's appeal to the Security Council led to state cooperation, and times when the Council was slow or declined to act. There were also times when it acted, but the state in question successfully resisted international pressure. In addition, the state may be able to launch its own diplomatic counteroffensive and win over powerful states, at which point the arrow of persuasion is reversed and international courts can come under inordinate strain, with deleterious consequences for their independence and neutrality.

---

[45] Payouts for police brutality in South Africa cost 120 million rand (more than US$16 million) between 2000 and 2003. Makhudu Sefara, "Police Brutality Cost Taxpayers R120m," *Sunday Independent* (South Africa), 8 February 2003, http://www.iol.co.za/index.php?set_id=1&click_id=13&art_id=ct20030208185859613B63086.

[46] Original emphasis. Antonio Cassese, "The Special Tribunal for Lebanon Six Months On: President's Report 2009," http://www.stl-tsl.org/x/file/TheRegistry/Library/presidents_reports/SixMonthReport_En.pdf.

[47] Caroline Tosh, "War Crimes and State Cooperation," IWPR Tribunal Update No. 476, 10 November 2006.

Even as international tribunals can be vulnerable to external political influence, they also enjoy an operational autonomy that allows them greater latitude to undertake probing historical investigations of past crimes. The most obvious contrast between domestic courts and international tribunals is that the latter are not constituted in the institutional framework of the nation-state. As a result, international courts do not face material conflicts of interest of the type described previously in South Africa. Although they do experience political pressure as overbearing as might be experienced by a domestic court, the external intrusions are of a dissimilar nature and do not affect historical inquiry in the same way. Because the nation-state is not in its usual place, the compulsion to engage in nation-building rhetoric or in nationalist mythmaking is not as acute as in national settings. Here we might acknowledge the wisdom of the authors of the statutes of the ICTY and the ICTR, who refrained from a direct mandate to "reconcile the nation" or to "build a national identity," as commonly found in the legislation establishing national truth commissions.

Although international courts are administered by an international bureaucracy, and even a highly politicized one, they are not subject to the bureaucracy of a nation-state with a recent criminal past. The ICTY and ICTR are sited outside of the countries where the crimes they are prosecuting took place and are administered and funded by the UN Security Council, to which they must report annually or biannually.[48] Vital financial assistance was forthcoming from the U.S. State Department and private foundations such as the Open Society Institute, and ICTY outreach programs have also been funded by the European Union.[49] Tribunals are staffed by citizens of many countries, the overwhelming majority of them from outside the country of concern and they do not generally have a previous connection to the conflict. The same cannot usually be said of legal actors in national justice institutions, in, say, Chile or El Salvador or South Africa. Gideon Boas (2007:292) develops this point with regard to judicial autonomy: "[International tribunals] are far more resistant to political influence because of the mélange of different legal and political cultures of judges and legal staff, and a trial will invariably be conducted before three independent judges from three different countries. That fact in itself lends greater protection to the goal of delivering justice independently and impartially."

Moreover, international tribunals are not bound by the legal conventions of any nation-state, which gives them more freedom to develop their own

---

[48] The ICTY president must report once per year, and the ICTR biannually.
[49] ICTY press release, "Support from the European Union to the ICTY," The Hague, 7 December 2000.

rules of procedure and evidence, which is the topic of the following chapter.[50] Nation-states do not have the jurisdiction to regulate the Rules of Procedure and Evidence of the ICTY and ICTR, nor can they tamper with them to suit their objectives in a particular case. International prosecutors have significant discretion in how they run their cases, and although they are under the authority of the chief prosecutor, they do not come under the formal authority of a national politician seeking reelection or legal counsel for the executive branch. It is claimed that this gives them more leeway to make independent decisions about legal matters, with potentially far-reaching political implications. For instance, Louis Arbour, former chief prosecutor for the ICTY and ICTR remains adamant that she issued the indictment for Slobodan Milošević in 1999 when she had the case to justify it, not because she was under international pressure:

> As ICTY prosecutor, it was my job to prosecute when it was possible. The Milošević indictment came after 80 days of NATO bombing. The indictment complicated the war aims, it did not assist them, since it made a peace process *less* likely. The EU and US could no longer negotiate with Milošević. He was removed from the diplomatic picture. I charged Milošević when I was ready with charges of crimes against humanity. He gave in 14 days later, whether he might not have without the indictment, I don't know.[51]

Even though the governments of Rwanda or the former Yugoslavia may be able to hamper investigations by destroying incriminating evidence, they cannot terminate the funding of an international court and close it down. They cannot impede a legal process quite as comprehensively as the Serb government did during the trial of radical Serb nationalist Milorad Ulemek and eleven others accused of the assassination of Prime Minister Zoran Djindjić.[52] Serb government interference was blamed for the resignation of one judge and the replacement of the entire prosecution team during the trial.[53] National governments cannot lift the indictment of military personnel accused of crimes against civilians out of an international tribunal and transfer the case to a military court, as occurs frequently in countries with a history of military dictatorship.[54]

---

[50]   The Rules of Procedure and Evidence (RPE) of the ICTY and ICTR state at Rule 89(A): "A Chamber . . . shall not be bound by national rules of evidence." Adopted 11 February 1994.

[51]   Seminar discussion at the Thomas J. Dodd Research Center, Storrs, CT, 17 October 2005.

[52]   Djindjić was assassinated for transferring Slobodan Milošević to The Hague for trial in what Moghalu (2008:64) deems "clearly a vengeance killing by Serb extreme nationalists." Ulemek and eleven others were found guilty of arranging the murder of Djindjić in a Belgrade court on 23 May 2007.

[53]   Nicholas Wood, "12 Serbs Guilty of Killing of Prime Minister," *New York Times*, 24 May 2007.

[54]   On Guatemala, see Sieder (1999, 2001), Wilson (1997).

National governments may pass amnesty laws or pardons that would effectively halt domestic criminal investigations of the kind just reviewed in South Africa, but international tribunals are not bound by national amnesties or other indemnity arrangements. The Bosnian Serb leader Radovan Karadžić filed a motion in July 2009 requesting the indictment against him be dismissed on the grounds of an alleged agreement with U.S. State Department representative Richard Holbrooke, but the Appeals Chamber found no provision in the ICTY Statute excluding an individual from its jurisdiction, reiterating that individuals accused of crimes against humanity "can have no legitimate expectation of immunity from prosecution."[55]

2.4. STATE INTERFERENCE AT THE ICTY AND ICTR

There are numerous ways in which nation-states influence and even distort the work of international tribunals. Space constraints do not allow me to delve deeply into all the debates regarding the geopolitics of international tribunals. Compelling and detailed accounts can be found in a collection of recent books by Pierre Hazan (2004), Kingsley Moghalu (2008), and Victor Peskin (2008), as well as in memoirs by tribunal staff such as Florence Hartmann (2007) and Carla Del Ponte (2008). In what follows, I can only give the broad brushstrokes and indicate how international political machinations have affected some aspects of the work of international courts.

At the most general level, states seek to influence the work of the tribunals through their powerful allies on the UN Security Council. The record points toward all states implicated in international trials having attempted this at some point, but some are more effective than others. Serbia lobbied effectively through the Russian ambassador to the United Nations, who missed few opportunities to register dissatisfaction with the ICTY during Security Council meetings. Russia went beyond mere expressions of disapproval in international fora, and in her memoirs, the ICTY chief prosecutor Carla Del Ponte (2008:113) quotes former NATO commander general Wesley Clark as informing her that the Russian agents had protected Tribunal indictees Mladić and Karadžić and warning her, "The Russians don't want you to succeed. They are with the Serb nationalists. They play a dirty game. They read all your mail. And they listen to all of your telephone conversations." The Russian ambassador and officials from the region made personal representations to the senior ICTY officials, threatening to cut off the Tribunal's funding at the Security Council if their demands were not met regarding various matters, including the treatment

---

[55] "Karadžić Trial Commences," *ICTY Digest*, No. 66, 26 October 2009.

of sensitive evidence and the handling of witnesses and indictees facing trial.

At a level beneath geopolitical maneuvering, the governments of Rwanda and the former Yugoslavia can and do obstruct the work of the *ad hoc* tribunals on practically a daily basis, to such an extent that one exasperated ICTY prosecutor told me, "The fact that we get anything done under these conditions is a minor miracle."[56] International tribunals do not possess their own police force, and they are beholden to states to enforce powers of search, seizure, subpoena, and – perhaps most important – arrest. As Del Ponte pointed out on more than one occasion, the arrest of two individuals indicted for genocide in Bosnia, Radovan Karadžić and Ratko Mladić, was not a high priority for successive governments in Belgrade.[57]

However, international tribunals are not completely lacking in avenues of recourse, and chief prosecutors persistently petitioned the UN Security Council, urging greater state cooperation in arrests and access to evidence and witnesses. Beyond the United Nations, the European Union has also played a vital role in reminding states of their obligations to cooperate. Former ICTY deputy prosecutor David Tolbert (2009:285) notes the fortunate position of the ICTY after 2003, when the "carrot" of accession to the European Union smoothed the execution of arrest warrants.[58] The European Union's policy of conditionality and its willingness to suspend talks compelled assistance from states of the former Yugoslavia with regard to handing over sensitive government documents and executing arrest warrants. This cooperation tended to be more forthcoming when governments changed, as in Croatia in 2002.

State noncooperation occurs in less visible ways, too. Obstructing access to evidence occurs offstage when states withhold or destroy reports, memoranda, internal documents, and other forms of incriminating evidence. They may also bury information by submitting it under protective measures. For example, Rule 70, "Matters Not Subject to Disclosure," of the ICTY and ICTR Rules of Procedure and Evidence permits a state to provide evidence to the Office of the Prosecutor on a confidential basis, to be used solely for the purpose of generating new evidence. The prosecutor must obtain the state's permission to disclose the information or its origin, and the Trial Chamber is prevented by Rule 70(C) from issuing an order for additional information, including further documents and witness testimony.

---

[56] Author interview, June 2007.
[57] See Peskin (2008:85–90) on Del Ponte's strenuous efforts to require states to arrest war crimes indictees Mladić and Karadžić.
[58] Tolbert also made this point some years previously in IWPR Tribunal Update No. 471, 6 October 2006.

There are other, less officially sanctioned ways to suppress evidence. Prosecutors in the Milošević case contended that Serb police transported more than one hundred corpses from Kosovo hundreds of miles into Serbia proper to remove traces of war crimes.[59] States have, as we will see in a moment, impeded prosecution witnesses from traveling to testify in Arusha or The Hague and have thus derailed the schedule of a trial. They have the ability to dismiss witnesses from state employment for testifying for the prosecution in an international trial. On a more sinister note, states have the capacity, through their intelligence services, to engage in subterfuge to undermine the work of the tribunals. They have been known to invent fake evidence, introduce false witnesses who give untrustworthy evidence, and plant counterfeit documents to distract investigators and prosecutors. Del Ponte (2008:245) catalogs the ways in which Croatian leaders from Franjo Tuđman onward "mounted an organized, covert effort to obstruct the tribunal's work." While presenting a polished veneer of cooperation, Croatian civilian and military intelligence services tampered with evidence, intimidated witnesses, leaked to the press the names of protected prosecution witnesses, and helped indictees escape arrest by providing false papers and erasing police files holding their fingerprints.

In the discussion that follows, I address the two most egregious and well-documented examples of state influence on the work of the ICTR and ICTY, and I assess their impact on the historical accounts written by the tribunals. At the ICTY, one issue that generated extensive media coverage concerned the Tribunal's handling of the minutes of meetings of the Supreme Defense Council (SDC) of the Federal Republic of Yugoslavia. This governmental body, made up of the presidents of Serbia, Montenegro, and Yugoslavia, had formal command and control over Bosnian Serb forces until 19 May 1992, after which time it continued to arm, supply, fund, and provide logistical support to Bosnian Serb forces through the regular Yugoslav army.

In March 2007, the international court that adjudicates disputes between states, the International Court of Justice (ICJ), issued a judgment that Serbia was not directly responsible for the 1995 massacre of more than seven thousand Muslims by soldiers of the Bosnian Serb Army (VRS) at Srebrenica.[60] The ICJ did find the government of Serbia, however, in contravention of its obligations under the UN Genocide Convention of 1948, for failing to use its influence

---

[59] "Milošević Denies Bodies Cover-Up," CNN.com, 23 July 2002, http://edition.cnn.com/2002/WORLD/europe/07/23/Milošević.trial/index.html?related.

[60] International Court of Justice, *Application of the Convention on the Prevention and Punishment of the Crime of Genocide (Bosnia and Herzegovina v. Serbia and Montenegro)*, Judgment, 26 February 2007. The International Court of Justice in The Hague is an international legal institution created under the aegis of the United Nations in 1945.

to prevent genocide and for failing to cooperate with the ICTY by arresting VRS General Ratko Mladić and Bosnian Serb leader Radovan Karadžić. In acquitting Serbia of direct involvement in the genocide, however, it became apparent that the ICJ had not seen crucial evidence already provided to its neighboring international justice institution less than a mile away, the ICTY.[61]

In the aftermath of the ICJ decision, former ICTY staff, including prosecutor Sir Geoffrey Nice and Florence Hartmann, former spokesperson for the Office of the Prosecutor, publicly denounced the Tribunal's decision to withhold confidential information from the ICJ.[62] The story that emerged in the press is as follows: in 2003, during the trial of Slobodan Milošević, the Serb government handed over to the ICTY highly sensitive minutes of sessions of the Supreme Defense Council held between 1992 and 1999, a period that included the high point of the war in Bosnia and Herzegovina. These sessions were attended by various high-ranking political and military leaders, and all seventy-four sessions were attended by Slobodan Milošević. Nice and Hartmann maintain that the SDC minutes contain evidence of the direct involvement of Serbia and Montenegro in the planning, funding, and directing of the war in Bosnia. The minutes revealed that Bosnian Serb Army (VRS) officers such as General Ratko Mladić, whom the ICTY has indicted for genocide, were members of the Federal Republic of Yugoslavia's Army (VJ), thus confirming the lines of command and control necessary to establish superior responsibility according to Article 7(3) of the ICTY Statute.

Claiming that their disclosure would prejudice national security interests, lawyers in Belgrade applied in 2003 for protective measures under the Tribunal's Rule 54 *bis* confidentiality rules to prevent parts of the documents from being publicly disclosed (and, most crucially, disclosed to the ICJ), so as to avoid paying potentially large financial reparations to Bosnia. The Trial Chamber upheld the Serb government's request to keep the SDC documents secret, accepting Serbia's argument that its vital national interest in the ICJ case could be admitted as a "national security interest," allowed under Rule 54 *bis*.

According to Hartmann (2008), a subsequent Appeals Chamber decision in 2005 found the earlier Trial Chamber's decision to be in error as a matter of law: protection from censure from an international legal institution such as the ICJ

---

[61]   Marlise Simons, "Genocide Court Ruled for Serbia without Seeing Full War Archive," *New York Times*, 9 April 2007, 1 and A6.

[62]   Letter from Geoffrey Nice to the International Herald Tribune, "Hidden from Public View," 17 April 2007; Florence Hartmann, "Vital Genocide Documents Concealed," Bosnian Institute, 21 January 2008, http://www.bosnia.org.uk/news/news_body.cfm?newsid=2341. On 14 September 2009, Hartmann was found guilty of contempt of court by the ICTY and fined seven thousand euros for revealing confidential information in this publication and in her 2007 book *Paix et Chatiment*. She is presently appealing her conviction.

cannot constitute a legitimate "national security interest."[63] Yet the Appeals Chamber considered that it would be unfair to reverse the decision after the fact, on the grounds that Serbia had acted on a legitimate expectation that sections of the SDC minutes would not be publicly disclosed. One lawyer from the Belgrade team was quoted as saying, "We could not believe our luck."[64] Hartmann (2008) concludes unforgivingly, "ICTY judges kept key material from the public for the sole purpose of shielding Serbia from responsibility before another court." Why would they act in this way? They did so to keep Serbia on board and not to capsize their working relationship by reneging on an agreement. Such was the Tribunal's dependence on Serbia's cooperation to function.

Although there is reason to be concerned about how the ICTY judges conceded too much ground to a state party, the events described here are relatively minor compared with the breakdown in cooperation between the Rwandan government and the ICTR and the ensuing consequences for the ICTR's impartiality. From the very beginning, the signs were not auspicious, as the Rwandan ambassador to the United Nations cast his vote against the statute creating the ICTR. Relations improved as long as the Tribunal indicted and convicted senior Hutu Power leaders, but they collapsed in June 2002, when the Rwandan government effectively shut down ongoing trials by preventing witnesses from traveling to Arusha to testify.

The trigger for this souring of relations was chief prosecutor Carla Del Ponte's determination to investigate RPF war crimes committed in 1994. Del Ponte (2008:225) gives her account of traveling to Rwanda to resolve the impasse and quotes President Kagame as saying to her, "You are destroying Rwanda. . . . If you investigate, people will believe there were two genocides. All we did was liberate Rwanda. . . . Don't touch. . . . Stop the investigation. . . . We will not allow you to do this." Despite Kagame's vehement opposition, Del Ponte remained committed to her "special investigations" of the RPF and was at the point of issuing indictments in 2002–3. The Tribunal's president, Navanethem Pillay, made a formal complaint to the UN Security Council that Rwanda was failing in its obligation to cooperate. The United Nations dragged its feet on the matter and only six months later issued a lukewarm statement encouraging Rwanda to cooperate more fulsomely with the Tribunal. The United States and other countries approached Kigali independently, urging cooperation. The Rwandan government subsequently lifted its moratorium on witnesses traveling to testify in Arusha.

---

[63] The content of the Appeals Chamber decision was confidential, and Hartmann was convicted in 2009 by the ICTY for contempt of court.
[64] Quoted in Simons, "Genocide Court Ruled for Serbia."

The Rwandan government then waged a full-scale diplomatic campaign against Del Ponte and won early backing from Britain's minister for international development, Clare Short, and the U.S. ambassador for war crimes, Pierre-Richard Prosper. Kofi Annan, UN secretary-general, declined to defend Del Ponte robustly, and the tide began to turn against her. When her four-year term as chief prosecutor of both the ICTR and the ICTY came up for renewal in September 2003, Rwanda had orchestrated enough international antipathy toward Del Ponte to have her removed as ICTR prosecutor, although she stayed on at the ICTY. There are various explanations for the Rwandan government's success in swaying international opinion, unseating Del Ponte, and blocking RPF investigations. Peskin (2008:210–12) lays great emphasis on the Rwandan government's ability to manipulate the guilt and shame felt at the United Nations and by the Western powers that failed to stop the genocide. Del Ponte (ibid.:231) attributes the volte-face in the U.S. position to a deal struck whereby the RPF would sign a bilateral agreement exempting U.S. citizens from prosecution by the International Criminal Court in exchange for a cessation of investigations of its own officers. The United Kingdom, like many countries, valued its development partnership with the Kagame regime, which was genuinely improving the living and working conditions of its citizens, even as it suppressed internal dissent and freedom of expression. The United Nations and other countries feared that prosecutions would destabilize the government and scupper peace negotiations to end a war in the Democratic Republic of the Congo that had already claimed millions of lives, a war in which Rwandan troops were embroiled.

Del Ponte's replacement as chief prosecutor at the ICTR, the Gambian national Hassan Jallow, has not to date issued any indictments against the RPF, even though human rights organizations continue to document extensive RPF crimes: Amnesty International estimates that between April and July 1994, RPF soldiers killed up to sixty thousand Rwandan villagers.[65] This civilian death toll would be considered staggering in any context other than Rwanda in 1994. Although RPF crimes are not as extensive as those of the Hutu Power regime, they constitute widespread and systematic crimes against humanity, and it is a central principle of international humanitarian law that all such crimes must

---

[65] Amnesty International [IOR 40/045/2006], "Appeal to the UN Security Council to Ensure That the Mandate of the International Criminal Tribunal for Rwanda Is Fulfilled," 12 December 2006, http://www.amnesty.org/es/library/asset/IOR40/045/2006/es/3da30076-d3ca-11dd-8743-d305bea2b2c7/ior400452006en.html. Human Rights Watch reports between twenty-five thousand and forty thousand civilian deaths, citing an investigation by the UN High Commissioner for Refugees. Human Rights Watch, "Rwanda: Tribunal Risks Supporting 'Victor's' Justice," 1 June 2009, http://www.hrw.org/en/news/2009/06/01/rwanda-tribunal-risks-supporting-victor-s-justice?print.

be treated equally. Such equal treatment before the law is still not the norm. In June 2008, Chief Prosecutor Jallow transferred the files of RPF suspects in the *Kabgayi* case to Rwanda for domestic prosecution in its ramshackle justice system.[66] Four officers were tried in relation to the 1994 executions of fifteen civilians, including the Roman Catholic archbishop of Kigali; other bishops and priests; as well as minors, including a nine-year-old Tutsi boy who had survived the genocide. In a trial that lasted only a matter of days, the two senior-ranking officers were acquitted. Two officers who had confessed to the murders were convicted and sentenced to eight years in prison, which was later reduced to five years on appeal, prompting Human Rights Watch to designate the trials a "political whitewash."[67] Lest we forget in our discussion of the limitations of international criminal tribunals, the *Kabgayi* case reminds us of the inability of some national court systems to deal adequately with mass crimes.

International indictments against the RPF have continued to roll out, and subsequent to the Bruguière Report, the Spanish judge Fernando Abreu Merelles issued indictments against forty top Rwandan military officers for genocide, crimes against humanity, and terrorism committed in 1994 in Rwanda and during Rwanda's military interventions in Zaire, and then, after the country's name changed in 1997, in the Democratic Republic of the Congo.[68] In a more recent development, the UN Office of the High Commissioner for Human Rights released a 550-page report titled *Democratic Republic of the Congo, 1993–2003* documenting "systematic, methodological and premeditated" attacks committed by the Rwandan army on civilians. The victims were predominantly women, children, the elderly and infirm who posed no military threat. The 2010 report concluded that "the apparent systematic and widespread attacks described in this report reveal a number of inculpatory elements that, if proven before a competent court, could be characterized as crimes of genocide (§31)."

---

[66] "Amnesty International . . . believes that the legal system in Rwanda is unable now to ensure that the right to a fair trial will be fully respected [and] urges the Security Council to instruct the ICTR not to transfer any cases to Rwanda until the problems with the national legal system are resolved." Amnesty International, "Appeal to the UN Security Council to ensure that the mandate of the International Criminal Tribunal for the Rwanda is fulfilled" 12 December 2006. [IOR 40/045/2006] http://www.amnesty.org/es/library/asset/IOR40/045/2006/es/3da30076-d3ca-11dd-8743-d305bea2b2c7/ior400452006en.html.

[67] Human Rights Watch, "Rwanda. Tribunal Risks Supporting 'Victor's Justice'" 1 June 2009. http://www.hrw.org/en/news/2009/06/01/rwanda-tribunal-risks-supporting-victor-s-justice?print.

[68] "Brussels Can Effect Arrest Warrants against RPF Suspects," Hirondelle News Agency, 18 July 2008, http://www.publicinternationallaw.org/warcrimeswatch/archives/wcpw_vol03issue24.html.

Despite the avalanche of compelling evidence of RPF mass crimes inside and outside Rwanda, at the ICTR in Arusha, the government in Kigali has managed to hold justice hostage and maintain impunity by derailing all attempts on the part of the Tribunal to achieve a semblance of even-handedness. Unless this changes, we can conclude only that the historical record produced by the ICTR is a partial one, as it has rendered an account of the crimes of just one side in the conflict, the losers.

2.5. THE POLITICS OF HISTORY IN INTERNATIONAL TRIBUNALS

National and international courts are both influenced by nation-states, and this can have an effect on their historical inquiries into the underlying causes of a conflict. The pressures these two types of courts face can be comparable or distinctive. National courts may be more prone to pressures resulting from the state's internal conflicts of interest and the tendency of national politicians and local media outlets to engage in historical mythmaking. International tribunals are not in the same position with regard to the nation-state, and this allows for a measure of autonomy but also makes international courts vulnerable to state interference, albeit through more external and diplomatic channels.

All international tribunals are not equally predisposed in this regard, however, and the ICTY and ICTR have had dissimilar experiences of state obstructionism and noncooperation. At the ICTY, the judges' decisions regarding the minutes of meetings of the SDC have been questioned by former insiders on the grounds that the Trial Chamber's decision not to publicly disclose the SDC documents was based on legally erroneous reasoning. In retrospect, the Appeals Chamber might have followed up its discovery of the legal error with a reversal of the earlier Trial Chamber position. This is what the Appeals Chamber was set up to do, and indeed it overturns incorrect Trial Chamber decisions and judgments on a regular basis.

While there is cause for concern, the main impact of the nondisclosure of the SDC minutes was not on the ICTY but on the ICJ in its ruling in *Serbia v. Bosnia*.[69] The responsibility for SDC minutes' not being reviewed in the Bosnia genocide case lies more with ICJ judges, who were apparently too timid to issue a formal request for disclosure of information from Serbia. The incident did not affect cases at the ICTY, nor did it affect the main trial in which SDC minutes were germane, namely the trial of Slobodan Milošević.

[69] Acknowledging that a genocide ruling at the ICJ may have increased the likelihood of successful subsequent prosecutions for genocide at the ICTY.

The ICTY judges had full access to the documents, and they formed a key part of their ruling on 16 June 2004 that a Trial Chamber "could be satisfied beyond a reasonable doubt that the accused was a participant in a joint criminal enterprise (that had) the aim and intention to destroy a part of Bosnian Muslims as a group."[70]

Events at the ICJ, however, did not prevent the ICTY from examining, in Slobodan Milošević's and subsequent cases, the trajectory of the war in Bosnia and the role of the government in Belgrade in arming, supporting, and directing the Bosnian Serb Army, nor from examining the factors underlying the conflict in the former Yugoslavia. State pressure on the ICTY has not, to my knowledge, prevented the ICTY from prosecuting all sides in the conflict or thwarted its capacity to, recalling David Tolbert's (2009:284) words, "undermine the national myths that have developed regarding the underlying conflict." The ICTY, as we will see in more detail, has challenged extremist nationalist myths in the Balkans, even as states have strived to restrict access to key information.

The most prevalent national myth, found on all sides of the armed conflicts dealt with in this book, was most clearly stated by historian and republic of Croatia's first president Franjo Tuđman, while on his deathbed: "Croatian men, who were liberating the country from evil, cannot be held accountable."[71] What has become clear from the weight of ICTY cases is a different picture entirely, one that contests an image of noble wars fought by heroes against a historical oppression so evil that their valiant acts cannot be subjected to the rule of law. Instead, trials in The Hague have shown that all sides committed terrible atrocities against innocent civilians, and they have documented the destruction of villages with no military significance and the slaying of noncombatants, including women, children, the aged, and the disabled, who were executed out of sheer prejudice and group hatred. Moreover, international trials have shown how radical nationalist politicians manipulated the past to construct an extremist vision of national destiny that led to a violent confrontation and, in some cases, economic and political ruin.

The same cannot be said of the ICTR, where the Rwandan government has so far succeeded in preventing any prosecutions of its own soldiers through intimidating tactics and a sustained diplomatic offensive at the United Nations, ultimately leading to the replacement of the only chief prosecutor determined to conduct investigations against them. The Kagame regime has thereby

---

[70] ICTY Trial Chamber, "Decision on Motion for Judgement of Acquittal," 16 June 2004; *Prosecutor v. Slobodan Milošević*, Case No. IT-02–54-T, §288.

[71] Quoted in Del Ponte (2008:246).

prevented the Tribunal from contesting a hegemonic historical mythology that represents the RPF as noble liberators who led the way to an ethnic reconciliation without reprisals. Meanwhile, the Rwandan government pursues its authoritarian agenda unchecked, ruthlessly crushing press freedom, freedom of association, and any meaningful discussion of ethnicity and the long-standing ethnic hierarchy in the country. It has censored all assessments of the economic and political oppression of Hutus that Hutu Power extremists were able to seize on and turn to their political advantage. The RPF version of history has been embraced in a credulous fashion by the international media, and even by seasoned commentators such as Philip Gourevitch of *New Yorker* magazine.[72] One of the few media outlets to confront the rosy picture of Rwandan reconciliation is the *Economist*, which wrote in 2009, "Throughout this region the basis of exclusion is the division between Hutu and Tutsi. . . . The current pseudo-democratic regime in Rwanda does not represent a substantial break with the past in this. Backed by Britain and America, President Paul Kagame manipulates the Hutu-Tutsi divide more subtly than his predecessors, but just as fatally."[73]

Although the ICTR has been cowed by the Rwandan government, it could have been otherwise, and we ought to be careful not to extrapolate from one regrettable case. A more autonomous tribunal might have been possible had Chief Prosecutor Del Ponte been as accomplished a diplomat as she was a courtroom prosecutor, and if the United Nations and powerful states such as Britain and the United States had compelled the Rwandan government to accept a fair and balanced tribunal that investigated the ruling party's crimes as well. That is a lot of ifs, but the fate of the Tribunal was not predetermined. All courts, be they national or international, are at risk of malign interference from national governments, although as we have seen, not in the same ways. The closer their proximity to states that lack established rule of law and strong and independent civil society movements, the more likely it is that politics will encroach on law. Even where such a democratic political and legal history exists, inappropriate political influence may still occur, as we saw in the Holocaust trials in France. The perennial tension between justice and political expediency is ultimately irresolvable, but it is still worth trying to fathom its (often hidden) undercurrents in national and international legal contexts.

[72] Philip Gourevitch, "The Life After," *New Yorker*, 4 May 2009, 37. This is one of the more uncritical pieces of reporting available on contemporary Rwanda.
[73] "Central Africa: Bloody History, Unhappy Future," *Economist*, 22 January 2009, http://media. economist.com/displaystory.cfm?story_id=12970793.

3

Contrasting Evidence: International and Common Law Approaches to Expert Testimony

The modern European law of evidence is fairly simple and rational: the law lets most everything in and trusts the judge to separate good evidence from bad. But American legal culture tends to distrust the judge; and . . . the system obviously trusts the jury even less that it trusts the judge. The rules of evidence grew up as some sort of countervailing force.

– Lawrence Friedman (2006:101), A History of American Law

3.1. A HISTORY OF HEARSAY

This chapter compares the rules of procedure and evidence of international criminal tribunals with those of Anglo-American courts, concentrating on the admissibility of historical evidence and expert witness testimony. In both national and international trials, experts called by the parties are the main conduit for historical evidence. The decision of judges to admit or exclude evidence in the courtroom goes to the heart of a legal system's understandings of probative value and fact, the building blocks of knowledge about an armed conflict. Although international courts are appreciably more lenient with respect to various types of evidence, including historical expert testimony, this varies according to the type of case and is most pronounced in trials of senior political leaders. Before addressing international criminal tribunals, however, it is worth reviewing conventional evidentiary practices in common law jurisdictions. A central defining feature of Anglo-American law is how it assiduously filters and evaluates evidence, and only by grasping this can one appreciate the sharp contrasts that exist with international criminal law.

A historical review of the role of experts in common law courts must start by acknowledging the ongoing struggle between judges and expert witnesses over at least the past three hundred years, with judges fiercely protecting their role as gatekeepers. One of the main ways they do this is through the hearsay rule, which prevents a court from accepting as true the testimony reported to a witness by a third party who is unavailable for cross examination by the court.[1] Historically, the hearsay rule has been one of the reasons most commonly invoked by common law courts to exclude expert witness testimony.[2] *Folkes v. Chadd* (1782) is widely considered the earliest precedent establishing the admissibility of expert evidence in English law. With the rising status of scientific knowledge during the Enlightenment, English courts heard more scientific or technical expert testimony, but with a distinct sense of unease and only within the boundaries delineated by judges. In nineteenth-century England, judges prevented experts from speaking about the "ultimate issue" in question in a case and issued dire warnings of the consequences that would follow if trial by jury were replaced with "trial by expert."[3]

The hearsay rule seems to have appeared in American courts in about 1820.[4] During the nineteenth century, U.S. courts applied a relatively accommodating martketplace test, whereby if consumers deemed expertise of value, then it was presumed reliable enough for the courts.[5] Yet this test did not proscribe those types of expertise such as palm reading, crystal-ball gazing, and water divination using a forked stick, which enjoy a fee-paying clientele and could therefore pass the marketplace test but that might not provide the soundest foundations for determining criminal guilt or innocence. In the twentieth century, the court's decision in *Frye v. United States* (1923) set the precedent for U.S. judges in their treatment of expert testimony. Although not always applied systematically, the *Frye* test substituted the intellectual marketplace for the commercial one, such that expert evidence became admissible only when it was based on the techniques that the scientific community conventionally perceived as valid at the time. As well as the general acceptance of an expert's theories and methods, *Frye* interrogated the credentials and the professional standing of experts brought before courts. *Frye* adopted a relativist stance on expert knowledge, evaluating historians and forensic scientists on their own terms rather than imposing the standards and conventions of one on the other.

---

[1] Rule 801 of the U.S. Federal Rules of Evidence defines hearsay as "a statement, other than one made by the declarant while testifying at the trial or hearing, offered in evidence to prove the truth of the matter asserted." Rules 803 and 804 provide twenty-eight exceptions to the hearsay rule, many for situations in which the declarant is unavailable to testify. For a fuller discussion of the hearsay rule, see Anderson et al. (2005:139, 305–10).

[2] Courts also employ a number of other criteria of admissibility, including the relevance of the evidence to the issue at hand and the reliability of the individual expert proffering evidence.

[3] Good (2008:48).

[4] Friedman (2006:102).

[5] Saks and Faigman (2005:106–7). This review essay serves as the basis for the subsequent discussion of *Frye* and *Daubert*.

Frye refused to create a hierarchy between forms of knowledge and instead adopted the techniques of each particular field; "Thus, rigorous scientific fields are judged using strict admissibility standards (because that is how they judge themselves), whereas fields lacking a rigorous tradition are judged using lax admissibility standards" (Saks and Faigman 2005:107). Problems frequently noted with *Frye* include the vagueness of the threshold of general acceptance in a scholarly community and the customary delay between the appearance of a fresh innovation and its general acceptance.

In U.S. courts, *Frye* has now been superseded by what some have called a "gatekeeping revolution" in judges' handling of expert evidence.[6] This began with the promulgation of new Federal Rules of Evidence in the 1970s. Rule 704 of the Federal Rules of Evidence allows experts to express "opinions and inferences" regarding the "ultimate issue" in a case, but they are precluded from testifying on the link between a defendant's "mental state" (*mens rea*) and the crime of which he or she is accused. The revolution culminated, however, in three Supreme Court cases, beginning with *Daubert v. Merrell Dow Pharmaceuticals* (1993). Collectively referred to as *Daubert*, these judgments imposed new and more rigorous tests of admissibility and shifted the onus onto judges to evaluate the expert evidence on the basis of the soundness of its methods and principles. *Daubert* reformulated "general acceptance" to denote modern scholarly standards of publication and peer review, and judges were instructed to consider the robustness of the research design based on indicators such as the error rate of a scientific technique. *Daubert*'s philosophical foundations were made explicit in Justice Blackmun's reliance on philosopher Karl Popper's theory of knowledge: "The criterion of the scientific status of a theory is its falsifiability, or refutability, or testability."[7] In contrast to *Frye*, scientific criteria of testability and falsifiability apply to all forms of expert testimony, not just to the scientific kind, thus creating a disciplinary hierarchy with science at its summit.[8]

The U.S. Supreme Court's endorsement of scientific realism sparked much debate among scholarly and legal commentators. Some reacted positively to the Court's unambiguous criteria for evaluation, and how it places the locus of decision making where it belongs, with judges.[9] Others are less ebullient, including Anthony Good, a British legal anthropologist with extensive experience as an expert witness in U.K. asylum courts. In the shift from *Frye* to *Daubert*, Good (2008:48–9) identifies a more general shift from

---

[6] Ibid.:108.
[7] *Daubert*, at 2.c., p. 11.
[8] A point later upheld by the U.S. Supreme Court in *Kumho Tire Co. v. Carmichael* (1999).
[9] Saks and Faigman (2005:109).

experience and tacit learning to a fixation with methodology and quantitative results. He doubts that any of the humanities disciplines (e.g., history) and few of the "soft" social sciences (e.g., social anthropology) can meet Judge Blackmun's falsifiability threshold. Overall, he counsels against what he sees as Anglo-American law's increasing concern with technique rather than with content of expert evidence and its "simplistic" notions of scientific objectivity and empiricism (Good 2008:48).

In terms of formal case law, there has indeed been a revolution in the rules of admissibility of expert testimony, but as legal realism taught us long ago, in daily practice, the consequences can be varied and unexpected. Legal scholars remain divided over whether *Daubert* signals a more or less permissive attitude toward expert evidence and whether this attitude varies depending on the type of court (whether civil or criminal) and the type of evidence (e.g., hard science versus more interpretative or experiential forms of knowledge). In terms of sheer numbers, it appears that more and more experts are being called by defense attorneys and prosecutors than ever before. Anderson et al. (2005:270) note an increasing reliance of U.S. courts on expert evidence directed toward the ultimate issue in a case, citing estimates that, by 1990, more than 70 percent of civil trials in the United States involved expert evidence.

As the trajectory of courtroom expert testimony has spiraled ever upward, so has the number of challenges and the incidences of exclusion. Saks and Faigman (2005: 120–2) refer to a substantial body of research indicating a dramatic upsurge in post-*Daubert* challenges to expert evidence. These challenges are not evenly distributed between civil and criminal courts. Ninety percent of objections are raised by defendants in civil trials and 70 percent of those are successful, an increase from the pre-*Daubert* figure of 50 percent. In criminal trials, in contrast, the success rate of defendant challenges to government evidence drops precipitously to 10 percent. Expert evidence introduced by defense counsel in criminal trials was excluded two-thirds of the time. These figures led Saks and Faigman (2005:122) to conclude that *Daubert* is less a "directive to conduct meaningful and sincere analyses of the substance of proffered expert advice, using rational criteria" and more "a vague call to arms against junk science in civil cases while keeping hands off the government's proffers in criminal cases."

The evidentiary chasm between civil and criminal courts goes beyond *Daubert* and is pervasive in Anglo-American law generally. Good (2008:55; 2007) draws attention to how the role of expert witnesses varies in different branches of law in the United Kingdom and closely correlates with the presence or absence of a jury. His research finds that U.K. civil courts are more willing to receive evidence from an anthropologist about context and culture than are criminal courts, which apply more restrictive rules of admissibility. This is relevant for our comparison of international and national criminal trials insofar as, as we have seen earlier, international criminal tribunals do not include juries, and pleadings take place before a panel of judges.

Digging deeper into judges' justifications for excluding expert evidence post-*Daubert*, one again encounters some surprises. *Daubert* factors such as error rate or testability of hypothesis do not feature prominently in judicial decision making. Many courts and entire U.S. states are still using the *Frye* test or vaguely articulated criteria regarding the qualifications of the expert and his or her testimony, which are conventional measures relatively unchanged from the pre-*Daubert* era. The most salient criterion used by U.S. judges to evaluate expert testimony remains the general acceptance test.[10] Judicial disregard for *Daubert* criteria can be explained in part by studies showing that U.S. judges are not particularly scientifically literate, or at least no more literate than the population at large.[11] As a result, many do not apply the principles laid down in *Daubert*, because they do not sufficiently comprehend scientific theory or method. In a survey of four hundred state court judges, Gatowski et al. (2001:447) found that only 4 percent of respondents could define an error rate. A mere 5 percent of respondents had a basic understanding of the scientific idea of falsifiability (444). This lack of knowledge is not confined to state court judges. To his credit, Supreme Court Chief Justice Rehnquist confessed his own imperfect grasp of falsifiability in his concurring opinion in *Daubert*. Even though post-*Daubert* judges have been awarded enhanced powers to manage expert evidence, research suggests that they are for the most part ill equipped to identify flawed research designs in social science evidence.[12]

This foray into the changing procedures and evidentiary rules helps us to comprehend why common law courts often struggle to address the history of mass crimes. In his discussion of the two trials of Ernst Zündel, Lawrence Douglas (2001) documents how Canadian court procedures and evidentiary rules impeded a thoroughgoing historical reckoning with the Holocaust. Zündel was indicted in the 1980s under Section 177 of the Canadian criminal code, which treats as an offense the willful publication of news that

---

[10] Gatowski et al. (2001:447–8).

[11] Cornelia Dean, "Scientific Savvy? In U.S., Not Much," *New York Times*, 30 August 2005, http://www.nytimes.com/2005/08/30/science/30profile.html?_r=1/.

[12] Kovera and McAuliffe (2000:584). This study also showed that judges held the discipline of psychology in fairly low regard. Evidence from psychological studies was excluded on the basis of a negative perception of psychology as a discipline rather than the specifics of the research design itself. My conjecture is that judges' disapproval of psychology is likely to extend to social science more widely.

an individual knows to be false and that "causes or is likely to cause injury or mischief to a public interest." Zündel, whom Douglas (2001:213) describes as an "an ardent neo-Nazi," founded and oversaw a publishing company dedicated to publications that denied the Holocaust. In the first Zündel trial, the presiding judge refused to take judicial notice of the Holocaust, thus diverting the trial unnecessarily into an inquiry into the truthfulness of established accounts of the Holocaust. Zündel's defense attorney Douglas Christie used the hearsay rule to object to, *inter alia*, survivor testimony; expert witness evidence from the historian Dr. Raul Hilberg; and the screening of the film *Nazi Concentration Camps*, made by the U.S. Signal Corps in 1945. Moreover, the hearsay concept became the "controlling trope" of Zündel's defense, according to Douglas (226). Historical studies were eventually admitted by the court, but only as hearsay exceptions, thus validating the indiscriminate attack on historical methodology conducted by the defense. The appellate court ruled that the film *Nazi Concentration Camps* ought to have been barred under the hearsay rule, as the film's narrator was not known and Zündel's conviction was overturned. In the second trial, Zündel was convicted again under Section 177, but the prosecution refrained from screening documentary footage of concentration camps and Hilberg did not return to testify.

In common law, it often seems that the best that historical and social science research can aspire to is to be considered admissible hearsay by a court, which is an exception to the usual rigorous courtroom standards. This does not always imply that admissible hearsay is inherently weak or of low probative value. Certain documents may be considered hearsay evidence; if corroborated, then they may be perceived as reliable and indicative and contribute to a cumulative effect. Nonetheless, in the trials analyzed by Douglas, historical expert witness testimony was generally considered secondary evidence of a relatively weak kind. Common law's evidentiary rules and standards developed to bolster the legitimacy of the courts may defeat a central purpose of certain trials, namely the integrity of the historical record of mass crimes. As Douglas concludes at the end of his account of the Zündel trials, law's jealous safeguarding of its own concepts of fact and evidence means that "criminal law often fails to do justice to the history it has been enlisted to protect" (255). The question then becomes, Do international criminal trials adopt different standards of evidence than standard criminal trials in common law courts, and if so, with what consequences? As we will see, historians and social scientists and other expert witnesses occupy a markedly different position in the international courtroom, one that potentially allows them more opportunity to influence the outcome of a case. This does not mean, however, that their evidence goes unchallenged or is simply taken at face value. Nor does it signify, perhaps more importantly, that expert witness evidence is necessarily granted a higher probative value than in the domestic courtroom.

3.2. THE FRAMEWORK FOR EXPERT EVIDENCE IN INTERNATIONAL CRIMINAL LAW

The Tribunal shall not be bound by technical rules of evidence.

– Article 19, Charter of the International Military Tribunal ("Nuremberg Charter," 1945)

When the International Criminal Tribunal for the Former Yugoslavia was first established in 1993, it possessed no rules of procedure or evidence. Into this vacuum stepped the U.S. State Department, which provided a draft set of rules of procedure, computers, trained personnel, and further logistical support. The Tribunal thus began with a set of rules of criminal procedure from the New York State Bar that set out a classically adversarial process and evidentiary regime. Although useful in furnishing a baseline, the ICTY's first Rules of Procedure and Evidence (RPE) quickly proved inappropriate to the task of trying violations of international humanitarian law and Tribunal judges set about amending them to suit their needs. The International Criminal Tribunal for Rwanda established a year later, in 1994, initially adopted the ICTY's Rules of Procedure and Evidence, and although the ICTR set up its own chambers committee to consider amendments to the RPE, it has largely taken its lead from the ICTY.

Expert witness testimony at the ICTY and ICTR is governed by Rule 94 *bis*, which authorizes either party to tender an expert statement after which the other party has thirty days to indicate whether it accepts the expert witness statement and wishes to cross-examine the witness and whether it challenges the qualifications of the witness and the relevance of his or her report, in whole or in part.[13] Behind the explicit terms of this rule lies a complex and evolving set of deliberations regarding admissibility of evidence in international criminal trials. As noted previously, the two *ad hoc* international criminal tribunals and the International Criminal Court are hybrid systems that combine elements of the adversarial process and the civil law tradition. Although the operating structure of international criminal trials is adversarial in that the prosecution case is the engine of the trial, nowhere are the courts more like the civil law system than in their approach to admissibility of evidence. Civil law courts place few constraints on evidence introduced in the courtroom and, crucially,

---

[13] Rule 94 *bis* of the ICTR RPE and ICTY RPE, adopted 10 July 1998.

do not automatically require thorough cross-examination of the author of a document or film tendered by prosecutors or defense counsel. As a result, the approach to evidence at the ICTY, ICTR, and ICC has been described as "flexible, liberal and unhindered by technical rules found in national and particularly common law systems."[14]

There is precedent in international humanitarian law for the lenient rules of evidence adopted by the ICTY and ICTR, and we can say that an inclusive (or less generously, a laissez-faire) approach to evidence has been an ingrained trait of international criminal law generally. Article 19 of the Charter of the International Military Tribunal (1945) allowed the Nuremberg tribunal to "apply to the greatest possible extent expeditious and non-technical procedure, and shall admit any evidence which it deems to be of probative value." Analogous wording appears in Rule 89(C) of the ICTR and ICTY: "A Chamber may admit any relevant evidence which it deems to have probative value," with the main grounds for exclusion being "if its probative value is substantially outweighed by the need to ensure a fair trial [Rule 89(D)]." Extensive case law now upholds international rules of evidence, such as the ICTY's 1998 trial decision in *Blaškić*, which held that, "barring exceptions, all relevant evidence is admissible, including hearsay evidence."[15]

In stark contrast to accepted common law conventions, international criminal courts operate without an explicit hearsay rule.[16] There is no concern that a jury might be misled, because there is no jury, and as in civil law courts, it is assumed that judges are competent to distinguish between reliable and unreliable evidence.[17] In *Tadić*, the ICTY Trial Chamber rejected a motion filed by defense counsel seeking to exclude hearsay evidence as a general rule, affirming that the judges were able, "by virtue of their training and experience, to hear evidence in the context in which it has been obtained and accord it appropriate weight. Thereafter, they may make a determination as to the relevancy and the probative value of the evidence," based on the

---

[14] Cryer et al. (2007:383).
[15] *Prosecutor v. Blaškić*, Decision on the Standing Objection of the Defense to the Admission of Hearsay with No Inquiry as to Its Reliability, IT-95-14-T, 21 January 1998, §§10–12. More recent case law upholding Rule 89(C) can be found in the Trial Chamber judgments in *Halilović* (§14) and *Blagojević and Jokić* (§20).
[16] The ICTY has defined hearsay evidence as "evidence of facts not within the testifying witness' own knowledge" (*Halilović* Trial Judgment §15). This is rather different from the standard common law definition cited earlier.
[17] In light of the studies cited earlier, we might be wary of this assumption. In the absence of evidence to the contrary, there is no reason to believe that international judges are any more competent than U.S. judges to differentiate a sound research design from a flawed one.

"context and character of the evidence in question."[18] The Tribunal would be guided in admitting hearsay evidence "by the truthfulness, voluntariness and trustworthiness of the evidence."[19]

Over time, the two *ad hoc* international criminal trials became more and more flexible in their rules and procedures regarding expert evidence. As noted in the previous section, the tribunals were created at a time when ever greater numbers of expert witnesses appeared in Anglo-American courts, and their own development has paralleled the wider trends. However, the primary motivation for change at the international tribunals was not evolving procedure in national courts; instead, it was the acute pressure applied on the tribunals from the UN Security Council to conduct shorter trials.[20] As noted in the previous chapter, some members of the UN Security Council, such as Russia, were inherently hostile to the tribunals, and even dependable supporters such as Britain and the United States reacted with alarm to the burgeoning financial costs of international justice. The ICTY alone consumed more than $64 million of the UN budget in 1998, and that jumped to $94 million in 1999.[21] Seeking to alleviate concerns, the UN secretary-general commissioned a group of international legal experts to review the operational efficiency of the two *ad hoc* tribunals and to make recommendations to reduce the length of trials.[22]

Meanwhile, at the ICTY, the pressure came to a head in 1998, when the Tribunal was swamped with an influx of indictees. With only three functioning Trial Chambers and approximately twenty-five indictees awaiting trial in the detention unit, it looked as if it would take upward of eight years to bring some of the accused to trial. Daryl Mundis, a legal officer then working for the Tribunal's president, Gabrielle Kirk McDonald, recalled her saying to him, "We have a problem, Daryl."[23] In subsequent discussions, Judge McDonald concluded that it was simply not possible to address the backlog of cases at

---

[18] *Prosecutor v. Tadić*, Decision on the Defense Motion on Hearsay, IT-94–1-T, 5 August 1996, cited in *Blaškić*, Decision on the Standing Objection of the Defense, §28. Neither the *Tadić* nor the *Blaškić* decision on the admissibility of hearsay evidence has been the subject of appeal.

[19] *Tadić* Trial Chamber, Decision on Defense Motion on Hearsay, §16.

[20] ICTY Judge Patricia Wald (2001:549) noted at the time that the "new Rules sharply respond to the problem of lagging trials."

[21] In 2008–9, the total budget for the ICTY was $342 million and the ICTR budget was $267 million. Official tribunal figures in 2010 are available at http://www.icty.org and http://www.ictr.org.

[22] Report of the Expert Group to Conduct a Review of the Effective Operation and Functioning of the International Criminal Tribunal for the Former Yugoslavia and the International Criminal Tribunal for Rwanda, U.N. Doc. A/54/634 (1999).

[23] Author interview, May 2006. For an assessment of the shift from common law to civil law practices, see Mundis (2001).

the Tribunal with the infrastructure and procedures in place at the time. The common law system conventionally requires a procession of witnesses to establish the authenticity, reliability, and probative value of each item of evidence. An arduous process at the best of times, testing the evidence was made even slower by the need for simultaneous courtroom translation and the translation of documents. Judges, ever keen to keep cases moving along expeditiously, were aware that a more civil law–oriented model would serve their purpose better because it would cede more authority to judges to manage their cases.

A number of amendments to the Rules of Procedure and Evidence beginning in 1998 (at the time of writing, forty-four revisions and counting) signaled a shift away from the common law adversarial model toward the civil law system and increased judicial control over case management – what Máximo Langer (2005:835) describes as the rise of a "managerial judging model." In early trials of the ICTR and ICTY, all expert evidence was led in the courtroom, and some expert witnesses did not even produce written reports but simply appeared for cross-examination. With continual revisions to the Rules of Procedure and Evidence, fewer and fewer of the accepted adversarial conventions of courtroom procedure were retained.

One such revision was the adoption of Rule 92 *bis*, on 1 December 2000, which permitted the submission of written statements in place of oral testimony.[24] Evidence could be admitted into a case without being led in the Trial Chamber and in the absence of cross-examination, although either adversarial party could object, request cross-examination, or seek to prove the evidence unreliable or prejudicial (92 *bis*, A.ii.b–c). Rule 92 *bis* lists six factors in favor of admitting evidence, two of which are relevant to submissions of expert witness reports, namely that which "relates to the relevant historical, political or military background" or "consists of a general or statistical analysis of the ethnic composition of the population in the places to which the indictment relates" (A.i.b–c). Judges may call witnesses and request further documentation regarding the credibility of evidence, although this occurs infrequently. The advent of Rule 92 *bis* gave prosecutors and defense attorneys significantly more latitude to submit voluminous quantities of expert witness evidence, especially in the form of scholarly reports, books, and articles, as well as nongovernmental organization reports, films, and videos. While the intent behind Rule 92 *bis* was to cut down on the number of witnesses taking up valuable courtroom time and resources, the documentary basis of cases

---

[24] Rule 92 *bis* of the ICTY RPE and ICTR RPE. For an extensive critical commentary on Rule 92 *bis*, see Langer (2005).

swelled to barely manageable proportions. At the outermost end of the continuum, in the *Kordić and Čerkez* case the prosecution tendered 2,721 exhibits, and the defense submitted 1,643 exhibits.[25]

3.3. THE ADVENT OF THE MANAGERIAL JUDGING MODEL

The managerial judging model gathered momentum at the ICTY when Judge Claude Jorda of France became the Tribunal's third president in November 1999, replacing Judge McDonald of the United States. Judge Jorda, who also sat on the Appeals Chamber of the ICTR, described his mind-set on assuming the leadership position:

> I came in with a program, a plan. I said the Tribunal is not doing very well. The trials are too long and we are not being exemplary in our work. We have a historic responsibility that concerns the whole of civilization. The common law system is not working very well and the Tribunal has to prepare the trials better. If we keep these methods, we won't make any progress. . . . [W]e need a more inquisitorial role for judges and more of a trial dossier approach to discipline the parties. It's still the OTP [Office of the Prosecutor] that prosecutes but a trial and appeal should not last more than 18 months."[26]

New civil law modifications and case management practices were additionally endorsed by Swiss prosecutor Carla Del Ponte, who took up the post of chief prosecutor of the ICTY and ICTR in 1999. Del Ponte, according to ICTY Senior Trial Attorney Mundis (2001:379), was a "strong proponent" of the civil law dossier approach, by which trial attorneys present entire evidentiary packages, including both incriminating and exculpatory evidence, in advance of a trial. In this environment, judges came to adopt a more bullish attitude toward the hearsay rule in the trial chambers of the ICTY and ICTR. In the 2000 *Blaškić* trial judgment, the ICTY Trial Chamber (§28) went a step further than admitting hearsay exceptions to maintain that "it is well settled in the practice and jurisprudence of this Tribunal that hearsay evidence is admissible." Also in 2000, the Rwanda Tribunal Trial Chamber ruled that hearsay evidence may be admissible even when it is not corroborated by direct evidence.[27]

During his tenure from 1999 to 2003, President Jorda promoted a civil law–style framework that permitted judges to actively supervise their cases in the

---

[25] Kordić and Čerkez (IT-95–14/2), Case Information Sheet, http://www.icty.org/x/cases/kordic_cerkez/cis/en/cis_kordic_cerkez_en.pdf.
[26] Author interview, May 2006.
[27] ICTR *Musema* Trial Chamber §43. Upheld in the Appeals Chamber §§36–8.

pretrial and trial phases.[28] In this period, ICTY senior legal officer Gideon Boas (2001:168) wrote that the "principle of expedition" became the "fundamental principle behind the rules and practice governing admissibility of evidence." New rules governing case management introduced by President McDonald in mid-1998 were aggressively implemented, thus shifting the axis of authority to run the proceedings from prosecutors to judges. For instance, Rule 65 *ter* (N), governing pretrial matters, requires prosecutors to file a witness list, a document list, and a list of contested matters and admissions and permits "the exclusion of testimonial or documentary evidence." Rules 73 *bis* and 73 *ter* allow judges to decide which witnesses to call and to limit the scope of their testimony. Rules 90(F) and 90(G) give judges control over the order and manner of witness cross-examination and the presentation of evidence to "avoid needless consumption of time." Trial Chamber decisions reinforced the general shift toward shorter prosecution cases, for instance, when the ruling in *Kordić* in October 2000 prohibited the prosecution from leading evidence on "peripheral and background issues" in its rebuttal of the defense case.[29]

Responding to sustained pressure from the UN Security Council to expedite trials, President Jorda unveiled his "completion strategy" for the ICTY on 10 June 2002, and the ICTR followed with its completion strategy on 14 July 2003.[30] Both were heartily endorsed by UN Security Council Resolutions 1503 (2003) and 1534 (2004).[31] The completion strategies called for the wrapping up of all investigations at the ICTY and ICTR by 31 December 2004, the end of all trials by the end of 2008, and the conclusion of all appeals by 2010. Only the first date was met, and as the other dates were pushed back, the tribunals' completion strategies came to dominate all aspects of their work. In daily practice, judges cited the completion strategy to justify paring down cases to what they deemed absolutely necessary. For example, at the ICTY they regularly ordered prosecutors to drop a specific number of indictments

---

[28] International criminal law became more like the French inquisitorial system just at the time that that system itself began to shift in a more adversarial direction. After the 2004 Outreau affair, the French judicial system was thrown into crisis, and there is now significant pressure to move toward a more accusatorial Anglo-American model of criminal law. The top French judge and advocate of judicial reform, Jean-François Burgelin, declared to *Le Figaro*, "The Napoleonic system has had its day" ("The French Judicial System: Exit Napoleon." *Economist*. 11 February 2006. p. 48).

[29] Mundis (2001:376).

[30] Report on the Judicial Status of the International Criminal Tribunal for the Former Yugoslavia and the Prospects for Referring Certain Cases to National Courts, UN Doc. S/2002/678 (2002). Completion Strategy of the International Criminal Tribunal for Rwanda. UN Doc. S/2003/946 (2003).

[31] For an analysis of the impact of the completion strategy for the ICTY, see Mundis (2005); Raab (2005:82–102).

or to cut their cases by a set figure, such as 25 percent or 30 percent.[32] When prosecutors protested the seemingly arbitrary numbers, judges ruled that any time spent addressing an objection would be subtracted from the time allotted to the party making the objection.[33]

The post-1998 evidentiary regime at the *ad hoc* tribunals allowed ever more scope to the parties to tender expert evidence on background and historical topics that would not be subjected to cross examination, unless the other side demanded it. Yet the principle of expedition driving the completion strategy worked in the opposite direction, conferring sweeping powers to judges to restrict the number of expert witnesses and to limit the scope of their testimony and cross-examination. In practice, what happened in any given trial depended in part on the nature of the case and the inclination of the particular judges on the bench. Overall, however, after 2004, prosecutors at the ICTY called background expert witnesses on a less frequent basis than before and in a more targeted fashion, in favor of a conventional crime-based approach. In the pretrial phase, the judges became accustomed to intervening to reduce the scope of prosecution and defense cases and to limit expert witness testimony and historical inquiry. In my reading of the trial transcripts, defense cases were usually handled with a lighter touch, even in the era of judicial management and completion strategies. The ICTY's defense counsel, for reasons that will become apparent in Chapter 6, became ever more reliant on expert witnesses, especially in cases involving senior military and political leaders. At the ICTR, the changes were less pronounced. The Office of the Prosecutor – having had more success in prosecuting genocide cases; having gained general acceptance for its account of Rwandan history; and having a historical expert witness, Alison Des Forges, who had the confidence of the judges – continued to rely to a great extent on historical expert testimony.

3.4. DISPUTING THE TREATMENT OF EVIDENCE IN INTERNATIONAL TRIBUNALS

At this point, it is worth pausing to gauge the opinions of various legal actors at the international criminal tribunals regarding their rules of procedure and evidence. The survey conducted for this book revealed a clear consensus between

---

[32] In an ICTY trial decision of 21 November 2006, judges gave the prosecution until 4 December 2006 to come up with a plan for reducing the scope of the indictment against Momčilo Perisić, former chief of general staff of the VJ (Yugoslav Army), by "at least a third." On 13 November 2006, the Trial Chamber slashed the time previously allotted to the prosecution in the Prlić case by more than a quarter to meet the timetable decreed by the Security Council.

[33] See *Prlić* Trial Chamber, Decision on Adoption of New Measures to Bring the Trial to an End within a Reasonable Time, 13 November 2006, §§18–22.

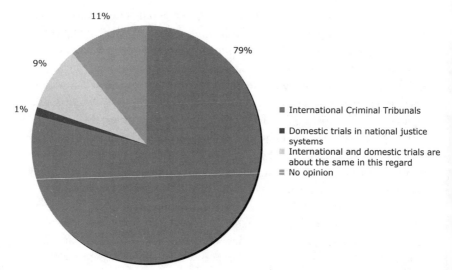

FIGURE 3.1. Which type of criminal trial is more likely to include historical evidence?

defense and prosecution attorneys on certain questions regarding evidence, and historical evidence in particular, in international criminal trials. At the most general level, by a wide margin, respondents perceived international trials as more likely to include historical evidence than national courts.

The flexible approach to evidence developed at the two *ad hoc* tribunals has been justified by international law experts on grounds of "the complex factual situations, large amounts of evidence and difficulties in obtaining it."[34] The same reasons have been given in the international courtroom itself: when the *amicus curiae* in the Slobodan Milošević trial objected to the eight-hundred-page report submitted by the prosecution, Judge Richard May replied, "It's the scale and complexity of these trials which require that one forms new forms of thinking in the ways of conducting trials away from the old common law oral model but, of course, ensuring that fairness is maintained."[35]

References to the scale and complexity of international criminal cases found favor with both prosecutors and defense lawyers in our survey. When asked to respond to the statement "When trials at the ICTY include historical evidence, they do so because the crimes were more complex than most conventional domestic crimes," a sizable majority (71 percent) of respondents agreed or strongly agreed, and only 18 percent of all respondents disagreed or strongly

[34] Cryer et al. (2007:383).
[35] Slobodan Milošević trial transcript, 26 May 2006, T21295–6.

disagreed.[36] Members of prosecution (65 percent) and defense teams (72 percent) agreed at about the same rate. Seventy-one percent of all respondents also agreed or strongly agreed with the statement "When trials at the ICTY include historical evidence, they do so because the crimes were more widespread and systematic than most conventional domestic crimes." Again, prosecutors and defense attorneys agreed or strongly agreed at more or less the same rate (65 percent and 72 percent, respectively).

Beneath these areas of agreement lies a sharp divergence of opinion between prosecutors and defense attorneys on other issues. Although some prosecutors chafed under the yoke of the managerial judging model, none of those interviewed for this book objected to the overall approach to admissibility of evidence of the ICTY or ICTR or claimed that the absence of a hearsay rule was unfounded or unfair. All represented the civil law modifications as beneficial. This included prosecutors from an Anglo-American trial background, such as Mark Harmon, the Senior Trial Attorney with the longest experience at the ICTY:

> The civil law elements of the ICTY are very positive. If I had to go through the common law process of leading evidence then I would have to lay the foundation for every single document that came before the court and establish its authenticity and call several witnesses per item . . . but here it's up to the judges to decide what weight they are going to give each item. . . . [W]e would be trying the Krajišnik case for ten years using strictly common law procedures, and the civil law system is fairer in many ways.[37]

The only reservation some prosecutors harbored was their uncertainty that judges read the voluminous amount of material they tendered and absorbed it in the way they expected. They worried whether an item of evidence would be held by judges as having probative force – a fact that becomes apparent only when the judgment is handed down, by which time it is too late for them to remedy the situation. As a result, their preferred strategy became repetition and reiteration, as explained by Ekkehard Withopf, former Senior Trial Attorney at the ICTY: "If evidence is tendered at the bar and it's not read out and discussed then there is a huge risk that it would not be valued as evidence by the courtroom. You don't know what they'll use, so you have to spell it out."[38] Given prosecutors' concerns, Rule 92 *bis* might not have reduced so appreciably the time spent by prosecutors in the courtroom presenting and reiterating written evidence submitted under the rule.

---

[36] Six percent were neutral, and 6 percent expressed no opinion.
[37] Author interview, May 2006.
[38] Author interview, June 2007.

The main opposition to the evidentiary regime at international criminal tribunals has undoubtedly come from the defense. Although defense attorneys generally embrace judicial case management in pretrial hearings, they find significant fault with ICTY and ICTR rules of evidence. All defense lawyers interviewed for this book raised questions regarding Rule 92 *bis*'s permitting the prosecution to submit written documents from expert witnesses when the witness is not examined and the credibility of sources is not sufficiently evaluated. Defense attorneys expressed concern that judges might accord written evidence not subject to challenge and cross-examination the same or greater weight as live testimony. They expressed profound concern that they might not be accorded the opportunity to cross-examine an author of a report or director of a film and that the hearsay evidence contained in a document or film might constitute grounds for finding their client guilty. Michael G. Karnavas, president of the Association of Defense Counsel at the ICTY, spoke for many, if not most, defense attorneys when he said:

> The ICTY is far too willing to admit irrelevant information and evidence from dubious sources. The judges allow everything and say 'We'll decide later' but as the Defense we don't know what they're going to give value to later, so we are concerned. They do not give us the full opportunity to test the evidence.[39]

Another ICTY defense counsel stated a similar position even more forcefully:

> When the Court decided to accept hearsay evidence and to basically ignore obvious perjury, the stage was set for a system that could not produce an accurate history of the events and likely not produce justice either. In my view this court is a failed experiment in international justice. It could have been so much better.[40]

The most trenchant disagreement came from lawyers from the U.S. and British legal tradition. For instance, when I asked Beth Lyons, defense counsel in a number of high-profile trials at the ICTR, whether she had objected to hearsay evidence brought by the prosecution, she replied:

> We protested all the time. Hearsay gets admitted – not only hearsay, but triple, quadruple hearsay. When you object, the judges rule: "It is admissible and we will decide the weight later." In our closing arguments, we have to reiterate our objections. Often, it appears that the prosecution witnesses are given a free rein when it comes to hearsay.[41]

[39] Author interview, June 2007.
[40] ICTY survey response, 2009.
[41] Author interview, July 2009.

The U.K. barrister Joanna Evans, part of the defense team of Ferdinand Nahimana at the ICTR, objected to the prosecutors' reliance on expert witness and background evidence in the trial (also known as the *Media Trial*):

> Most domestic criminal justice systems have developed organically over time and include safeguards which reflect the respective legal history and culture. In many instances, certain procedural measures are a direct result of the need to prevent the repeat of specific miscarriages of justice. By contrast, the international criminal process is a fusion of different legal systems and sometimes this mix has resulted in a situation where neither the safeguards of the civil or the common law system apply. In our trial, one of the most significant sources of evidence was a prosecution expert witness who repeated a large amount of information from other sources. For much of this information, original sources were not provided and there was no meaningful way for the defense to test its authenticity or context. In the common law system, there would have been the opportunity to exclude much of that evidence and I imagine that in the civil law system the investigating judge would have played a far more proactive role in examining its provenance and reliability. At the ICTR however, it could feel that you had fallen down the gap between the two systems, thereby losing any meaningful protection against a miscarriage of justice. On occasions it felt like trial by NGO [nongovernmental organization].[42]

Even if one accepts the viewpoint advanced by defense attorneys that the rules of admissibility at international tribunals are imperfect, it is not immediately apparent why this should disadvantage the defense more than the prosecution. After all, it could be argued that both have the right to call their own preferred experts and to tender reports, books, and whatever material they wish. As noted earlier, defense counsel have become as reliant as prosecutors on background expert witnesses, and perhaps more so at the ICTY. Both retain the privilege, which they exercise frequently, to object to expert witness testimony or Rule 92 *bis* written evidence on the grounds that it is irrelevant, unreliable, or based on untested hearsay. And there are times when the judges accept and uphold their objections and limit the testimony of an expert or demand that the cross-examination be redirected.

Why, then, do defense lawyers become so exercised by the evidentiary regime of international criminal law? In my estimation, defense attorneys resent being deprived of one of their most potent weapons in common law criminal cases, the hearsay rule. Yet defense objections also raise legitimate concerns regarding fairness and due process. Defense attorneys counter the argument that the evidentiary rules cut both ways by pointing out that

---

[42] Author interview, July 2006.

this neglects the special role of the defense in exercising quality control against what they perceive as the kitchen-sink approach of the prosecution. Diana Ellis, Queen's Counsel (QC), and defense counsel for Ferdinand Nahimana at the ICTR, explains why the lack of admissibility rules conventionally found in English courts tilts the proceedings in the prosecution's favor:

> Trials at the ICTR are adversarial. It is the role of the judges to determine issues of admissibility of evidence in accordance with the rules of the court. The applicability of the rules leads to the exclusion of evidence in certain circumstances. Where issues of admissibility arise they are determined before the evidence is given. Under an inquisitorial system no such rules exists and the judges, at the conclusion of the trial, weigh up the weight to be attached to a particular piece of evidence. It was our experience that, possibly due to the fact that not all the judges were familiar with a system in which rules govern the admissibility of evidence, the court refused to address the issues of admissibility during the trial process. This allowed the prosecutor to place before the court large amounts of material which should have been excluded. It denied the defense the opportunity of challenging the content or determining the provenance of much of the evidence.[43]

Judges' views are more varied than those of the opposed parties and largely divide along the fault line of civil law versus common law systems. Judges from inquisitorial civil law systems, such as former ICTY president Antonio Cassese, tend to defend the Tribunal's evidentiary rules robustly. In his book *International Criminal Law*, Cassese (2003:421–3) concedes nothing to defense objections to international rules of evidence and specific procedures and goes so far as to acerbically mock them at one point. Judges from common law countries, in contrast, have tended to be more circumspect and willing to openly express their misgivings. Judge Gabrielle Kirk McDonald (2000:570) who initiated the program of revisions to the ICTY's and ICTR's evidentiary rules in 1998 while president of the ICTY, acknowledged that the "admission of hearsay . . . violates the rights of the accused under internationally recognized standards." The widely respected ICTY Judge Patricia Wald (2004:473) sees the rules of evidence as "the most troublesome aspect of ICTY proceedings," elements of which threaten "to squander the ICTY's most precious asset – its reputation for fairness and truth seeking." A number of judges, including Wald (2001b:552), have expressed grave doubts about the admission of critical

43 Author interview, July 2006.

material without the ability to directly question the witness allowed under Rule 92 *bis*:

> Nuremberg and Tokyo left a clouded legacy as to whether, and how much, live witness testimony can be legitimately dispensed with in a criminal trial. The civil law is certainly more flexible on the point than our own. But how much is too much? As the ICTY moves further away from the Anglo-American model . . . ICTY judges . . . have still to preserve an overall aura of fairness in the proceedings. . . . A paper trail is one thing, a paper trial quite another.

Other judges from common law countries have been won over as a result of their experience of the international legal courtroom. Although the existing rules may not give a clear indication of outcomes, most international judges express a confidence in the fairness of established courtroom practice and judicial discretion. Navanethem Pillay, a South African who served as a judge at both the ICTR and the ICC, observed:

> In international law, hearsay is not inadmissible and the evidence does not have to be corroborated. This causes anxiety on the part of the Defense and they raise strong objections. However, if the prosecution's evidence is not corroborated, then we don't rely on it unless it is reliable. Because of the rules of evidence, for example allowing hearsay, a large body of evidence is allowed in, that's the only way to try crimes that are widespread and systematic. There is just no other way to try large-scale crimes.[44]

Judge Pillay's comments raise an important rejoinder to defense objections, insofar as they draw attention to the unusual size and complexity of the cases brought before international criminal tribunals, an issue touched on earlier in this book. We could add to this line of reasoning the point that hearsay exceptions are allowed on a daily basis in Anglo-American courts in certain types of cases. In U.S. courts, it is now standard practice to admit multiple hearsay witnesses in child sexual abuses cases, including teachers, social workers, health professionals, and others.[45] Courts have widely recognized that, in these special kinds of cases, the usual constraints do not apply, and courts must work with lower-than-normal expectations of testimonial evidence from victims. Racial and gender discrimination cases often consider evidence from experts on broader gender or racial inequality in employment or education. This practice was perhaps most famously employed in the U.S. Supreme Court

---

[44] Author interview, June 2007.
[45] See Marsil et al. (2002).

case *Brown v. Board of Education of Topeka* (1954, 1955). Thurgood Marshall, legal counsel for the National Association for the Advancement of Colored People, used psychological studies to prove that the segregationist doctrine of "separate but equal" meant that, in practice, African American children internalized a sense of inferiority, thus violating the Constitution's Fourteenth Amendment equal-protection clause.[46] More recently, it has generally been accepted that trials involving organized crime or complex financial schemes necessitate more flexible rules of evidence and procedure, and there has been much debate over the past ten years about the degree to which terrorism trials in national courts ought to deviate from established criminal law procedures.[47]

The question is, then, whether charges of crimes against humanity and genocide require similar evidentiary permissiveness, given that the crimes are usually committed in very complex scenarios that involve extended histories of discrimination along religious, ethnic, racial, or national lines and that the cases involve immense amounts of evidence and greater-than-usual obstacles to obtaining that evidence. For some, the answer is categorically yes, and indeed, they feel that the tribunals have not moved far enough away from common law practices. Gideon Boas, senior legal officer during the long, "monstrously broad"[48] and immensely complex trial of Slobodan Milošević, takes the view that "the greatest mistake of international tribunals is that they were created as adversarial legal systems. This is the single most important reason why international trials are often incoherent and unmanageable."[49] Indeed, one could say that Boas's entire account in *The Milošević Trial* (2007) of the four years he spent in the Trial Chamber is a meticulous and closely argued elucidation of that thesis.

[46] See Kluger (1976); Patterson (2001).
[47] In the United Kingdom and other countries, the debate about the nature and form of terrorism trials has been going on for much longer. Since 2001, the legal and scholarly literature on how to try terrorists in national courts and military commissions is now substantial, but one might start with Choi (2007), Robertson (2005), and Wedgewood (2002). More recently in the media, there has been a discussion of the implications of the Obama administration's stated desire to try suspects in U.S. criminal courts. Charlie Savage. "Trial without Major Witness Will Test Tribunal System." *New York Times.* 1 December 2009. A18.
[48] Boas (2007:xvii).
[49] Author interview, June 2006.

4

Does History Have Any Legal Relevance in International Criminal Trials?

4.1. INTRODUCTION

Criminal Courts exist for the purpose of establishing individual accountability – not . . . to provide an official history. To the extent that a historical record is integral to individual trials, it may be said that this is incidental to the work of the ICTY, but it is not its primary purpose.

> – Ralph Zacklin, UN Assistant Secretary-General
> for Legal Affairs (2004:544)

These chambers have produced histories that are not only credible and readable, but *indispensable* to understanding the origins and course of the 1990s conflicts in the former Yugoslavia.

> – Robert Donia (2004:2), ICTY Expert Witness

Is historical debate incidental or indispensable to international criminal trials? Without a doubt, the historical record left by international criminal trials is indispensable for historians and political scientists seeking to comprehend an armed conflict. No student of the Balkans or Rwanda can afford to ignore the Tribunals' judgments and the new evidence revealed in the trials, from insider and eyewitness testimony to telephone intercepts and the massive archives of government documents detailing the operation of local, regional, and national political institutions before and during the conflicts. Yet the reverse is not exactly true: historical accounts produced by historians and political scientists are not always indispensable to international criminal trials. The majority of trials have proceeded without academic experts, and no accused has ever been convicted on the basis of historical evidence alone. It is possible to recognize this and still claim that historical evidence has been relevant to the Tribunals' work and, in certain kinds of cases, might even approach the threshold of indispensable. Understanding how and why requires a close examination of how historical evidence has become legally relevant during trials, in contrast to the stance adopted by Hannah Arendt during the Eichmann trial. What specifically legal rationale is there to call a historian to testify as an expert witness in a trial? What are the motivations of legal actors when they introduce historical evidence and when they seek to exclude it?

As noted earlier, prosecutors and defense attorneys are not compelled by any statutory mandate to write history. Nor are they necessarily committed to the inherent value of historical reflection for its own sake. However, all parties to a trial have an interest in advancing the most persuasive legal argument possible, and some have come to see historical evidence as assisting them in that goal. As a number of prosecutors and defense lawyers have come to realize, the complexity of history in the Balkans and the Great Lakes region of Africa is such that it can lend itself to virtually any legal argument. Historical argumentation is not merely rhetorical window dressing but can become an integral part of the legal objectives of either or both parties. Even though they may strive for objectivity and neutrality, background experts ultimately serve in furtherance of the legal aims of one party or the other in the trial. That is, their presence is a function of the adversarial process, and in this regard, their role is analogous to that of experts in the domestic adversarial criminal courtroom.

If the introduction of historical evidence is a function of the adversarial process, then evaluating the role of a historian or social scientist ought to begin with what the parties intend to achieve when they engage an expert witness, and the following two chapters scrutinize prosecutors' strategies at the ICTY. The discussion begins with the *Tadić* trial in which prosecutors explored the past extensively but asserted only a weak causality between past and present, and it ends with the trial of Slobodan Milošević in which prosecutors claimed a direct relationship of cause and effect. In the *Milošević* trial, ICTY prosecutors brought historical evidence to bear on the ultimate issue in the trial: the question of whether there existed special intent to commit genocide on the part of the accused. History was truly at the center of the *Milošević* trial. This chapter and the next also tell a story of the rise and fall of prosecution's history telling during the ten years from 1996 to 2006. Once it was apparent that the limits of history had been reached, prosecutors largely abandoned grand histories of nationalism in favor of more targeted and specific microhistories, and that shift in tactics is detailed in the following chapter. Sweeping historical metanarratives then became largely the province of the defense, and Chapter 6 analyzes the role of defense expert witnesses in ICTY trials. The arc of historical testimony is less pronounced at the ICTR, where the prosecution won early acceptance from judges for its version of Rwandan history.

4.2. THE *TADIĆ* TRIAL: AN EXTENDED LECTURE ON HISTORY

Day 1 of Tadić Trial, 7 May 1996.

PRESIDING JUDGE [MCDONALD]: Is it possible for you . . . to tell us, starting from the beginning and taking us to the end, the changes in terms of the ethnic composition in different areas, but beginning from the fourteenth century? Is that possible for you to do? Maybe you do not even understand my question because I am not much of an historian, although I actually majored in history . . . but American history.

DR. JAMES GOW [EXPERT WITNESS]: Overall I think the purpose of the evidence . . . is to set the events of 1991 and afterwards in their military-political context. In order to do that I have been reviewing some of the factors which went to create the Yugoslav states which dissolved in 1991, and that has meant making reference not only to the fourteenth century but to the fourth century . . . to give a sense of the way in which the territories which went to make up the federation which dissolved came to be.[1]

As the first-ever war crimes trial by a truly international tribunal got under way, prosecutors and defense counsel reported a pressing need to instruct judges about the historical and political context of the crimes. The Balkans historian and ICTY expert witness Robert Donia (2004:1) writes, "When the trials began, most judges were wholly unfamiliar with the history and culture of the region in which the alleged crimes were committed." The ICTY judges were nominated and elected by the UN General Assembly and then appointed by the secretary-general. The first group came from more than thirty countries, none from the former Yugoslavia. Few were knowledgeable about the Balkans before they arrived at The Hague. Donia (2004:1), commenting on his experience as ICTY expert witness in the 1997 *Blaškić* trial, remarks: "My presentation was more an extended lecture on regional history than court testimony as it might take place in an American court, where a judge would neither need nor welcome such an extensive background portrayal."

Although extended testimony on historical matters by expert witnesses is not commonly encountered in domestic courts, Tribunal judges were receptive to a primer in local history, in part because it allowed them to defend themselves from charges made by defense teams that the international judges lacked the requisite knowledge of the political and social circumstances to adjudicate

---

[1] *Prosecutor v. Duško Tadić*, Case No. IT-94-1-T (hereinafter *Tadić*), Trial Transcript, 7 May 1996, T123–4.

crimes committed in the region.[2] In addition, Tribunal judges were encountering crimes on a scale they had never seen before, and they were asking themselves, How could such extensive violations occur? The former ICTR Judge Navanethem Pillay elucidated the judges' position by stating: "We judges agreed that you can't avoid this question of history of Rwanda, otherwise it's just one ethnic group killing another ethnic group with no reason why. History is necessary for an understanding of why the conflict occurred. Our first judgment – *Akayesu* – did this."[3] The conclusion that the systematic violence was senseless and without discernible motivation was unacceptable to Trial Chamber judges, which led them to wrestle with the historical complexities of Rwanda and the Balkans. In our survey of former prosecution staff, defense lawyers, and expert witnesses, we found across-the-board support for the view that historical context rendered the widespread violations meaningful: 63 percent of respondents in our survey either agreed or strongly agreed with this statement: "Without historical context, individual criminal acts do not appear to make sense."[4] Of interest is the overlapping consensus between prosecutors and defense attorneys who agreed or strongly agreed with the statement at approximately the same exact rate, 61 percent and 60 percent, respectively.[5]

The first trial at an international criminal tribunal began in May 1996, and concerned the crimes of Duško Tadić, a Bosnian Serb part-time traffic policeman charged with persecution and crimes against humanity. On the very first day of the proceedings, the prosecution called a background expert witness, Professor James Gow of the Department of War Studies at King's College, London, who took the stand for three-and-a-half days. His testimony began in the most introductory and straightforward fashion imaginable. As a bored Tadić removed the headphones bringing him a simultaneous Serb translation, Gow explained that the Socialist Federal Republic of Yugoslavia comprised six republics and two autonomous provinces, and he produced maps showing the ethnic composition of provinces in the 1981 and 1991 censuses.[6]

---

[2] For instance, defense counsel argued that judges were not competent to hear the case in the *Brđanin* trial because they were unfamiliar with the history and culture of the former Yugoslavia, an assertion dismissed in *Prosecutor v. Radoslav Brđanin*, Case No. IT-99-36-T, Trial Chamber Judgment, 1 September 2004, §§44–5.

[3] Author interview, May 2006.

[4] Twenty-six percent either agreed or strongly disagreed, 9 percent were neutral, and 1 percent expressed no opinion.

[5] As might be expected, expert witnesses surveyed endorsed the statement even more fulsomely, and 77 percent agreed or strongly agreed.

[6] Tadić was not the only one bored by the prosecution's extended history lesson. Court Television, which had a negotiated a contract to show the entire proceedings, ended its live coverage after only one month of the trial.

He described the topography of the country and the languages spoken and the Latin and Cyrillic scripts used, and he outlined the different histories of Catholicism, Islam, and Greek and Russian Orthodoxy over the centuries.[7]

The defense team called as its expert witness the anthropologist Dr. Robert Hayden, whose testimony offered a different interpretation of one aspect of Yugoslav history: Tito's 1974 Yugoslav Constitution, in granting the right to self-determination of peoples (*narod*), referred not to separate sovereign nations but to separate ethnic groups that would remain within a federal Yugoslavia. Hayden's testimony gave support to the defense's theory that the 1991–5 Yugoslav conflict was an internal civil war rather than an international armed conflict and that the crimes were subject to domestic national courts rather than international humanitarian law.[8] This argument mattered greatly because, as the Trial Chamber later noted, "the extent of the application of international humanitarian law from one place to another in the Republic of Bosnia and Herzegovina depends upon the particular character of the conflict."[9] International law has historically assumed greater jurisdiction over war crimes committed in an international armed conflict, and Article 2 of the ICTY Statute on "Grave breaches of the Geneva Conventions of 1949" applies only where an armed international conflict exists. Thus, the very jurisdiction of the Tribunal over a sizable proportion of the alleged crimes hinged in part on a question of historical interpretation.[10]

The ICTY's first judgment was handed down on 7 May 1997, reinforcing the jurisdiction of the Tribunal and establishing key precedents of both a legal and a historical nature.[11] The *Tadić* Trial Judgment (hereafter, *Tadić*) represented the first conviction for crimes against humanity by a truly

---

[7] See *Tadić* Trial Transcript, 7 May 1996, 80–9.

[8] See *Tadić*, Trial Transcript, 10 September 1996, 5594–7.

[9] *Prosecutor v. Duško Tadić*, Trial Chamber Judgment, IT-94-1-T, 7 May 1997 (*Tadić* Trial Judgment), §571.

[10] Gow's view that the republics were sovereign nations and the conflict was international in character seemed to prevail in the historical section of the *Tadić* Trial Judgment (§65). Yet later on the in the judgment, at §§607–8, the judges (Presiding Judge McDonald dissenting) stated that, because of the complex relationship between the Republika Srpka and the Federal Republic of Yugoslavia, the Bosnian conflict did not meet all the criteria for an international armed conflict, and Article 2 of the ICTY Statute did not apply to the entire conflict. The issue was settled in the *Tadić* Appeals Judgment, which categorically classified the armed conflict between Bosnian Serbs and the central authorities of the Bosnian government as an international armed conflict (*Prosecutor v. Duško Tadić*. IT-94-1-A, Appeals Chamber Judgment, 15 July 1999, §162).

[11] The jurisdiction of the ICTY was established in an interlocutory decision: *Prosecutor v. Duško Tadić a/k/a "Dule,"* Decision on the Defence Motion for Interlocutory Appeal on Jurisdiction, Case No. IT-94-1-AR72, 2 October 1995.

international tribunal.[12] It is worth observing two things regarding the judgment at the outset: first, it starts with sixty-nine pages of extended Balkan history. It would be well-nigh inconceivable for a national court to open a decision with such an extended historical treatise. Second, the judgment's historical account is based entirely on expert-witness testimony presented to the Trial Chamber (§54).

Tadić described Bosnia as a multiethnic political entity with no single dominant group, situated as it was at the shifting frontier of the Ottoman Empire and the Austro-Hungarian Empire. A Serb population was concentrated along its northern and western borders to protect Hapsburg lands from the Ottoman Turks, whose occupation resulted in a large Muslim population (§56). The judgment notes that Serbs, Croats, and Muslims are all Slavs who speak the same language; therefore, it is "inaccurate to speak of three distinct ethnic groups" (§56). During the course of the nineteenth century, the idea of a single state of southern Slavs was advanced by Croat intellectuals, whereas Serb nationalists pursued Greater Serbia, which aspired to integrate all lands inhabited by Serbs into a Serb state (§§85–96). After World War I and the disintegration of the Ottoman and Austro-Hungarian empires, these incompatible ideas were fused to create the Kingdom of Yugoslavia in 1929 (§59).

Yugoslavia, however, was the result of "an uneasy marriage of two ill-matched concepts and in the interwar years the nation experienced acute tensions of an ethno-national character" (§59). During World War II, a ferocious armed conflict raged in Bosnia, large parts of which were annexed by the pro-Nazi Croatian state. Prijedor, where Tadić's crimes occurred, saw prolonged fighting between Croatian Ustaše forces, Serb nationalist Chetniks, and communist partisans led by Marshal Tito. Croatian government officials pursued strategies that would later be termed *ethnic cleansing*, and in 1941, the Ustaše killed up to 250,000 Serbs. At the end of the war, the Ustaše army was handed over to Tito's partisans, who summarily executed approximately one hundred thousand prisoners of war (§§61–3).

Despite this bitter legacy, relations among Croats, Muslims, and Serbs were relatively harmonious in the aftermath of World War II (§64). No ethnic atrocities were documented between 1945 and 1990, although this was in part due to the suppression of nationalism and religion by Tito's socialist regime. A nationalist resurgence began in 1974, as a new Yugoslav constitution devolved powers to the governments of the republics (§68). In 1980, President Tito died, and the 1980s economic crisis generated more appeal for nationalist policies

---

[12]   The Nuremberg trials were multinational in formation and composition and established by the victors in World War II.

(§§70–1). Communism, the ideology that had suppressed nationalist political organization for four decades in Eastern Europe, came crashing down in 1989.

The *Tadić* Trial Judgment wrote the historical run-up to the conflict in Bosnia as the backdrop to a tragic play. Yet nowhere does the language of *Tadić* suggest that historical events brought about the 1991–5 conflict in Bosnia. The judgment's historical narrative does not lead inexorably toward ethnic cleansing and war, as other outcomes were possible. According to the Tribunal, the first precipitating factors or triggers to the Bosnian conflict only came in 1989, the year of the six-hundredth anniversary of the battle of Kosovo, which occupies a central place in Serb nationalist history. Mass rallies at which politicians such as Slobodan Milošević delivered inflammatory nationalist speeches (§72) were held to commemorate the battle. The judgment rejected the explanation that the ethno-nationalist violence of the 1990s was a product of lingering animosities from World War II, also known as the "ancient-hatreds" view. Although the Trial Judgment recognized centuries of conflict in the Balkans, it laid greater emphasis on a relentless propaganda campaign in the 1990–1 period for inciting fear among the populace. *Tadić* documents how the Serb-controlled media in Bosnia pounded out the same unrelenting message that Serbs were about to be overwhelmed by Ustaše Croats and fundamentalist Muslims and had to join the JNA in an all-out war. Broadcasts from Belgrade featured Serb extremists such as paramilitary leader Zeljko "Arkan" Raznatović, who declared that World War II was not over, and they featured fictitious "news" reports about Croat doctors sterilizing Serb women and castrating Serb boys (§§88–93).

The *Tadić* Trial Judgment contained two errors worth mentioning because they persisted in later trials and judgments. First, *Tadić* states, "In March 1992 Bosnia and Herzegovina declared its independence" (§78), but no such declaration of independence was issued, formal or otherwise.[13] It would have been reckless in the extreme for Bosnia and Herzegovina to have declared independence at such a delicate moment in the political negotiations. Such an act, had it actually occurred, would have made the Bosnians appear as provocateurs in a tinderbox scenario. Second, *Tadić* gave short shrift to the international dimensions of the Balkans conflict and the role played by the

---

[13] This error was repeated in the *Simić* and *Kordić* indictments and Trial Judgments. The correct version of events is contained in the *Brđanin* Trial Judgment §§63–4, which describes the proclamation of an independent republic by the Serbian assembly on 9 January 1992. A referendum for independent statehood was held in Bosnia on 29 February and 1 March 1992. *Brđanin* records no declaration of independence by Bosnia but notes that the European Union recognized Bosnia as an independent state on 6 April 1992, and the United States did so on 7 April.

European states. The Judgment reported the official recognition of the Republic of Bosnia and Herzegovina by the European Union of the Republic "in April 1992" (§78), but it neglected to assess the impact that recognition had on negotiations to avert war of Germany's recognition of Croatia and Slovenia on 15 January 1992. Some have argued that external recognition came too early, preempting and undermining the Badinter Advisory Commission set up by the European Union to consider applications for recognition of independence.[14] The Federal Republic of Germany granted its endorsement at a time of extreme tension and instability, and thereby, it is argued, fanned the flames of nationalist indignation and contributed to the descent into armed conflict. This may or may not have been a significant factor, but the Trial Chamber might have at least addressed the matter.

As a final comment, it is worth remarking on the weak historical causality contained in *Tadić*: the past carries little causal or determinative weight. Any sense of an inevitable cascade of events enters into the analysis in 1989; only at that point did the Tribunal consider that a nationalist conflagration in the Balkans had become unavoidable. *Tadić* contradicts nationalist explanations that accord great significance to incidents that occurred in 1941 or even in 1389. The Tribunal openly critiques extreme nationalist histories for manipulating the "remote history of Serbs" (§91). For Serb nationalists (i.e., the majority of the Serb population), historically constructed memories and narratives of World War II are not remote history. Instead, many nationalists perceive a constant and unbroken line from Kosovo and the Field of Blackbirds in 1389 to the Ottoman Empire through to World War II and the present day. In *Tadić*, the Tribunal rejected such *longue durée* nationalist narratives. Overall, even as historical inquiry featured prominently in early trials, it was granted low determinative value by the judges, and prosecutors only hinted at a faint causality. This began to change as lawyers realized the potential advantages that historical and contextual narratives might accord them.

4.3. FRAMING THE CRIMES AND THE BATTLE FOR THE FIRST PARAGRAPH

A trial at the ICTY is usually more akin to documenting an episode or even an era of national or ethnic conflict rather than proving a single discrete incident.

– ICTY Judge Patricia Wald (2001:535, 536–7)

---

[14] See Hillgruber (1998:508).

The lengthy lecture on history that characterized the *Tadić* Trial Judgment
was not repeated in any subsequent judgments, but it set a precedent, and all
ICTY and ICTR judgments since have opened with a paragraph or section
setting out the historical context of the crimes. Judge Claude Jorda, former
president of the ICTY and a judge at the ICC, recognized the unusual format
of international tribunal judgments:

> In an international criminal trial, a judge needs to examine four items: 1.
> Elements of the crimes: what happened; 2. Criminal responsibility: who was
> responsible for the crimes; 3. Whether there was an international armed
> conflict and did the crimes constitute breaches of international law; 4. Exam-
> ination of the context and history. But if you look at the ICTY and ICTR
> judgments, they are written in the reverse order, beginning with context. I
> know, I am in part responsible, since I have signed them![15]

The format of Tribunal judgments has resulted in what the former ICTY
research officer Andrew Corin terms "a battle over the first paragraph."[16] Why
might the parties contest so vigorously the opening paragraph of a judgment?
In large part, prosecutors and defense lawyers take their cue from judges, and
whatever seems to resonate with judges resonates even louder with them. If a
Trial Chamber begins every judgment with a section on history and context,
then this must be essential, relevant information. An opening historical section
also presents opportunities that lawyers are quick to comprehend, with both
sides hoping to gain a rhetorical advantage by situating the ensuing findings
regarding the alleged crimes in the historical framework that best suits their
arguments. Prosecutors have exploited this opening to "frame" the crimes, that
is, to construct a cognitive framework that organizes scattered acts, statements,
and events and thereby inculcate a certain disposition or set of feelings toward
them.[17] In *Ways of Seeing*, a classic text of art criticism, John Berger (1972:27–
8) considers why paintings are often reproduced with words around them.
He selects as a paradigmatic example Vincent van Gogh's *Wheatfield with
Crows*, painted in Auvers-sur-Oise in July 1890. He reproduces the picture
once, then asks the reader to look at it for a moment and then turn the
page.

[15] Author interview, May 2006.
[16] Author interview, May 2006.
[17] Turković (2003:53), writing about the ICTY, refers to how "[t]he Prosecutor frames judges'
and public sensitivity which later, when it is the Defense's turn to present its part of the case,
may be difficult to change." I should make clear that in this present discussion, I am not using
"framing" in the sense of "to incriminate an innocent person with false evidence" but instead
in the sense of inculcating a sensitivity or predisposition toward the evidence.

IMAGE 1. *Wheatfield with Crows*, by Vincent Van Gogh. Courtesy of Van Gogh Museum Amsterdam (Vincent van Gogh Foundation).

The picture is reproduced again, but this time with the words written underneath: "This is the last picture that Van Gogh painted before he killed himself." Berger remarks: "It is hard to define exactly how the words have changed the image, but undoubtedly they have. The image now illustrates the sentence" (28).

As the viewer first beholds the painting, the raw sensory data is instantly organized by higher-order visual processes to provide an awareness of structure and composition. From there, the viewer may go on to have thoughts about Van Gogh's corpus of paintings, to make comparisons with other impressionist paintings of the time, and so on. Yet once we are told that *Wheatfield with Crows* was the last canvas Van Gogh painted before shooting himself in a field outside Paris, the image takes on a new and poignant meaning. It presents a window onto his state of mind in the moments before he committed suicide, as well as his personal, visual epitaph. In this way, the image irreversibly loses some of its immediate visual authority and is subordinated to a broader thesis about Van Gogh's life and work. Even if we later learn that the last-painting thesis surrounding *Wheatfield with Crows* is entirely conjectural (although it was painted in the final months of Van Gogh's life, we simply do not know whether it was his final painting), it is hard to mentally expunge the information and return to the less charged perception of the painting held moments earlier. In a sense, the damage has already been done.

Historical information presented in an international criminal trial frames the crimes in a way similar to the words accompanying a painting by furnishing a high-order meaning and thereby changing the beholder's perception of the raw, as-yet-unprocessed data. The alleged crimes cease to be disconnected from one another as prosecutors use a narrative framework to create an ordered sequence of events. As with the painting, the alleged crimes lose some of their authority and are integrated into arguments constructed either by the defense or by the prosecution. History then becomes a prism through which the courts view and apprehend the alleged crimes.

It is important not to overstate the role that historical evidence can play in transforming judges' perceptions of alleged crimes, as historical and political context occupy the lowest rung of causality and determinacy.[18] In standard Anglo-American criminal law, causality is carefully defined by a series of legal precedents established over centuries that delineate and qualify the concept. In early international trials, prosecutors generally advanced only the weakest of causal claims on the basis of historical evidence. There exists no criminal law term that accurately encapsulates historical or contextual causation; the legal concept that comes closest is "proximate cause," but this is a civil law term denoting a cause that is legally sufficient to result in liability. This lacuna in criminal law necessitates the minting of new terms such as *indeterminate cause* or *distant macrocausation* or *umbrella causation*. Although the nebulous nature of historical causality might instinctively lead one to dismiss its legal relevance, in fact this characteristic may be its greatest asset. Making a claim of a causal connection between events is a highly circumscribed area that is regulated by established legal principles and courtroom conventions that allow very little room for maneuver by prosecutors. Because historical claims are not advanced as forcefully as other parts of the prosecution case, and because everyone understands that they imply only indeterminate and indirect causality, they are less rigorously interrogated by judges. In this way, chronologies that lay out a chain of events connected by an indeterminate causality and conclude with the alleged criminal acts appeal to prosecutors because such narratives stand a greater chance of eluding standard courtroom constraints.

Indirection is one of the main attractions of historical context for prosecutors, and it opens up a conduit of information and intimation that would otherwise be closed off. In analyzing the testimony of historian Henry Rousso, expert witness in the Holocaust trial of Maurice Papon, Richard Evans (2002:337) correctly observed that, "although the historians were only asked to provide broad generalizations about the historical context, they were by implication acting as witnesses on the character of the accused. A slippage from context to person was unavoidable, even though the historians were not presenting formal evidence on the latter at all." For the prosecution, the slippage from

---

[18] It should be noted that many contemporary historians would reject out of hand such language of causality and determination and instead place more emphasis on context, subjectivity, and *mentalité*. I am grateful to Saul Dubow for underscoring this point.

context to person inherent in historical testimony is an oblique way of casting the character of the accused in a negative light without overtly doing so, in a manner that is both subtle and deniable. Contextual information silhouettes the character of the accused without shining a light on the subject directly.

In a standard Anglo-American criminal trial with a jury, such a historical narrative could sway opinion against the accused and therefore be ruled inadmissible. However, what is the effect on international judges? Does framing using historical narrative produce its intended effect on trained legal professionals? The indeterminate nature of the causation implied in historical framing makes measuring its impact difficult, and the degree to which judges are actually influenced by it is unclear. Overall, respondents to our survey perceived judges as positively disposed toward historical testimony introduced by the prosecution. When asked, "How receptive are ICTY judges to the testimony of historians serving as expert witnesses called by the Prosecution?" 21 percent of all respondents thought judges were highly receptive and 59 percent somewhat receptive, for a total of 80 percent. Only 3 percent thought judges were unreceptive, and none thought judges were highly unreceptive.[19] In practice, judicial receptivity varies on a case-by-case basis, depending on the particular proclivities of the bench. Some judges from academic or diplomatic backgrounds came to the Tribunal with little or no criminal courtroom experience, and this group may be more susceptible to framing kinds of arguments. Judges at the ICTY and ICTR never abandoned their practice of opening judgments with a section on history and context, and as long as that was the case, many prosecutors continued to call historical expert witnesses and to seek an advantage from this practice, however intangible.

4.4. HISTORICAL AND SOCIAL SCIENCE ANALYSIS IN THE OFFICE OF THE PROSECUTOR

Looking behind the scenes at the research and analysis occurring inside the Office of the Prosecutor, we find that there were organizational changes that, over time, enhanced the ability of prosecutors to integrate historical and contextual evidence into their cases. In particular, two new structures for analysis were created in late 1997 that accentuated the role of contextual information and analysis: the Military Analysis Team and the Leadership Research Team (LRT), the latter being most relevant to our discussion of historical debates at the ICTY. Until that point, investigators – the majority of whom were

---

[19] Seventeen percent expressed no opinion.

former police officers – were divided into eleven teams according to "perpe-trator group." Seven teams investigated Serb crimes and four were tasked with investigating Croat, Muslim, and Albanian crimes.[20] According to some of the academic researchers, police team leaders did not know how best to use their expertise and instead gave team members routine tasks and sent them on mundane errands.

The Military Analysis Team and LRT emerged out of the Strategy Team, led by Johan "J. J." Du Toit, a former deputy attorney general in South Africa. The Strategy Team contained a subunit, the Special Projects Unit, that com-prised investigators and analysts who documented the personal background and business and social networks of high-ranking military and political lead-ers, one of the first being General Radislav Krstić. The LRT's leader for the twelve years from February 1998 to the end of 2009 was Dr. Patrick J. Treanor, a historian of Russia and Eastern Europe. He was previously employed as a senior historian in the Office of Special Investigations at the U.S. Depart-ment of Justice, the office tasked with identifying Nazi war criminals to be deported or extradited from the United States. Treanor started with twelve staff members and embarked on a hiring program. By its high point in 2004, there were more than thirty members of the LRT. Treanor sought out professionals with regional expertise who could speak the local languages and could read documents directly without the need for translation. He sought professionals with appropriate training, and a sizable percentage of LRT staff had graduate degrees, mostly in history and the social sciences. The LRT brought numer-ous regional specialists into the Office of the Prosecutor, and over time, it overcame an internal institutional resistance to hiring staff from countries of the former Yugoslavia.

The main function of the LRT was to respond to requests for informa-tion from Senior Trial Attorneys (known as STAs), who after the arrival of Chief Prosecutor Del Ponte, took over from police investigators in directing the investigations.[21] The LRT members assisted prosecuting attorneys from the initial stages of a case to its conclusion; that is, from the writing of the indictment through the pretrial, trial, and appeal stages. Staff performed a

---

[20] Although there were originally eleven teams, this had been reduced to four by the time all the indictments were issued in 2004. On the limitations of the ethnic organization of the investigation teams, see Hoare (2008:8–9). It seems somewhat ironic that the ethnic, national, and confessional divisions of the Balkans reproduced themselves at the level of an international justice institution. This might be a feature of criminal investigation organizations more generally. The U.S. Federal Bureau of Investigation (FBI) divides its organized crime division along ethnic or regional lines, listing the following categories: "Italian Mafia, Eurasian, Balkan, Middle Eastern, Asian and African," http://www.fbi.gov/hq.htm.
[21] Senior Trial Attorneys were assigned, usually two or three per case, to present the case against the accused in the Trial Chamber.

more analytical role than police investigators, authoring background reports on a specific topic or issue. With their knowledge of the culture and language of the former Yugoslavia, they furnished historical and political analyses that advanced and shaped the prosecution's thesis in the trial. Their most noteworthy contributions came in cases involving high-ranking military and political leaders. As Treanor explained: "LRT and MAT [Military Analysis Team] were best equipped to read the archives and documents and develop what was known about the political and military structures on the basis of the documents. We developed the factual basis for those structures in the leadership cases."[22] The LRT's members also did the spadework on the social and political context of the accused. With prominent political leaders such as Slobodan Milošević, Radoslav Brđanin, and Radovan Karadžić, they compiled compendious reports on their roles, responsibilities, and powers (both *de facto* and *de jure*) in the political organizations and institutions they operated in, as well as their informal family ties, business relationships, and political networks.

Not all STAs turned to the LRT for research assistance, but the ones who did found that the interaction often transformed their understanding of the case. Treanor remarked, "When we appeared in the Trial Chamber, defense counsel would say, 'You're just crafting your expert reports to fit the prosecution arguments, aren't you?' but actually it was the other way around."[23] Treanor claimed that the LRT assisted STAs in developing their "theory of the case,"[24] defined as the "particular line of reasoning . . . the purpose being to bring together certain facts of the case in a logical sequence and to correlate them in a way that produces in the decision-maker's mind a definite result or conclusion favored by the advocate."[25] In lay terms, the theory of the case is the overarching story that aligns individual facts and amalgamates them into a coherent whole. It integrates the how (i.e., what happened) with the why (i.e., the motives behind what happened). In leadership cases, Treanor emphasized, prosecuting attorneys were familiar with all the legal dimensions of the case, but they needed help with identifying the overarching narrative. Treanor's claim was borne out in qualitative interviews with STAs and in the survey.

Furthermore, the LRT also serves as a kind of institutional memory in the Office of the Prosecutor. According to Treanor, "[W]e remind them what the

---

[22] Author interview, November 2009. Treanor made the comments included in this book in his personal capacity, and these comments do not necessarily represent the views of the ICTY or the United Nations.
[23] Author interview, November 2009.
[24] Author interview, June 2006.
[25] Garner, Bryan A., ed. 2006. *Black's Law Dictionary*.

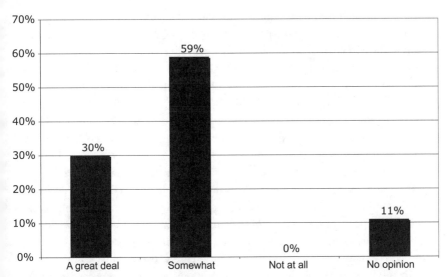

FIGURE 4.1. To what degree have Prosecutors used historical evidence in the Trial Chamber to assist in creating their theory of the case?

theory is and how it is relevant as the witnesses come up."[26] Continuity in the overall vision became an issue because STAs did not always follow cases from the beginning to their conclusion, and a new STA could be assigned to a case at any point in the legal proceedings. The LRT and Military Analysis Team staff constituted the main point of contact with external expert witnesses for the prosecution. Senior Trial Attorneys would design the commission, directing the consultant expert to undertake as discretely as possible a task that would be of use in the courtroom. The LRT staff assisted in the selection of expert witnesses, in reviewing experts' reports, and in preparing experts for cross-examination. Staff also pursued sensitive negotiations with high-level fact witnesses from the Balkans. Whereas STAs often struggled to forge a personal connection with witnesses and win their trust, LRT staff from the Balkans were more effective in persuading senior insiders to testify against the accused.

Members of the LRT accompanied STAs into the Trial Chamber, and a number of STAs confirmed that they were an invaluable source of local knowledge. Former ICTY prosecutor Sir Geoffrey Nice offered fulsome praise for the contribution of LRT staff: "[LRT analyst and University of Amsterdam professor] Nena Tromp-Vrkić was one of the most important members of our prosecution team. She played an invaluable role in identifying two of the most important pieces of evidence for the prosecution in the Milošević

[26] Author interview, June 2006.

trial: the Kula Camp video and the Supreme Defense Council minutes and accompanying stenographic records. Having her beside me in the courtroom was indispensable.... Members of the LRT had all the knowledge of the society and history."[27] Once the technology was in place to transmit court proceedings throughout the building, LRT members could watch trials from their desks and send comments and potential questions down to STAs in the Trial Chamber. What kind of LRT input mattered during cross-examination? Treanor responded: "The defendant is the leading expert on the context and history. If we are not careful, he is going to run rings around us."[28] Former ICTY Senior Trial Attorney Susan Somers confirmed Treanor's assessment: "You need someone from LRT in court with you, to help redirect a witness, to give you that expert piece of knowledge; otherwise you could end up looking uninformed."[29] In the ICTY courtroom, LRT staff proved invaluable in the cross-examination of defense witnesses, especially as prosecutors had little time to prepare for cross-examination of defense witnesses.[30] With little or no prior disclosure by the defense regarding their witnesses, prosecutors could undertake only limited groundwork in advance, as Susan Somers explained: "We didn't know what was coming in the defense case and we had little time to prepare. We needed someone beside us who knew the history and context and was an area expert. This was not a murder on the streets of Miami."[31]

When asked about the kind of contextual information that LRT staff could provide to STAs, research analyst Dr. Andrew Corin offered the example of understanding the intent of a politician making a speech.[32] On 26 October 1991, Bosnian Serb leader Radovan Karadžić addressed a mass rally at Banja Luka and referred to the need to create a state in which there would be no "traitors." Corin explained that an STA needed to be aware of the range of possible interpretations available to listeners at that rally, which required a thorough understanding of the historical background. References to "traitors" resonate in Serbian literature, notably in *The Mountain Wreath* (*Gorski Vijenac*), an epic poem written by the Montenegrin ruler Petar II Petrović-Njegoš

---

[27] Author interview, February 2009.
[28] Author interview, June 2006.
[29] Author interview, April 2009.
[30] Although prosecutors and defense counsel are both required by Rule 65 *ter* (F)(G) to provide details of their cases and lists of witnesses, in practice, the pretrial process demands more of the prosecution, to its perpetual chagrin. Daryl Mundis spoke for many STAs when he said, "We file a 150-page pretrial brief with footnotes and they (defense counsel) file 8 pages contesting everything we set out, without saying which issues they contest and why" (Author interview, May 2006).
[31] Author interview, November 2009.
[32] Author interview, May 2006.

(1813–51), and familiar to every Serb secondary school student.[33] Published in 1847, it was a virulent nationalist tract celebrating Montenegro's independence from Ottoman rule. For Branimir Anzulović (1999:54) it constituted a "hymn to genocide" because it labeled Muslims as "traitors" and commended the legendary eighteenth-century massacre of Montenegrin Muslims who refused to convert to Christianity. Only those familiar with the local cultural repertoire would detect such historical and literary references. Ample evidence has come to light showing that the language of Njegoš was part and parcel of the Bosnian conflict; for instance, the UN Commission of Experts quoted a Serb secret police officer in charge of concentration camps in Prijedor labeling his Muslim detainees as "traitors."[34]

The practical value of the LRT to prosecutors rose exponentially beginning in 2001–2 as an avalanche of government archives from the region arrived at the Tribunal. The LRT staff, in concert with STAs, played a central role in obtaining documents from Bosnia and Herzegovina, Croatia, and Serbia and Montenegro, as well as material from police stations and municipalities overrun by opposing military units. The LRT staff cataloged and combed through the documents and then explained to STAs how the knowledge gleaned might be applied in their cases. They became the experts on these documentary collections and, as we will see in more detail in the following chapter, began appearing as expert witnesses themselves in the Trial Chamber. Dealings between researchers and attorneys were not always harmonious, however, and LRT member Predrag Dojcinovic reported intermittent tensions: "LRT staff know a little too much about context and history and sometimes they try to impose their views and say how a case should be argued. But they don't know about the law, or anything about forensic evidence, or what purpose a fact witness serves. Let the STAs run the case – they know what they need – provided, of course, that the STAs have a fully developed awareness of the contextual evidence needed to try political and military leadership cases."[35]

The LRT and Military Analysis Team represent investigative units of a kind that is only rarely found in domestic criminal justice systems, and then in

---

[33] Two years after the interview with Corin, a *New York Times* article maintained that Karadžić modeled himself on Vladika Danilo, the Montenegrin bishop and sovereign who put Muslims to the sword in *The Mountain Wreath*. Aleksandar Hemon, "Genocide's Epic Hero." *New York Times*, 27 July 2008, http://www.nytimes.com/2008/07/27/opinion/27hemon.html?pagewanted=1&_r=3.

[34] 1992 Final Report of the UN Commission of Experts Established Pursuant to Security Council Resolution 780 (1992), UNSC S/1994/674/Add.2 (Vol. 1), 28 December 1994, Annex V, Prijedor Report, Part 1, Section IX, p. 8.

[35] Author interview, June 2007.

an attenuated form.[36] One would not expect such a presence of historians, political scientists, and linguists in national criminal investigation teams. Nor to my knowledge has any structure like them been created thus far in any other international criminal tribunals, which have tended to rely more on external experts as consultants. There are drawbacks to this latter approach. In terms of internal organizational dynamics, a team of thirty well-trained professional staff members possesses more institutional clout than a single expert who is external to the organization, no matter how highly that expert is regarded. In-house regional experts are more able to integrate themselves into the prosecution cases from the outset and therefore elevate the position of historical and cultural analysis.

4.5. GENOCIDE AND THE UNEXPECTED RIGORS OF SPECIAL INTENT

Actus not facit reum nisi mens sit rea (The act is not blameworthy unless the mind is guilty).

– Latin maxim

The Chamber considers that intent is a mental factor which is difficult, even impossible, to determine.

– *Akayesu* (ICTR Trial Chamber), §523

At certain exceptional junctures at international criminal tribunals, prosecutors have come to view historical evidence as indispensable to their line of argument. In the discussion that follows, the grand sweep of Balkans history – what I call a "monumental history"[37] – occupies center stage in an international criminal trial, as prosecutors sought to prove the genocidal intent of the accused, in this instance, former Yugoslav President Slobodan Milošević. They turned to historical evidence in a state of frustration bordering on desperation with the high threshold set by international judges for proving special intent to commit genocide. Genocide is, above all, a crime of intent; that is, the material elements of the crimes under consideration can be identical to other crimes

---

[36] And perhaps may be comparable to the investigation teams set up to deal with terrorism or organized crime in countries of Western Europe and North America.

[37] Friedrich Nietzsche (1997) used the term *monumental history* in his essay "On the Uses and Disadvantages of History for Life." I am using the term quite differently, to refer to the grand, sweeping narratives presented in the courtroom that covered centuries and focused on leaders, institutions, empires, and intellectuals. Continuity in these narratives was provided by a collective national identity and group mind-set. They could be contrasted with microcontextual social histories that described how individuals moved through their daily lives.

against humanity (e.g., murder, deportation), but genocide is distinguished by the special intent to destroy a protected group, in whole or in part, as such.

The category of genocide was of immense political significance to the Tribunals, whose very existence was premised on declarations from nation-states, the United Nations, and human rights organizations that genocide had occurred in Rwanda and the former Yugoslavia. Samantha Power (2002:481–6), noting the "coincidence of imagery between the Bosnian war and the Holocaust," describes how during 1992–3, claims of genocide committed in Rwanda and during the breakup of Yugoslavia were essential to galvanizing international support for both Tribunals. The Report of the UN Commission of Experts concluded that the events at Prijedor in Bosnia were unquestionably crimes against humanity and would likely be "confirmed in court under due process of law that these events constitute genocide."[38] European Union politicians such as German Foreign Minister Klaus Kinkel made impassioned speeches invoking the specter of genocide in Bosnia. Accusations that Serb military units were conducting genocide in Kosovo in 1999 formed a major justification for the North American Treaty Alliance military intervention.[39] Human rights organizations, at the pinnacle of their influence in modern times, sent letters to President George H. W. Bush, UN Secretary-General Boutros-Boutros Ghali and other world leaders, urging them to fulfill their obligations under the UN Genocide Convention to prevent and punish the crime of genocide.[40]

Over the following seventeen years, references to genocide resounded in the halls of the United Nations whenever the two *ad hoc* Tribunals' annual performance and budgets were reviewed.[41] Tribunal judges themselves consistently elevated the status of genocide by calling it "the crime of crimes" in their judgments and decisions.[42] Despite the prominence of genocide, the ICTY's record of prosecuting genocide is quite distinct from the ICTR, where, as noted in Chapter 2, prosecutors obtained early genocide convictions (*Akayesu* and *Kambanda*, both in 1998) that were upheld on appeal. In its 2006 decision in the *Karemera* trial, the ICTR took judicial notice of the 1994 genocide and rendered it a "fact of common knowledge," and thus, like the "laws of

---

[38] 1992 Final Report of the UN Commission of Experts Established Pursuant to Security Council Resolution 780 (1992), UNSC S/1994/674/Add.2 (Vol. 1), 28 December 1994, Annex V, Prijedor Report, Part 1, Section X, "Conclusions," p. 9.
[39] Scharf and Schabas (2002:67).
[40] Helsinki Watch (1993:398–409).
[41] See the annual reports submitted to the UN Security Council and General Assembly by the presidents of the ICTY and ICTR.
[42] For example, at the ICTY: *Jelisić* Appeals Judgment, p. 64, ¶2; *Stakić* Trial Judgment §502. At the ICTR, see *Kambanda* Trial Judgment, §16; *Serushago* Trial Judgment §15.

nature," beyond further legal dispute.[43] At the time of writing in 2010, seventeen years after the ICTY was founded, there is still no standing conviction for commission of genocide in the former Yugoslavia that has been upheld on appeal. Vidoje Blagojević's guilty verdict was overturned by the Appeals Chamber, and General Radislav Krstić's conviction for genocide was reduced to the lesser charge of "aiding and abetting" on appeal. The Bosnian Serb Army leaders Vujadin Popović and Ljubiša Beara were convicted on 10 June 2010 of committing genocide at Srebrenica and Žepa in eastern Bosnia, but these convictions have yet to be upheld by the Appeals Chamber.

Given the emphatic accusation of genocide in the Balkans, how should we understand the numerous ICTY verdicts over the past ten years that rejected the charge of genocide? First, it is worth reiterating that proving genocide in a court of law demands higher proofs than in the media or the court of public opinion. The available evidence for genocide in the former Yugoslavia is not as legally compelling as in Rwanda.[44] Chief Prosecutor Carla Del Ponte's plea bargaining strategy, which may or may not have been justifiable according to the broader aims of the Tribunal, nonetheless deprived the Trial Chamber of individuals indicted for genocide such as Biljana Plavšić. Prosecutors have also committed strategic errors, for instance, by rolling all three indictments (Bosnia and Herzegovina, Croatia, and Kosovo) together against Slobodan Milošević, to create one enormous and protracted trial in which the accused died before the verdict. Finally, two of the most senior-level indictees for genocide in Bosnia, Ratko Mladić and Radovan Karadžić, remained at large until 2008, when Karadžić was apprehended on a Belgrade bus while disguised as a natural health guru.

One seldom-noted reason for the paucity of genocide convictions at the ICTY is the degree to which prior expectations (held by human rights organizations, the media, politicians, and others) of swift and uncomplicated genocide verdicts were not based on a realistic assessment of international criminal law. Legal, political, and social science analyses can diverge widely on the question of whether genocide was committed in a locale, and the requirements of the law are much more stringent than any of the others. Despite widespread adoption of the 1948 Convention on the Prevention and Punishment of the Crime of Genocide,[45] there had been no prosecutions for genocide by an

[43] *Prosecutor v. Édouard Karemera, Mathieu Ngirumpatse, Joseph Nzirorera,* Case No. ICTR-98-44-AR73(C), Decision on Prosecutor's Interlocutory Appeal of Decision on Judicial Notice, 16 June 2006, §§22–35.

[44] Former ICTR legal adviser Kingsley Moghalu (2008:64) writes, "while what happened in Rwanda in 1994 was clearly genocide, it was a matter of debate whether ethnic cleansing in the Balkans constituted the ultimate crime."

[45] The Convention on the Prevention and Punishment of the Crime of Genocide was adopted by Resolution 260 (III) A of the UN General Assembly on 9 December 1948.

international tribunal until the late 1990s.[46] Up until that time, international case law on crimes against humanity was meager and furnished little guidance on key legal questions. With the establishment of the ICTY and ICTR, novel categories of international criminal law required pioneering judicial reasoning to apply them to ethnic, racial, religious, and national conflicts in places like the former Yugoslavia and Rwanda.

Because genocide had not been tried before in an international court, the threshold of proof had never been firmly established. The truth was that, until the late 1990s, no one really knew for certain how an international court would interpret the main elements of the crime. Even though there was ample evidence of massive violations against civilians in Bosnia and else-where in the former Yugoslavia, it was hard to anticipate how judges would decide questions such as, What constitutes a protected social group under the UN Genocide Convention of 1948? What evidence is required to prove an alleged perpetrator's special intent to destroy a designated group? How does international criminal law define "in whole or in part"? Genocide as a crime possesses unique legal aspects that are not always evident in the myriad usages by journalists, politicians, and human rights organizations.

The definition contained in the UN Convention on the Prevention and Punishment of the Crime of Genocide accords genocide a qualitatively different character from most other crimes against humanity, in that it must be directed at an individual because of his or her membership in a collective grouping.[47] In Article 2, genocide is defined as "acts committed with intent to destroy, in whole or in part, a national, ethnical, racial or religious group, as such."[48]

---

[46] Recall that the judgment of the Supreme Court of Israel on 26 May 1962 against Adolf Eichmann was for complicity in a "crime against the Jewish people." In 1997, two Serb Nationals were convicted of genocide in the German national courts: Novislav Djajić (Appeals Court of Bavaria, 23 May 1997, 3 St 20/96) and Nikola Jorgić (Düsseldorf Supreme Court, 26 September 1997, 2 StE 8/96).

[47] Some crimes against humanity, such as persecution, also contain a group dimension. On the international law of genocide I have relied on Cassese (2003), Kittichaisaree (2001), and Schabas (2009). For more general histories of the idea of genocide, see Staub (1994); Weitz (2003). Thomas Cushman (2009), Michael Freeman (1991), and Martin Shaw (2003) provide excellent reviews of theories of genocide.

[48] Article 2 of the Genocide Convention states in full:

"In the present Convention, genocide means any of the following acts committed with intent to destroy, in whole or in part, a national, ethnical, racial or religious group, as such:

(a) Killing members of the group;
(b) Causing serious bodily or mental harm to members of the group;
(c) Deliberately inflicting on the group conditions of life calculated to bring about its physical destruction in whole or in part;
(d) Imposing measures intended to prevent births within the group;
(e) Forcibly transferring children of the group to another group."

Whereas the vast majority of criminal acts require only two individuals, where one commits a proscribed act against the other, in the crime of genocide, it is conventionally held that the victim is both the individual and at least one of four designated collective groups: a national, ethnic, racial, or religious group, as such. The prosecution therefore shoulders a greater burden when proving genocide rather than other crimes against humanity. Demonstrating that the accused is guilty of genocide requires showing that he or she committed a proscribed act (*actus reus*), which means demonstrating that the victim(s) belonged to a national, ethnical, racial, or religious group as designated in the Genocide Convention. If the victims are not members of the aforementioned groups, if the existence of the victim's group identity is indeterminate, or if the group has a stable identity but one that is not national, ethnic, racial, or religious, then the category of genocide cannot be applied. On these criteria, the destruction of political and economic groups has historically been excluded from the category of genocide.[49]

The most unique element of the crime of genocide is *dolus specialis*, meaning "special intent," defined as "a particular state of mind or a specific intent with respect to the overall consequence of the prohibited act."[50] In legal parlance, the required mental aspect to convict is called *mens rea*, or "criminal intent," but the crime of genocide goes well beyond standard criminal intent to require special intent.[51] As the former ICTY president Antonio Cassese (2003:167) writes, "in addition to the intent necessary for the commission of the underlying offence (murder, rape, serious bodily assault, expulsion from a village, an area of a country, etc.) a discriminatory intent is required, namely the will to discriminate against members of a particular national, ethnic, religious, racial or other group." Yet even discriminatory intent is not sufficient on its own to prove genocide, as it must also be shown that the perpetrator was aware that the acts were part of a wider plan to exterminate members of a national, ethnic, racial, or religious group specifically on the basis of their membership in a group ("as such"). For an act of murder or forced removal to

---

[49] In Mexico, "political groups" are included in the definition of genocide contained in statutes, leading to genocide charges against former Mexican President Luis Echeverría for the shooting of student demonstrators in 1968. See "Mexico Charges Ex-President in '68 Massacre of Students," *New York Times*, 1 July 2006.

[50] *Prosecutor v. Radislav Krstić*, Trial Chamber Judgment (*Krstić* Trial Judgment), IT-98-33-T, 2 August 2001, §571 (quoting Report of the International Law Commission on the Work of its 48th sess.), 6 May–26 July 1996, U.N. GAOR, 51st sess., Supp. No. 10, at 88. U.N. Doc. A/51/10 (1996).

[51] Literally, Latin for "guilty mind." *Black's Law Dictionary* (Garner, ed., 2006) defines *mens rea* as "The state of mind that the prosecution, to secure a conviction, must prove that a defendant had when committing a crime; criminal intent."

be considered genocidal, there must exist a plan or policy of group destruction beyond the act itself, as well as an explicit awareness of the genocidal consequences of each particular act. This complex layering of intent in genocide gives it a particular character as a category of international criminal law.

The added element of special intent thwarted prosecutors at the ICTY for more than a decade and constitutes one of the main reasons they struggled to secure genocide convictions. There were several trials in which the prosecution seemingly presented a compelling case for genocide, only to have judges reject the charge on the grounds that special intent had not been proved. One of the first was the trial of Goran Jelisić, and at least initially, there was reason to believe that he might be found guilty of committing genocide. Self-proclaimed commander at the Luka camp in 1992 in Brčko, Bosnia, Jelisić called himself the "Serb Adolf." He admitted that he had come to the camp to kill Muslims, whom he called "balijas" or "Turks." Frequently, he boasted of the number of Muslims he had killed (reported by eyewitnesses in the trial, at various times, as 68, 83, and 150). He made Muslims sing Serb songs in front of the Serb flag before beating and cold-bloodedly executing them. Prosecutors presented undeniable evidence of Jelisić's murders plus corroborating testimony from eyewitnesses that indicated a discriminatory state of mind. Did not such a pattern of behavior meet the threshold of genocidal intention?

In its 14 December 1999 judgment, the Trial Chamber found Jelisić guilty of fifteen counts of crimes against humanity and sixteen counts of violations of the laws of war, including the murder of thirteen persons, and he was sentenced to forty years in prison.[52] However, he was acquitted of genocide.[53] The Trial Chamber acknowledged that the material element for the crime of genocide was present (§100), as was discriminatory intent, because Jelisić had so openly expressed his hatred for Bosnian Muslims, a group that qualified for protection under the Genocide Convention. Yet it had not been proved beyond reasonable doubt that the accused possessed a special intention beyond the immediate bigotry and personal prejudice motivating his crimes.

The Trial Chamber justified its conclusions in a number of ways. It noted that Jelisić was a "disturbed personality" (§105) who acted arbitrarily and did not kill according to any "precise logic" (§93). Instead, he selected the names of his victims at random from a list. Other detainees he released, again randomly (§94). Most crucially, the prosecution had not established to the judges' satisfaction that there was a wider genocidal plan to destroy Muslims at Brčko that

[52] *Prosecutor v. Goran Jelisić*, Trial Chamber Judgment (*Jelisić* Trial Judgment), IT-95-10-T, 14 December 1999.
[53] Upheld by the Appeals Chamber in 2001.

was conducted concurrently with Jelisić's individual criminal acts. Without a wider policy of extermination, prosecutors were prevented from showing that Jelisić had acted with awareness of how his individual acts furthered a larger genocidal policy or plan. Prosecutors therefore could not prove that Jelisić had acted under superior orders or through an established chain of command (§98). In the absence of any evidence of superior orders, it was possible that he exceeded his powers and acted independent of a coordinated policy or plan. Claude Jorda, the presiding judge in the *Jelisić* case, gave weight to the "crime of state" aspect in his personal reflections on the Trial Chamber judgment:

> This was a difficult case and we had lengthy discussions. He spread terror in the camp. He would put Muslims heads in the gutters and then shoot them. But my view is that genocide is a crime of the state. An individual does not just wake up in the morning and say, "I'm going to commit genocide."[54]

The lead prosecutor Geoffrey Nice offered a rather different perspective on the verdict:

> *Jelisić* was an example of a paradigm case to ascertain whether a low level perpetrator could be indicted, tried and convicted of genocide, or whether there was a ceiling in the chain of command below which convictions were not possible. Given that the crime of genocide was in the armory of the prosecution at the ICTY, it was entirely appropriate and understandable for Louise Arbour to indict Jelisić for genocide, as a test case. The court denied genocide in the judgment, but a strictly legal decision had been clouded by political considerations. We heard later on from a judge that the prosecution had proven the case against Jelisić, but that the judges wanted to save a genocide conviction for a bigger fish.[55]

When one such big fish was apprehended and brought to The Hague for trial, it looked as if a genocide conviction might be forthcoming from the Tribunal. Bosnian Serb General Radislav Krstić was one of the first high-level indictees to be arrested in the region – by NATO in 1998.[56] In August 2001, Krstić was convicted of leading the Bosnian Serb Army (VRS) as it committed genocide against the Bosniak population of Srebrenica between 10–19 July 1995, when the Drina Corps methodically slaughtered more than seven thousand Muslim men and boys.[57] Counsel for Krstić filed a notice of appeal, and on 19 April 2004, the ICTY's Appeals Chamber quashed the

---

[54] Author interview, May 2006.
[55] Author interview, February 2009.
[56] For a detailed account of the *Krstić* trial, see Hagan (2003:156–72).
[57] *Krstić* Trial Judgment, §§644–5.

genocide conviction and found Krstić guilty of the lesser charge of aiding and abetting genocide. The Appeals Chamber ruled that the first judgment was correct to find that genocide had in fact occurred in Srebrenica, that General Krstić had been aware of the intention of some members of the Main Staff of the Bosnian Serb Army to commit genocide, and that he had done nothing to prevent the use of men and resources under his command to facilitate the genocidal killings.[58] However, the Appeals Chamber found that the Trial Chamber had not fully established that General Krstić was aware of General Mladić's intention to execute the Bosnian men captured outside Srebrenica.

In these two early cases, prosecutors had satisfied the material elements (*actus reus*) of genocide, and they had proved in *Krstić* that a genocidal plan was carried out at Srebrenica, but in each instance, a potential genocide conviction had fallen at the final hurdle of special intent. This became an ingrained pattern in trial judgments in cases alleging genocide at the ICTY, including those of Milomar Stakić (2003), Vidoje Blagojević (2005), and Momčilo Krajišnik (2006). As a result, ICTY judgments generated controversy, with international law commentators such as Mark Osiel (2009b:117) criticizing the evolving jurisprudence on genocide as "arcane" and "thoroughly estranged from how others understand it."

The reasoning of ICTY judges was vindicated at another international court in The Hague, the International Court of Justice (ICJ), which in 2007 rejected Bosnia's claim that Serbia had committed genocide, finding no conclusive evidence of special intent to destroy Bosniaks as a group in whole or in part. The ICJ judges set the threshold of special intent thus: "The additional intent must also be established, and is defined very precisely. It is often referred to as a special or specific intent or *dolus specialis*.... It is not enough that the members of the group are targeted because they belong to that group, that is because the perpetrator has a discriminatory intent. Something more is required."[59] The ICJ did find that genocide had occurred at Srebrenica in 1995, however, and that Serbia had violated its obligation under the Genocide Convention in not preventing genocide and in not arresting and extraditing Bosnian Serb Army General Ratko Mladić.

The ICTY prosecutors were left to ponder the unexpected outcomes of successive genocide trials. It had been proved in two separate international courts that genocide had occurred at Srebrenica in eastern Bosnia, but judges

---

[58] *Prosecutor v. Radislav Krstić*, Case No. IT-98-33-A, Judgment of Appeals Chamber, 19 April 2004, §§135–9.

[59] International Court of Justice, *Bosnia and Herzegovina v. Serbia and Montenegro. Judgment of 26 February 2007*, p. 70, ¶187.

refused to accept that any of the accused on the stand had actually committed genocide themselves. As the ICJ judgment declared, "something more was required." Up until 2010, those found to have culpability had been only accessories to the crime of genocide. For instance, the Trial Chamber found that Vidoje Blagojević had provided "practical assistance" to those committing genocide at Srebrenica but did not share their criminal responsibility because it was not shown that he had "knowledge of the perpetrators' intent to kill those captured."[60] Who, then, had intended to commit genocide? Were Bosnian Serb leaders Radovan Karadžić and General Ratko Mladić the only ones who possessed the requisite level of special intent?

Prosecutors sought a way through this impasse, asking concretely, What do the Tribunal's judges require in the way of conclusive proof of special intent beyond reasonable doubt? In the absence of a direct written order from the political or military leadership, or both to exterminate all members of a group (unavailable even to Nuremberg prosecutors fifty years earlier), prosecutors had to build a circumstantial case in which specific intent could be inferred from actions and the context of those actions.[61] Prosecutors had to show evidence of acts conforming to genocidal *actus reus*, the existence of a widespread genocidal plan, and that the accused was fully aware of how the individual acts furthered the actually existing plan of group destruction.[62] That is a long chain of inferences, and ICTY judges were clearly unwilling to infer a great deal, unlike their ICTR counterparts in Arusha.

For a finding of genocide, ICTY judges require not only standard intent, as commonly understood in criminal law, but also what they referred to in the *Stakić* Trial Chamber judgment as a "surplus of intent."[63] What might constitute this ineffable "surplus of intent"? One senior prosecutor who wished to remain anonymous expressed uneasiness with the interpretation of special intent that had emerged at the ICTY: "In proving intent, normally all you have are the actions in and around an individual, the circumstances, since you can't get into someone's head. Usually there is no smoking gun, so what else is there apart from their actions? Judges are looking for a kind of evidence that does not exist."[64] The same prosecutor then offered an intriguing reflection on how

---

[60] *Blagojević* Trial Judgment §736, 742, 745.
[61] As the *Brđanin* Trial Judgment states, the "existence of specific intent required for the crime of genocide must be supported by the factual matrix" (§976).
[62] See *Stakić* Trial Judgment, §561. "In order for Dr. Stakić to be held responsible for complicity in genocide, it must be proved that genocide in fact occurred."
[63] *Stakić*, §520.
[64] Author interview, May 2006.

the judges' understanding of the requisite level of special intent ventured into other, more inscrutable domains of intention and desire:

> Sometimes you hear the term "conscious desire" as a way of proving intent. This is an unfortunate choice of words. . . . Conscious desire is almost like motive but in most criminal trials you don't have to prove motive . . . and in a military context it's not really relevant when a soldier is under orders. Judges have taken the view that they will not find special intent unless they see more than just committing or assisting a crime. . . . That is too strict a theory and it requires the prosecution to prove malice, or evilness as a motive for actions.

Such comments provide a valuable window into prosecutorial thinking during the 1998–2010 period. In rejecting the genocide counts brought before them, ICTY judges did seem to be looking beyond intent to "conscious desire," to motive, or to malice aforethought. At the end of the *Krstić* Trial Judgment, the judges ventured as far as to refer to the "insane desire" of Krstić's superior officer General Mladić "to forever rid the Srebrenica area of Muslim civilians" (§724). This statement seems to raise special intent to a level bordering on motive. Conventionally, *intent* refers to what an individual intended to do (e.g., commit murder), whereas *motive* refers to the reasons or motivations for which he or she committed the act (e.g., take revenge for a previous attack) and is not usually necessary to prove guilt in common law crimes.[65] The accepted ICTY jurisprudence also notes "the irrelevance and 'inscrutability' of motives in criminal law.'"[66] The prosecution contested the Chambers' enhanced interpretations of special intent, to no avail. In their appeal against the *Jelisić* judgment, prosecutors had argued that the bench had erroneously drawn from civil law system formulations of intent to elevate it to an unacceptably high threshold of conscious desire.[67] The Trial Chamber had surpassed

---

[65] In Anglo-American criminal law, intent refers to the knowledge that an act or sequence of acts will have a certain definable consequence (e.g., the death of the victim). In the international criminal law of genocide, this idea is preserved, and special intent is understood as "a psychological nexus between the physical result and the mental state of the perpetrator" (*Akayesu* Trial Judgment, §518).

[66] *Prosecutor v. Goran Jelisić*, Case No. IT-95-10 (Appeals Chamber), 5 July 2001, §49 – "the necessity to distinguish specific intent from motive. The personal motive of the perpetrator of the crime of genocide may be, for example, to obtain personal economic benefits, or political advantage or some form of power. The existence of a personal motive does not preclude the perpetrator from also having the specific intent to commit genocide." Citing the *Tadić* Appeals Judgment, §269. The *Brđanin* Trial Judgment reiterated this view at §696.

[67] *Jelisić* Appeals Judgment, §42.

common law understandings of intent to arrive at a concept akin to the German civil law category of *Absicht*, according to the prosecutor's brief.[68]

Are prosecutors justified in their perception that the bar for special intent was set too high at the ICTY? This requires a complex answer. First, it does seem that Anglo-American and civil law courts treat the question of intent differently. Criminal trials in the United States and the United Kingdom are generally held in front of juries rather than a panel of judges, and as a result, specific intent tends to be more plainly formulated, with judicial appeals to "common sense" and "ordinary language."[69] For instance, in the 1985 case in England of *R. v. Moloney*, Law Lord Bridge clarified how judges should direct juries dealing with crimes of specific intent, namely by avoiding "any elaboration or paraphrase of what is meant by intent, and leav[ing] it to the jury's good sense to decide whether the accused acted with the necessary intent."[70] English courts, Lord Bridge continued, could infer specific intent on the basis of the foreseeable consequences of an act or acts. Using Lord Bridge's reasoning, prosecutors would have had an easier task of fulfilling specific-intent criteria and securing convictions of perpetrators such as Krstić and Jelisić for directly committing genocide.

However, the situation is more complex than prosecutors admit. Although a standard U.S. criminal law textbook states, "The law does not recognize motive in most instances: *mens rea* suffices," the same textbook does grant a place for motive, saying that it "might aid in proving *mens rea*" (Samaha 1999:226). Moreover, in criminal and civil cases where racial or ethnic discrimination is alleged, commentators acknowledge that in U.S. legal history, "racial motivation is next to impossible to prove" (Brandwein 2007:262). As a result, twentieth-century U.S. jurisprudence has imposed an "animus standard" for establishing discriminatory intent in cases alleging ethnic, racial, and gender discrimination, employing a standard of proof that is quite comparable to international tribunal judges' threshold of conscious desire.[71]

Second, judges at the ICTY and ICTR have not always distinguished special intent and motive in a consistent manner. When asked directly in interviews, international criminal judges will uphold the accepted jurisprudence, clearly

---

[68] *Jelisić* Appeals Judgment, §42n74. *Absicht* corresponds to the criminal category of *dolus directus*, or direct intent. For a discussion of *mens rea* and *Absicht* in international criminal law, see Badar (2005).

[69] See Lacey (1993) on the ambiguities in the concept of intention despite attempts by judges to simplify the language of *mens rea* in British criminal law.

[70] (1985) 1 A.C. at p. 926, cited in Harris (1993:229).

[71] See, for example, U.S. Supreme Court case *Guardians Assn. v. Civil Svc. Comm'n*, 463 U.S. 582 (1983), indicating in a Title VI case that a plaintiff may establish discriminatory intent by presenting evidence of discriminatory animus.

separating specific intent from motive. However, Tribunal decisions and judgments have allowed ambiguity to slip in. For instance, the *Blaskić* Appeals Judgment endorsed the relevance of motive to determining special intent as follows: "Motive is also to be considered in two further circumstances: first, where it is a required element in crimes such as specific intent crimes, which by their nature require a particular motive."[72] The first genocide conviction at an international criminal tribunal, *Akayesu* (ICTR), confused matters when it introduced "ulterior motive" into the definition of special intent.[73] Subsequent ICTR judgments also conflated and confused motive and intent by referring to an "ulterior purpose" and "ulterior motive" to destroy a group during discussions of intent.[74] A passage from the *Musema* Trial Judgment gives a flavor of this: "The perpetration of the act charged, therefore extends beyond its actual commission . . . to encompass the realization of the ulterior purpose to destroy the group in whole or in part."[75] Muddled thinking on this issue is not only confined to the two *ad hoc* international criminal tribunals; it can be found throughout the history of the genocide concept, and Alexander Greenwalt (1999:2278–9) documents the trouble the committees drafting the Genocide Convention in 1948 experienced in trying to differentiate the categories of intent, special intent, and motive.

Third, and perhaps ironically, the prosecution itself has contributed to the confusion surrounding special intent, as when it used the expression "conscious desire" in early genocide trials. The prosecution's pretrial brief in *Krstić* stated that the accused and his coperpetrators "consciously desired their acts to lead to the destruction of part of the Bosnian Muslim people as a group."[76] Once they grasped the deleterious ramifications of the concept of conscious desire, prosecuting attorneys generally avoided it wherever possible.

In the concrete daily practice of planning their case strategy, the deductions prosecutors made appear comprehensible: the burden of proof for special intent does look a lot like conscious or willful desire, bordering on motive. We may never know whether the majority of ICTY judges actually view special intent in this way. What matters for understanding the strategies adopted by

---

[72] *Prosecutor v. Tihomir Blaskić*, Appeals Chamber Judgment, IT-95-14-A, 29 July 2004, §694.

[73] *Akayesu*, §522. "The perpetration of the act charged therefore extends beyond its actual commission, for example, the murder of a particular individual, for the realisation of an ulterior motive, which is to destroy, in whole or part, the group of which the individual is just one element."

[74] See *Akayesu* Trial Judgment, §522; *Musema* Trial Judgment, §165; *Rutaganda* Trial Judgment, §60.

[75] *Musema* Trial Judgment, §165.

[76] Prosecutor's pretrial brief pursuant to Rule 65 *ter* (E)(i), 25 February 2000, ¶90, cited in *Krstić*, §569.

the prosecution is that many ICTY prosecutors believe that judges raise special intent to a higher level of conscious desire. As we will see in the subsequent section, this prompted some STAs to underscore historical factors in building an inferential case for special intent. When presented with the statement, "Prosecutors lead historical evidence in the Trial Chamber in order to give a sense of the motivation for the crimes," 57 percent of all those surveyed agreed or strongly agreed, 14 percent were neutral, and 24 percent disagreed or strongly disagreed.[77] When disaggregated, the figures show a more variegated picture, with 73 percent of respondents from the Office of the Prosecutor and 69 percent of expert witnesses (both prosecution and defense) either agreeing or strongly agreeing with the statement. Only 29 percent of defense team members agreed, however. For the great majority of prosecutors surveyed and interviewed, historical evidence speaks to the motivations and mental state of the accused, as vividly illustrated in one of the most notorious international criminal trials conducted thus far.

4.6. MONUMENTAL HISTORY AND A "SURPLUS OF INTENT" IN THE TRIAL OF SLOBODAN MILOŠEVIĆ

I recognize that this trial will make history, and we would do well to approach our task in the light of history.
— Chief Prosecutor Carla Del Ponte, at the start of the trial of Slobodan Milošević[78]

"It's rubbish.... I don't know what you're talking about."
— Presiding Judge Richard May to Slobodan Milošević 24 July 2003 (T24866)

Widely denounced as a "fiasco," where the accused, Slobodan Milošević, "derailed the trial" and made "a political mockery of the proceedings by casting them as a show trial,"[79] the *Milošević* trial is nonetheless instructive, as it represented the high-water mark of historical debate at the ICTY. Here, we see the greatest role for a grand, sweeping metanarrative of history that led inexorably to the alleged crimes of the accused. The *Milošević* trial is simultaneously the best demonstration of how extensive use of historical evidence can

---

[77] Three percent expressed no opinion
[78] *Prosecutor v. Slobodan Milošević*, hearing, 12 February 2002, Transcript 8, cited in Boas (2007:112).
[79] Moghalu (2007:67–8). Boas's (2007:110) book on the trial says as much, though in more careful terms, criticizing the prosecution for over-indicting and "trying to prove too much," and for its application for combining the three indictments that made the trial an enormous process beset by "significant case management problems."

be functional to the prosecution's thesis and why it represents a risky strategy, especially when a high-profile defendant is representing himself before the court.

The trial of Slobodan Milošević commenced with saturation media coverage and tremendously high expectations. It was, after all, the trial of a former European head of state who had thumbed his nose at the United States, the European Union, and NATO and had skillfully played diplomatic games to his political advantage. Perhaps more substantially, Milošević had been the most powerful political and military actor in the former Yugoslavia. He was the architect of an armed conflict that, according to conservative estimates by statistician Jakub Bijak and ICTY demographer Ewa Tabeau (2005:207), left more than one hundred thousand dead in Bosnia and Herzegovina alone, and the majority (54 percent) of fatalities were civilians. As president of Yugoslavia and then Serbia and Montenegro, Milošević had held a position of superior responsibility, exercising effective control over the Yugoslav National Army that played a central role in the Balkans' conflicts of 1991–5.

In the media and more widely, the success of the trial seemingly hinged on a successful genocide conviction. Yet when the mammoth four-and-a-half year trial of Milošević commenced on 12 February 2002, no genocide count was included in any of the three indictments for Kosovo, Croatia, and Bosnia. A genocide charge with respect to Bosnia alone was introduced by Chief Prosecutor Carla del Ponte in late 2002, against the advice of some of her own senior prosecutors, who, along with a number of prominent international criminal law scholars, feared that the charge would be impossible to prove.[80] There was no direct evidence of an executive order or written blueprint for genocide, and the prosecution conceded during the trial, "[T]here is little direct evidence to that precise effect, such as a specific order to commit genocide signed by the accused or a confession by him."[81] The case for special intent was therefore inferential and circumstantial, but as we have seen, ICTY judges had thus far found fault with various prosecution arguments for special intent that were based on circumstantial evidence. The prosecution could find little support for its case in preceding Tribunal trials: although the judges had ruled that genocide had occurred at Srebrenica in *Krstić*, they made no finding regarding the alleged complicity or involvement of Milošević in the massacre. As the prosecution's case unfolded, Tribunal reporting agencies fretted that

---

[80] Moghalu (2007:66). See Scharf and Schabas (2002:129–30) for a skeptical view of the genocide charge.

[81] *Prosecutor v. Slobodan Milošević*, Decision on Motion for Judgment of Acquittal, IT-02-54-T, 16 June 2004, §121.

genocide would not be proved against Milošević because the "burden of proof [was] too high."[82]

Prosecutors asked where they might identify the mystery ingredient that would show a surplus of intent beyond all reasonable doubt. Might a compelling historical narrative help them demonstrate the requisite degree of special intent to the satisfaction of ICTY judges? In the eyes of some STAs, a historical review of nationalist ideology might assist them in providing additional and compelling evidence of the surplus of intent that judges seemed to be looking for. Milošević's foremost adversary in the trial, the British barrister Geoffrey Nice, was one such prosecuting attorney. Having previously served as a prosecutor in *Jelisić*, Nice already had a bitter experience of the judges' elevated threshold for special intent, and moreover, he was personally inclined to attach value to the history and culture of the region.

The prosecution's theoretical armature rested on historical arguments, from the beginning to the end of the Milošević trial. Its thesis was this: special intent to commit genocide was not accidental but the culmination of a century-old ideological program to carve a Greater Serbia from the patchwork of minorities in the Balkans. Genocidal acts in the 1990s were motivated by an impassioned commitment to an extreme Serb nationalist ideology stretching back into the nineteenth century. Serb nationalism's long-held animus toward other ethnic, national, and religious groups sanctioned individual acts of malice and indicated a conscious or willful desire to destroy protected groups in whole or in part, as such.

While premeditation is not required to make a finding of genocide, for acts to be considered genocidal, they must be carried out in furtherance of a genocidal policy or program that is known and understood by the actors in advance:[83] the ICTR's *Kayishema* Trial Judgment states plainly that for the crime of genocide to occur, *mens rea* must be formed before the commission of the genocidal acts (§91). During the *Kayishema* trial, the prosecution produced a substantial amount of evidence of premeditation, showing how massacres were prearranged months in advance by mayors who distributed lists of Tutsis.[84] Likewise at the ICTY, the case for guilt was assisted if it could be shown that violent

---

[82]   Stacey Sullivan, "Milosevic and Genocide: Has the Prosecution Made the Case?" Institute for War and Peace Reporting, 18 February 2004.

[83]   *Krstić* Trial Judgment, §572: "Article 4 of the Statute does not require that the genocidal acts be premeditated over a long period."

[84]   See *Kayishema* Trial Judgment, §309. *Kayishema* also states: "the massacres of the Tutsi population indeed were meticulously planned and systematically coordinated by top level Hutu extremists in the former Rwandan government at the time in question" (§289).

criminal acts were in furtherance of a long-standing aspiration for a monoethnic state. One member of the LRT and the Milošević prosecution team, Dr. Nena Tromp-Vrkić (2009:5–6), elucidated her understanding of the historical salience of nationalism: "A [criminal] plan often derives from ideological concepts conceived in the past. The plan as charged in the indictments against Milošević developed over decades, even centuries. A proper understanding of such an ideology applied contemporaneously is best achieved, or perhaps can only be achieved, when placed in a broader historical context."

Greater Serbia is an idea conventionally traced back to certain currents in Serb nationalism in the mid-nineteenth century. In 1844, the Serb Minister for Internal Affairs Ilija Garašanin produced a founding document titled *Načertanije* (defined variously as "Program," "Outline," or "Principles") that proposed a Greater Serbia, understood as a plan to expand the Serbian state into all territories inhabited by Serbs.[85] The category of "Serb" applies to those who speak any variant of the "Štokavian dialect," regardless of their religion and including members of the Orthodox, Catholic, and Muslim faiths.[86] The ideological genealogy of Greater Serbia had already been presented during the *Tadić* trial (§§85–96), and prosecutors would rehearse the same historical evidence in each subsequent trial of Bosnian Serb political or military leaders, reading out the relevant sections of the *Tadić* Trial Judgment.[87] Prosecution cases against Bosnian Serbs generally followed the same format: an overarching argument would be built on nationalist Serbs' pursuit of a Greater Serbia. Then prosecutors would turn to the operational level and the "Six Strategic Goals" announced by Radovan Karadžić to the Bosnian Serb Assembly in 1992, which laid out, *inter alia*, a policy to separate Serbs from Muslims and Croats, to establish a corridor between Semberija in Serbia and Krajina in Croatia, and to overrun the border on the Drina River and set a new one along the rivers Una and Neretva. Then prosecutors would scrutinize the local and individual levels, presenting the minutes of meetings of assemblies and municipalities, and lead evidence on the actions and words of the accused. In this way, prosecutors went beyond the indeterminate, umbrella causation of *Tadić* to assert a direct causality between past and present.

[85] According to many historians of the Balkans, in its draft form, the treatise originally called for unity of South Slavs, but Garašanin altered its intended purpose.

[86] Drawing from nineteenth-century linguists such as Vuk Stafanović Karadžić, and maintained by modern proponents such as Vojislav Šešelj. See Šešelj's elucidation of Greater Serbia during the Milošević trial on 25 August 2005, Trial Transcript 43215.

[87] For instance, when cross-examining defense expert witness Dr. Nenad Kećmanović in the trial of Blagoje Simić, 12 November 2002, Trial Transcript 12108.

The standard recipe for trying leaders several steps removed from criminal acts assumed a new and special prominence in the *Milošević* trial, in that the historical argument about Greater Serbia became a central plank in the prosecution's thesis regarding special intent. History performed clear and identifiable functions in the trial, anchoring the prosecution's arguments for special intent. As Boas (2007:90) notes: "The Prosecution case theory revolved around Milošević's espousal of and aspirations for a Greater Serbia." This first became evident in the combining of the three indictments against Milošević. In 2000–1, there were originally three separate indictments and as we just saw, none included a charge of genocide. When Geoffrey Nice became lead prosecutor in mid-2001, the indictment for events in Kosovo in 1999 was complete, and the Bosnia and Croatia indictments were still pending but near completion. Intensive discussions took place about whether prosecutors should proceed with Kosovo alone or combine all three into one vast trial. According to members of the prosecution team, Nice advanced the view that the trial should leave a historical record for posterity, and this justified combining the Bosnia, Croatia, and Kosovo indictments. In late 2001, the prosecution used a historical justification when petitioning the court to combine the indictments, claiming that all three fell under "the same transaction in the sense of a common scheme, strategy or plan, namely the accused Milošević's overall conduct in attempting to create a 'Greater Serbia' – a centralized Serbian state encompassing the Serb populated areas of Croatia, and Bosnia and Hercegovina, and all of Kosovo."[88] The plan to create a Greater Serbia was the organizing principle integrating the three elements of the case. The connection between an overarching plan and special intent was spelled out in the Appeals Chamber judgment in *Jelisić*: "in the context of proving specific intent, the existence of a plan or policy may become an important factor."[89]

Even though historical debates raged in the courtroom during the *Milošević* trial, I should make clear that historical evidence was only one element in the prosecution's case for special intent. While it did construct a scaffolding for the prosecution case, the history of the former Yugoslavia gained relevance from its combination with other forms of evidence that pointed toward the accused's superior responsibility for atrocities committed by official agents of the Socialist Federal Republic of Yugoslavia (then from April 1992 onward the Federal Republic of Yugoslavia) and by Bosnian Serb forces and paramilitaries. This evidence included minutes of meetings such as those of the Supreme

---

[88] *Prosecutor v. Slobodan Milošević*, Case No. IT-99-37-PT, IT-01-50-PT, IT-01-51-I, Prosecution's Motion for Joinder, 27 November 2001, §113, cited in Boas (2007:91).
[89] *Jelisić* Appeals Judgment, 5 July 2001, §48.

Defense Council, as well as electronic intercepts of telephone conversations with Bosnian Serb leader Radovan Karadžić confirming that Belgrade was supplying funds, arms, and equipment to Bosnian Serbs.

4.7. DEBATING SERBIAN NATIONALISM IN THE TWENTIETH CENTURY

The prosecution commissioned Dr. Audrey Helfant Budding as its historical expert in the *Milošević* trial, and her primary role was to develop a thesis on a long-standing Serb mind-set that could speak to the mental elements of the crime of genocide. Budding was eminently qualified: she had worked at the U.S. embassy in Belgrade in the 1980s and then obtained a Ph.D. from Harvard University (her dissertation is titled "Serb Intellectuals and the National Question"). Her expert report, titled "Expert Report: Serbian Nationalism in the Twentieth Century: Historical Background and Context," claimed the existence of a collective Serbian "national mind-set" (Budding 2003:1, 14), under the direct influence of the Serb National Academy in Belgrade that performed the role of articulating "Serb national thought" (1, 4, 17, 20). Budding's theoretical approach was informed by the foremost modern critic of nationalism, Ernest Gellner (2), who famously defined nationalism as a political principle that maintains that the political unit (i.e., the state) must be congruent with the national or cultural unit, or both (e.g., the Serb nation). For Gellner, nationalism was also a sentiment, usually of indignation, that often led to intense confrontations with neighbors (where one's conationals may unfortunately reside) and internal minorities (who may not share the dominant national culture). In Gellner's theory, nationalism raises cultural prejudice and intolerance to the level of a state ideology.

According to Budding, nationalist tensions in twentieth-century Yugoslavia were held in check by the rules of the game – the game being the state of the Federal Republic of Yugoslavia, which was created by a political compromise between various nations and in which Serbs assumed the a role of stewardship. The weakening of Yugoslav unity, hastened by the political decentralization occurring in the late 1960s, early 1970s, and late 1980s, became the basis for the mobilization of all "nationally-minded Serbs" who perceived that the rules of the game had been violated (58): "More specifically, the weakening of Yugoslav unity immediately and dramatically focused the attention of nationally-minded Serbs *within* Serbia on the position of Serbs outside Serbia" (14). Yugoslavia was an inherently unstable political bargain, and an economic crisis coupled with the failure of the political system to contain the mounting pressures triggered an outbreak of nationalist sentiment: "Serbian,

Croatian and Slovene nation-state ideologies were always incompatible with a multinational Yugoslav state – but it was system failure that catapulted these ideologies from relatively marginal status to political prominence" (48). Budding remarked on the decisive role of the accused in the rapid rise of extreme nationalist politics: "Milošević's policies and rhetoric . . . helped these forces move from marginal to dominant political positions" (60).

Under examination by Geoffrey Nice, Budding proposed a directly causal relationship between nineteenth- and twentieth-century nationalist ideology: "The idea of collecting all the people in one state is not in any way unique to Serbian nationalism. It's really the principle that's central to all nationalisms, that cultural and political borders ought to coincide. In my view, this element of Serbian nationalism became particularly destructive and self-destructive at the end of the twentieth century *because* Serbs in the course of the nineteenth century had sought a unified state."[90] In her use of the word *because*, nationalism becomes a historical vector, bearing conflict and destruction through the various epochs. In the Trial Chamber, the prosecution's objective in calling Budding to the stand became apparent: the foundations for genocidal *mens rea* were embedded in a Serb national mind-set. In the prosecution's theory of the case, special intent and extremist nationalist ideology are both mind-sets; the former is criminal and the second is historico-political. They are bound together insofar as the crimes contained in the indictments were an extension of the nationalist project to defend and enlarge Greater Serbia. Budding clarified her understanding of the connection between nationalism and the dissolution of the Yugoslav state when she explained "the emergence of a Serbian national mind-set" as

> a set of beliefs related to the Serbian question in Yugoslavia, and a central component of that belief was that if Yugoslavia was not to exist as a unified state, as a state that might unite all Serbs, then Serbia ought to attempt to protect or unite, if not all Serbs, at least as many Serbs as possible. This phenomenon is very visible in the period of Yugoslavia's dissolution. (T24823)

Then came Slobodan Milošević's turn to cross-examine the expert witness. Although Milošević had attended law school in Belgrade, he had no prior courtroom experience, but he could still be a wily cross-examiner. He began by attacking Budding's methods and denouncing what he saw as historical reductionism: "[T]he historian blames Serbian nationalists for using Garašanin's *Načertanije*, as she writes in her report, from the Second World War, claiming

---

[90]   23 July 2003, Trial Transcript 24826 (emphasis added). Budding testified at the ICTY over two days from 23–24 July 2003. All transcript references in this subsequent section refer to those days.

Muslims, Montenegrins as Serbs or blaming Vuk Karadzic for counting as Serbs everyone who uses the Stokavian dialect. That is a projection of a historical situation onto another period which amounts to the gravest methodological mistake in the science of history" (T24866–9). At this point, Presiding Judge Richard May intervened on behalf of the expert witness, calling the accused's assertion "absolute nonsense" (T24866).

Undeterred, Milošević accused Budding of bias in her selection of historical sources, which to his mind did not include enough Serbian historiography (T24872) and omitted relevant historical events such as the oppression of Serbs by the Ottoman Empire (T24877) and the murder of Serbs by "fascist" Albanian guerillas during World War II (T24859). Milošević also made reckless and unfounded allegations, for instance claiming that Budding had portrayed Serbs as "primitive and wild," which prompted Judge Richard May to intervene and prevent him from proceeding further (T24876). This was courtroom theater at its most dramatic, with the accused folding his arms scornfully, engaging in epic scowling, and using his derisive wit to thwart the proceedings wherever possible. His methods melded the serious and outlandish, and he deployed scurrilous tactics that would have led to the disbarring of any defense counsel who had the temerity to use them. One ICTY legal officer commented, almost admiringly, "Contemptuous, indignant, swaggering and self-righteous, he's made this *his* trial in every sense."[91] Milošević took full advantage of the stage to advance his own version of history and to score political points with the audience watching the spectacle on television in Serbia, a service underwritten by U.S. taxpayers.

In cross-examining Budding, Milošević comingled a flurry of references to European high-romantic philosophers such as Herder and Fichte (T24899–24900), with febrile conspiracy theories, for example that Garašanin's *Načertinaje* was actually the creation of a British diplomat based in Istanbul called "David Urkvart" (T24917), all the while making esoteric points about distant Balkans history that only a specialist (or extreme nationalist) could hope to follow. The judges simmered openly, their frustration boiling over on several occasions during the two days of Budding's testimony and cross-examination. Judge May turned off Milošević's microphone three times after the accused ignored his request to cease listing authors and books not referred to in the expert report (T24875, T24881). To her credit, Budding maintained her dignity and composure during the unpleasant cross-examination. She stoically defended her report and refused to be drawn into futile debates, such as

---

[91] Julian Davis Mortenson, "A Week at the Trial of Slobodan Milosevic," *Slate*, 16 September 2005, http://www.slate.com/id/2126142.

regarding the role of international actors like the Vatican in the disintegration of Yugoslavia and whether the Balkans conflict represents "a clash of civilizations" along the lines of Samuel Huntingdon's thesis (T24855). She allowed the accused to hold forth and advance his own historical thesis of Serb oppression and valiant resistance. She accepted some of his interpretations and did not oppose claims that were peripheral to her report. Unlike a number of other expert witnesses, she did not react to Milošević's provocations, but the experience seemed to have scarred Budding. She never returned to the ICTY, left academic history, and declined requests to comment on her experience on the stand.

4.8. DID GREATER SERBIA CONSTITUTE A PLAN TO COMMIT GENOCIDE?

Even if Milošević was unable to demolish the prosecution's main historical expert witness, later in the trial he managed to raise serious doubts regarding the prosecution's thesis on nationalism and Greater Serbia. He called the bombastic Serb nationalist politician Vojislav Šešelj as his defense historical expert witness, and Šešelj, brushing aside judges' attempts to rein in his testimony, lectured the Trial Chamber about how he and his Serb Radical Party were the main advocates of Greater Serbia. This had never been a goal of the accused, who "had nothing to do with it."[92] Milošević mocked Geoffrey Nice's reliance on Greater Serbia as the "red thread bringing all parts of the case together," adding for rhetorical flourish that "even Franz Kafka would feel that he did not have [a] great imagination compared to this."[93] Milošević railed that prosecutor Nice had made "vague and incredible nebulous arguments." Moreover:

> I did not organize these three separatist movements in Croatia, Bosnia, and Kosovo in order to create a Yugoslavia in which all Serbs could live in one state when Yugoslavia has been existing for 70 years. Is there any logic in this? This is insulting to the average intelligence of an average man![94]

Debates over the exact significance of Greater Serbia in the politics of the former Yugoslavia confused the judges, who eventually lost track of exactly what Greater Serbia meant in the prosecution's argument and specifically whether it conformed to an ideology of malice and extermination or whether

[92] 25 August 2005, T43215; see also Boas (2007:90).
[93] 29 November 2005, T46688–9.
[94] 25 August 2005, T43230.

it merely justified a common garden variety land grab. This was not helped by the fact that the prosecution's use of Greater Serbia varied during the trial. At the beginning of the trial, Greater Serbia was the common factor that compelled the joining of the three indictments, but over the course of the trial, it was applied to the Croatia and Bosnia indictments, but not to Kosovo, making the prosecution case "inconsistent," according to Boas (2007:91). Toward the end of the trial, Judge Robinson noted that the prosecution's position had backed away from its reliance on Greater Serbia to an "extended Serbia," a reduced, and less ideologically motivated notion.[95]

The prosecution's historical thesis suffered a major setback when Geoffrey Nice "acknowledged that the words 'Greater Serbia' never fell from the accused's lips . . . to our knowledge."[96] How could the prosecution have relied so heavily on a notion that the accused had never actually uttered in public? Lacking any evidence that Milošević had ever publicly espoused a Greater Serbia, it is hard to understand why the prosecution team would have made it the centerpiece of its theory of special intent. To be fair, Slobodan Milošević had regularly exploited nationalist sentiments to advance his political career, and he had promoted many of the key tenets of Greater Serbia ideology, even in the ICTY Trial Chamber. For example, he adopted a skeptical position toward Bosnia and Herzegovina and Kosovo as viable national entities that could function without Serb stewardship.[97] According to the accused, Muslims of Bosnia, converted to Islam only "to avoid terror and violence by Turkish authorities," were essentially "Serbs" (T24897), and even up to the mid-twentieth century, many Slovene and Bosnian Muslims still identified as "Serbs" (T24847).

Despite these unanswered questions, the Greater Serbia thesis was accepted by judges more or less as the prosecution intended in the Trial Chamber's "Decision on Motion for Judgment of Acquittal" of 16 June 2004 under Rule 98 *bis*. Also known as an interim judgment, this decision makes known the judges' determination of which counts are irredeemably unsubstantiated and those for which the evidence offered up to that point carries enough probative value that the Trial Chamber could potentially convict. The judges asked, "Is there evidence upon which a Trial Chamber could be satisfied that the Accused was a participant in the joint criminal enterprise and that he shared the required intent of its participants?" (§248). The bench answered in the

[95] 29 November 2005, T46708.

[96] 29 November 2005, T46723.

[97] 24 July 2003, T24920 and T24948, when he claimed U.S. diplomat Christopher Hill called Kosovo "Disneyland."

affirmative, finding that Slobodan Milošević was the "Leader of All Serbs," citing as evidence the following:

> Mr. Babic testified that the Accused was the leader of the Serbian people in Yugoslavia, and the people in Knin saw him as the protector of the Serbs in Yugoslavia. Ambassador Galbraith testified that he believed that the accused "was the architect of a policy of creating Greater Serbia and that little happened without his knowledge and involvement." (§249)

Most crucial of all was the Trial Chamber's determination of whether Milošević was criminally responsible for genocide in Bosnia: "a Trial Chamber could be satisfied beyond reasonable doubt that the Accused was a participant in the joint criminal enterprise, found by the Trial Chamber . . . to include the Bosnian Serb leadership, and that he shared with its participants the aim and intention to destroy a part of the Bosnian Muslims as a group. . . . On the basis of the evidence as to – (1) the overall leadership position of the Accused among the Serbian people, including the Bosnian Serbs in Bosnia and Herzegovina; (2) the Accused's advocacy of and support for the concept of a Greater Serbia" (§288).

With its arguments vindicated in the 2004 interim judgment, the prosecution team adhered to the historical component of special intent right up to the end of the trial. In early 2006, Geoffrey Nice consulted his prosecution team on the prosecution's closing arguments and asked what should serve as the starting date for the historical discussion. Nice recommended beginning with the Field of Blackbirds in Kosovo in 1389 and tracing the connections through the following six hundred years until the crimes of Slobodan Milošević. Some applauded this approach, and one member of the prosecution team remarked, "Geoffrey Nice was the only Senior Trial Attorney who understood the importance of history."[98] Others were uncomfortable with the strategy. Another team member objected, "No one can be prosecuted for what someone else did in 1389."[99] Closing arguments were never delivered, due to the ill health of the defendant, who would die of hypertension only weeks before judgment was passed.

4.9. IS HISTORICAL EVIDENCE RELEVANT FOR PROVING MENS REA IN GENOCIDE CASES?

Reading international criminal law textbooks, one might get the impression that the law emerges perfectly formed like Pallas Athena from the head of Zeus, but it is more like a misshapen piece of iron, beaten on the anvil by

---

[98] Author interview, May 2006.
[99] Author interviews, June 2006 and June 2007.

many different blacksmiths. In the reformulations of special intent to commit genocide in international criminal law, we get a sense of law as a dynamic and, in some ways, even contingent process, shaped by rules and core principles to be sure but also refashioned by the changing strategies of the legal actors. In advance of the trials at the ICTY and ICTR, no one knew what the burden of proof for special intent to commit genocide was, and ICTY prosecutors, seeking a way through the impasse, adopted a variety of conscious strategies designed to convince judges.

When asked a year or so after the *Milošević* trial had ended whether the prosecution had taken too historical an approach, Leadership Research Team member Nena Tromp-Vrkić replied: "No. You have to leave a record. We only had one historical expert report by Audrey Budding plus Ton de Zwaan's so we were not obsessed with history. Milošević based his defense heavily on historical arguments. What were we supposed to do, ignore that? It is a misconception that one is introduced to the detriment of the other. You can present both crime-based evidence and historical context."[100] Although the prosecution ostensibly succeeded in having its position on Greater Serbia accepted as it intended, it would be the last time that an ICTY prosecution team constructed the rationale for *mens rea* on historical foundations and so wholeheartedly embraced historical inquiry and debate. Other prosecuting attorneys are drawn into historical discussions, but they enter into them reluctantly and tread more carefully than before. Over time, most prosecutors retreated to a more conventional crime-based methodology based on documents and fact-witness testimony, an approach with less exalted intellectual ambitions perhaps but also less risk of malfunctioning.

Even though 2004 represents the high-water mark (or nadir, depending on your point of view) of historical argumentation by the prosecution at the ICTY, the notion that that historical evidence is needed to prove genocidal special intent is still widespread at the Tribunal and among expert witnesses. In our survey, we asked respondents, "Is historical evidence relevant for proving *mens rea* in genocide cases?" My expectation was that there would be a strong division of opinion, in which prosecutors would agree with this statement and defense lawyers would categorically oppose it, but instead there was a statistically significant consensus between respondents on the question (Figures 4.2 and 4.3).

Breaking the figures down showed that respondents from the Office of the Prosecutor were more inclined toward viewing historical evidence as highly or somewhat relevant for special intent (81 percent) but not by an overwhelming

[100] Author interview, June 2007.

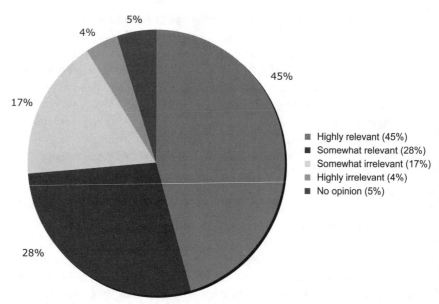

FIGURE 4.2. Is historical evidence relevant for proving *mens rea* in genocide cases (all respondents)?

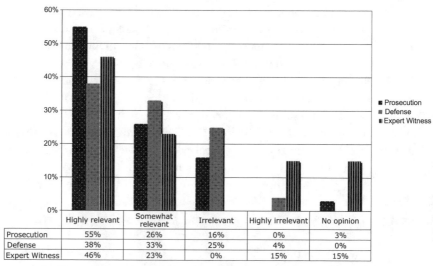

FIGURE 4.3. Is historical evidence relevant for proving *mens rea* in genocide cases? (Prosecution, Defense, and Expert Witness).

margin over defense counsel (71 percent) or expert witnesses for both prosecution and defense (69 percent).

These raw figures require further deliberation, particularly with regard to the stated views of the defense. Conceivably as a result of the judgment in *Tadić*, the Rule 98 *bis* decision in the *Milošević* trial and other decisions and judgments, the relevance of historical evidence in genocide trials has become widely accepted at the Tribunal. Yet even that would still beg the question, Why would the defense subscribe to this view, especially given its willingness to object energetically to many other aspects of the Tribunal's thinking and procedure? We have seen in this chapter how prosecutors incorporate historical evidence into their case, but what is the appeal for defense attorneys? Chapter 6 addresses this topic in detail, but perhaps defense teams perceive an advantage in the ICTY judges' fastidious application of special intent. Greenwalt (1999:2294) finds that the ICTY's conceptualization of special intent "invites obfuscation by defendants, allowing them to escape genocidal liability through their manipulation of ideology and hierarchy."

Recounting the history of nationalist ideologies in the former Yugoslavia, then, may allow defense greater latitude to lead evidence that sews generalized uncertainty about superior responsibility – especially given the exceedingly complex nature of Balkan history. All national histories are multifaceted, intricate, and hotly debated, but there are moments when the former Yugoslavia seems to be in a category all of its own. Virtually any argument can be made from the convoluted history of twentieth-century Yugoslavia, including many that refute the more deterministic version of nationalism advanced by the prosecution. In the aftermath of the *Milošević* trial, a more indirect and complex relationship would develop between history and criminal intent at the Tribunal.

5

From Monumental History to Microhistories

5.1. THE RISING TIDE OF JUDICIAL FRUSTRATION

After the trial of Slobodan Milošević, there was a precipitous decline in historical debate at the ICTY, as the managerial judging model gained traction and transformed the way in which prosecutors presented evidence in trials. The cracks had already started appearing during the interminable *Milošević* trial itself, and the ICTY's completion strategy resulted in more pressure on prosecutors to reduce the size of their cases, from the number of municipalities included in the indictment to the number of witnesses called in a trial. Aware of the growing impatience at the UN Security Council, and admonished by the Tribunal President Jorda, Trial Chamber judges openly vented their frustration with the historical contest playing out before them. During the day and a half of Audrey Budding's testimony on 23–24 July 2003, Judge Richard May interrupted the proceedings fifteen times, encouraging the parties to "move on" or "go on" and asking repeatedly, "What is the question?"[1]

Judge May's irritation was primarily directed at the disruptive defendant but at times implied a broader disdain for any historical deliberations, as when he scolded Milošević for lingering over the finer points of Serbian nationalism in the early twentieth century: "You have spent the best part of three hours arguing with the witness mainly on, as far as I can see, totally irrelevant matter."[2] The matter would seem irrelevant for the trier of fact, perhaps. This exchange and others like it provide a glimpse into why the ICTY held such low approval ratings in the former Yugoslavia. Historical events that were precious, and even bordered on sacred, to the local population were often seen as "totally irrelevant matter" by judges at the international criminal tribunal, and they could claim the attention of the court only when they were germane

[1] *Milošević* Trial Transcript, 24 July 2003, T24911.
[2] *Milošević* Trial Transcript, 24 July 2003, T24932.

to determining a specific point of law or fact. Judge May's replacement, Judge Patrick Robinson, expressed his ennui even more candidly with the defendant: "I want to make it clear I'm not interested in this. . . . Did you hear what I said? I said I'm not interested in a general discussion on Greater Serbia."[3]

A similar pattern of judicial frustration with extended treatises on Balkan history can be found in other ICTY trials as well, some of them even preceding *Milošević*. During the testimony of an historian expert witness in the trial of Milomir Stakić, Judge Wolfgang Schomburg pointedly reminded both the prosecution and the defense: "It was on purpose that I asked both parties in the beginning not to start history with the tribes in the 5th and 6th century. It doesn't make sense at all. . . . I have to ask you, concentrate yourselves first of all on this limited time and the limited area."[4] By 2005–6, Senior Trial Attorneys at the ICTY had obviously internalized the judges' proclivities: "Judges are now critical of the Office of the Prosecutor for our historical references, that we spend too much time proving the larger context. Now they say, 'Why don't you get to the point?'"[5] According to another STA, "[J]udges are tired of lots of evidence" – not only historical evidence but also what they see as repetitive testimony from eyewitnesses and victims.[6]

5.2. LOST IN TRANSLATION

In response to the overt signals from judges, STAs began to limit the scope of expert witness testimony. This shift not only was externally driven but also was related to the problems that many attorneys experienced when handling expert-witness evidence in the courtroom. Expert historians and social scientists, no matter how high their standing in their chosen field of academic or scholarly inquiry, often struggled in the transition to the courtroom, with its adversarial process and uniquely legal ways of knowing. For their part, prosecutors seldom attempted to clarify explicitly to the court their understanding of the relationship between legal standards of proof on the one hand and the knowledge produced by scholarly methods and theories on the other hand. During defense cross-examination, experts were often left alone to defend the integrity of their techniques and conclusions.

The absence of adequate preparation of experts for the court experience could be identified long before the expert took the stand. Interactions between

---

[3] 29 November 2005, T46731.
[4] 24 April 2002, T2127–8. Judge Schomburg was an early innovator of a model of historical evidence that emerged in the *Brđanin* trial.
[5] Author interview, May 2006.
[6] Author interview, May 2006.

experts and prosecuting attorneys were first initiated when the STAs commissioned an expert witness to undertake a discrete task and made available the necessary documents to write an expert report. Then staff from the ICTY's Leadership Research Team (LRT) would review and fact-check their expert report meticulously, so that every claim was footnoted with a list of relevant documents and that overall it met the criteria of, in the words of one LRT staff member, "verifiable, falsifiable and defensible in the Trial Chamber."[7] Staff ensured that each claim was supported by authenticated sources and matched the information and documents held by the LRT.[8] However, all the emphasis was on the product (the expert report) rather than the person. Experts received little in the way of training by the Office of the Prosecutor regarding courtroom conventions or legal criteria for weighing facts and evidence. In my interviews, I encountered no evidence of attorneys "coaching" prosecution or, for that matter, defense experts.[9] Many experts without prior courtroom experience reported feeling overwhelmed, having not anticipated the vehemence of the assault on their professional credentials, expertise, research methods and conclusions. Defense attorneys would trawl through the expert's curriculum vitae, probing for any weak spots and reading out critical reviews of their scholarly work, and their attacks frequently bordered on *ad hominem*. Equally, defense experts under cross-examination faced identical efforts by prosecutors to discredit them. For lawyers, this was all just routine procedure, simply "testing the witness," but for scholars, it was unlike anything they had experienced in a seminar setting.

As Figure 5.1 shows, when asked to rate the degree to which contextual expert witnesses called by the prosecution were appropriately prepared for courtroom testimony, a majority of prosecutors thought that their own experts were appropriately prepared. Defense lawyers were less impressed with the prosecution's experts, but as we will see in the subsequent chapter, they did not rate their own experts a great deal higher. Expert witnesses ranked their own courtroom performance more highly than defense lawyers but offered a less confident appraisal of their own preparation than did prosecutors.

When expert witnesses were asked to rate their experience of a criminal justice system before their involvement with the Tribunal, 8 percent reported it as

---

[7] Author interview, May 2006.
[8] There was a limit to this review process, and at no point in my interviews did I encounter the suggestion that expert reports were written or improperly guided by staff from the Office of the Prosecution.
[9] Sadkovich (2002:40) asserts that historians serving as prosecution and defense experts have been "coached" by the prosecution and the defense, but he gives no evidence for his assertion. Advance coaching may, of course, occur, but it is not my impression that it is widespread.

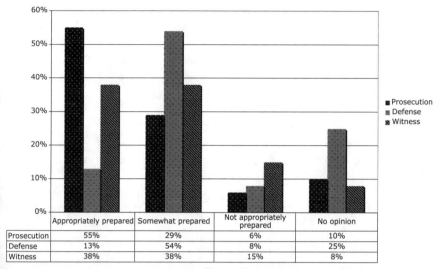

	Appropriately prepared	Somewhat prepared	Not appropriately prepared	No opinion
Prosecution	55%	29%	6%	10%
Defense	13%	54%	8%	25%
Witness	38%	38%	15%	8%

FIGURE 5.1. The degree to which contextual expert witnesses called by the Prosecution have been appropriately prepared for testimony in the courtroom.

excellent; 45 percent, very good or good; and a substantial percentage, 46 percent, fair or poor. With nearly half of experts having little or no meaningful experience of a criminal trial, a sizable number were ill equipped to translate their knowledge of a topic into the inimitable idiom of law. When such experts found themselves in a Trial Chamber setting governed by discriminating rules and procedures, scholarly knowledge was often lost in translation.

These points are illustrated concretely in looking closely at one instance of expert testimony, that of the Dutch sociologist Dr. Ton Zwaan, prosecution expert witness in the *Milošević* trial. Zwaan, of the Center for Holocaust and Genocide Studies at the University of Amsterdam, submitted an expert report titled "On the Aetiology and Genesis of Genocides and Other Mass Crimes Targeting Specific Groups." His 2003 report cataloged the general features of genocide and detailed four historical cases – Armenia, the Holocaust, Cambodia, and Rwanda. Zwaan was instructed by prosecutors to omit all reference to genocide in the former Yugoslavia, presumably on the grounds that only judges can determine the ultimate issue in a trial. In delineating the common features of genocides, however, the implications for the former Yugoslavia were apparent to all. The examination of the expert by the Principal Trial Attorney Geoffrey Nice was a classic example of prosecutorial framing of the crimes; he laid out the universal attributes of genocide without straightforwardly applying them to the situation in hand.

Nice's direct examination of the genocide expert over two days on 20–21 January 2004 teased out those elements of the report that indicated Milošević's culpability. For instance, genocidal crimes were not spontaneous outbursts but "top-down affairs." They were orchestrated by the state and dependent on the decisions of senior political and military officials (T31170–5). When asked by Nice about leaders' involvement in the detailed planning of a genocide, Zwaan answered:

> The top leadership usually only makes very general decisions and thereby gives other people the means and the organization and sometimes also the money and the armed force to organize the process in a more detailed way, in a more realistic way. We know, for instance, that Hitler, to give that example, never witnessed any genocidal acts himself, nor did he ever write down an order "kill all Jews," but we can be very certain especially in discussions with Himmler and others, that he must have stated the order, that is "kill all the Jews." (T31178)

Even if not overtly stated, the implications of this point were obvious for the criminal responsibility of former president Milošević. Zwaan went on to elucidate the role of ideology and propaganda in galvanizing "collective historical memory," dehumanizing the enemy, and creating a sense of common objectives in the civilian population (T31181).

When it came time for the defendant's cross-examination, the hazardous nature of the prosecution's framing strategy was quickly exposed. Milošević immediately exploited the distinction between legal and social science definitions of genocide and declared that, at the ICTY, "the legal meaning is the only essential one" (T31184). Using an argument very similar to the incompatibility theory outlined in Chapter 1, Milošević cited Zwaan's lack of legal training and pronounced that he had nothing meaningful to say to a court of law on the matter of genocide. Although it was galling to watch a defendant who had so openly flouted the authority of the international criminal tribunal extol the virtues of *ius cogens* and the inviolability of customary international law (T31221), Milošević raised a point worthy of deliberation. Zwaan was instructing the court on the concept of genocide without the prosecutor's having first prepared the ground for his expert testimony. Zwaan was alone in the task of disentangling legal definitions of the term from empirically based social science analyses of preceding genocides, and he represented a solitary figure as he defended the value of nonlegal disciplines: "I'm not a lawyer, and I'm not discussing legal matters here. And ... I think you should realize, Mr. Milošević, you are a lawyer, but there are different disciplines, like history and social sciences, and they operate on different principles than legal matters"

(T31217). Slobodan Milošević then turned to how Zwaan's testimony on historical genocides applied to the former Yugoslavia and whether he had Bosnia and Herzegovina in mind when drawing up the report. Zwaan denied any covert connection, but Milošević had succeeded in drawing him into a discussion about genocide in Bosnia that was unsubstantiated – Zwaan's rejoinders were not backed by any sources or documents and were therefore likely to be steeply discounted by judges.

Further, the accused sought to provoke the witness, asking for his views on Dutch involvement in slavery, apartheid, and "political violence" history (T31190–2), the kind of questions that Budding had deflected by replying that they were not in her report. Milošević accused the expert of selectivity and bias, asking why he had glossed over the pro-Nazi sympathies of Bosnian Muslim leaders and minimized "the scale of the genocide of the Serbs" during the World War II (T31198). Zwaan floundered and inexplicably defended the Muslim leader Alija Izetbegović, claiming that most Bosnian Muslims were not anti-Semitic at the time. He had allowed himself to be dragged into an irrelevant debate that he was bound to lose, falling for the time-honored defense tactic of eliciting the appearance of bias in the expert witness. During one heated exchange on the involvement of Bosnian Muslims in the Waffen-SS during World War II, Zwaan's composure abandoned him entirely and his riposte was full of animus: "You have been discussing now genocidal practices and intents of Croatians in history and also of Bosnian Muslims in history, but if I may quote yourself, you were talking just a few minutes ago about the dirt in front of your own door. Maybe we should discuss that. Thank you" (T31204). Zwaan's flare-up, understandable as it might have been, violated fundamental tenets of courtroom protocol, most important of which was the principle of the impartiality of the expert witness. The *Brđanin* trial judgment articulated the core principle thus: "In evaluating the evidence of the witnesses that gave evidence *viva voce*, the Trial Chamber has considered their demeanor, conduct and character as far as this was possible. . . . The credibility of the witness depends upon their knowledge of the facts upon which they give evidence, their disinterestedness."[10]

With his prosecution expert in a downward spiral, Geoffrey Nice intervened and redirected the witness, asking him to adhere to his report and the "method by which genocidal crimes are committed" (T31207). The judges, clearly uncomfortable with the turn the expert's testimony had taken, halted the proceedings and conferred. On emerging from their huddle, they asked the witness "whether that situation [in Bosnia and Herzegovina] has not somehow

---

[10] *Brđanin* (Trial Chamber), §25.

influenced the character of your report, perhaps even at the subconscious level" (T31208). Zwaan, obviously flustered, embarked on a meandering discourse on the ultimately unknowable nature of the subconscious. Judge Robinson interrupted him and spelled out what was at stake in his answer: "It would diminish the quality of your report if the report were tailored somehow to meet those characteristics" (T31209). In this incident, we can see the drawbacks of the prosecution's framing strategy, as the defense found it relatively straightforward to claim that the expert testimony was tainted with innuendo and therefore not objective or reliable.

In his redirect, Geoffrey Nice tried to salvage his expert's testimony. Zwaan recovered somewhat to offer lucid insights into how the historical legacy of World War II had never been properly discussed in socialist Yugoslavia and how there had been no real recognition of wrongs or admission of responsibility. Old memories that were part truth and part myth festered, having never been dismantled in a transparent public debate (T31242). Yet the damage to the witness's credibility had already been done. His hand forced by the defense cross-examination, Nice concluded by tackling the question of Bosnia that he had been avoiding for two days. He asked, "Did conditions for genocide exist in Bosnia?" – to which the witness replied in the affirmative. Without a moment's delay, Judge Robinson balked at the expert's determination of the central issue at stake in the trial: "Your report doesn't deal with Bosnia and Herzegovina, but here you're giving an answer that relates specifically to Bosnia and Herzegovina" (T31247).

Overall, Zwaan's testimony represented a lost opportunity that was all too common in international criminal trials. It had begun auspiciously: here was a well-informed expert in the academic field of genocide studies who had crafted a high-quality report that distilled the latest academic research on the methods and motivations for states to commit genocide. Fault lay more with the prosecution team that had not fully prepared the expert for Milošević's hostile cross-examination, although there is, of course, the question of whether one could ever be fully primed for such an experience. Perhaps more importantly, the prosecution had not assisted the court in understanding the bearing historical and social science analyses of genocide might have on legal understandings of the crime. Even accepting the preeminence of the legal definition of genocide, there was still room for a detailed exposition of the role of leaders in genocidal processes. Moreover, prosecutors did not fully anticipate how omitting Bosnia could leave their witness vulnerable to the accusation that his report contained a hidden agenda. One might conclude that Nice did not address Bosnia straightforwardly because he was looking to the indirect effect that a framing strategy might provide. Seeking the rewards of allusion and insinuation, the prosecution was instead strategically outflanked by the defense. The hapless expert witness was caught in the middle, left to do all the explaining himself. For their part, the judges were not hoodwinked by either party, and they observed the adversarial gamesmanship with a growing sense of restlessness and discomfort. It was not the tendering of historical or contextual evidence *per se* that aggravated them; it was the misappropriation of such evidence.

5.3. THE END OF MONUMENTAL HISTORY: THE *BRĐANIN* TRIAL

The courtroom drama described here was not the only time when prosecutors mishandled contextual and historical witnesses in the *Milošević* trial or in other trials.[11] Despite this, the judges' Rule 98 *bis* decision in *Milošević* in June 2004 sanctioned the prosecution's view that the history of the idea of Greater Serbia could be considered evidence of a long-standing and specific intention to commit genocide. The jurisprudential success of monumental history was short lived, however, and was reversed only a few months later on 1 September 2004, when the Trial Chamber acquitted Bosnian Serb leader Radoslav Brđanin of genocide (hereafter, *Brđanin* Trial Judgment or *Brđanin*).[12]

Brđanin was president of the Autonomous Region of the Krajina's (ARK) Crisis Staff, and vice president of the Bosnian Serbian state created in 1992 called "Republika Srpska." The indictment charged him with taking a leading role in the ethnic-cleansing operation that removed the non-Serb population from areas designated as part of the Serb state. Brđanin was charged with two counts of genocide, five counts of crimes against humanity, two counts of violations of the laws of war, and three counts of grave breaches of the 1949 Geneva Conventions. Looking to prove genocide, prosecutors relied on elements of the historical arguments and documents presented in the trial of Slobodan Milošević, albeit in a much less pronounced role: the Senior Trial Attorney Joanna Korner advanced the position on a number of occasions that Bosnian Serbs had waged a war of aggression that was motivated in significant part by an overarching plan to create an ethnically homogenous Greater Serbia (T24552–3, T24576). Brđanin's special intention to commit genocide, it was argued, was formulated in the particular circumstances of Yugoslavia in the late 1980s and early 1990s, but it drew sustenance from the

---

[11] See, for instance, the testimony on political propaganda of the prosecution's expert witness Renaud de La Brosse in the *Milošević* trial, 19–20 May 2003.

[12] *Prosecutor v. Radoslav Brđanin*, Case No. IT-99-36-T, Trial Chamber Judgment, 1 September 2004.

historically constituted ideology of Serbian nationalism. The defense, as we
will see in the subsequent chapter, countered with a monumental history of
its own.

The Trial Chamber found Radoslav Brđanin guilty on a number of counts,
including persecution, deportation, torture, and willful killing, and the court
sentenced him to thirty-two years' imprisonment.[13] In acquitting him of genocide, complicity to commit genocide, and extermination as a crime against
humanity, the Trial Chamber stated that criminal acts such as deportation and
murder were committed not to destroy Bosnian Muslims and Croats as groups,
in furtherance of a genocidal plan to create a Greater Serbia, but to control
territory and to impose an ethnic division of states. The "Six Strategic Goals"
promulgated in 1992 by the Bosnian Serb leadership was less a blueprint for
genocide than "a plan to seise [*sic*] and control territory, establish a Bosnian
Serb state, defend defined borders and separate the ethnic groups within BiH
[Bosnia and Herzegovina]" (§76). The judgment, more than any other before
it, also amalgamated the historical evidence of both prosecution and defense
experts, breaking with the reliance up until then on the prosecution's versions
of Balkans history.

The *Brđanin* Trial Judgment contained reasoning that would severely
diminish the value of historical testimony for the prosecution case. As ever,
this reasoning dealt with the grounds on which judges would be willing to
infer specific intent to commit genocide (§§969–91): "Where direct evidence
of genocidal intent is absent, the intent may still be inferred from the factual
circumstances of the crime. Where an inference needs to be drawn, it has
to be *the only reasonable inference available on the evidence*" (§970). That is,
prosecutors have to show that the intent to destroy a group in whole or in
part is the sole intent that one can reasonably infer from the evidence, a very
high burden of proof indeed. The Trial Chamber maintained that there were
other possible inferences that could conceivably be drawn from the acts of the
accused, namely that the accused intended to forcibly displace non-Serbs to
clear and hold specific territory, not to destroy the group in whole or in part
(§§977–9).

By sharply limiting the type of inferences that would be allowed, the *Brđanin*
Trial Judgment conveyed the unmistakable message that historical discussions
of Greater Serbian nationalism would not assist prosecutors in proving the
"surplus of intent" (*Stakić* Trial Judgment §520) required to make a finding
of genocide. The judges' emphasis on the factual circumstances of the crime
militated against contextual and interpretative forms of evidence. To achieve

---

[13] Reduced to thirty years on appeal.

their desired objective, the prosecution's focus needed to be narrowed to the point that it barely ventured outside the immediate circumstances of the actual crimes. Coinciding as they did with the added imperatives of the ICTY's completion strategy, these jurisprudential developments reduced the incentives for prosecutors to integrate contextual and historical expert witnesses into their cases, at least in the way they had been integrated up to that point.

5.4. WEAVING THE WEB OF CONTEXT

Historical evidence was put to a range of uses by the prosecution in the ICTY Trial Chamber, from the broad brush strokes in *Tadić*, which contextualized events and asserted only a weak causality between them, to the grand, monumental history of the Slobodan Milošević trial, where the inherent chauvinism of a nationalist mind-set was held up as the motivation for modern-day crimes. Yet, as we have just seen, compendious and generalizing histories did not sit well with judges. Connecting distant historical events to the present, though useful for familiarizing international jurists with the context of crimes, became problematic as soon as the prosecution introduced an element of causality. As the message sunk in, prosecutors had recourse to a more cautious and limited role for historical reports and expert testimony. Specifically, they adopted two strategies with greater frequency in the post-*Brđanin* era. First, they commissioned external historians to assist them in admitting documents in the courtroom. Second, they called internal historian experts from their own Office of the Prosecutor at the ICTY. As a consequence, prosecution narratives spanning centuries of Balkans history and culminating in the armed conflicts of the 1990s largely disappeared from the Trial Chamber and were replaced by a more modest use of historian expert witnesses. However, one could argue that the demise of grand historical inquiry led to advantages elsewhere, at least insofar as specific microhistories were more suited to the narrow legal aims of the prosecution.

In the early ICTY trials, from 1997 to 1999, STAs normally tendered documents at the bar themselves, without involving expert witnesses. Later, courtroom practice evolved whereby prosecutors would call an expert witness, often a historian, to address documents that featured in the prosecution case. These included the minutes of the Serb Assembly of Bosnia and Herzegovina, as well as statements and decrees by regional executive councils and municipal authorities. Two documents appeared in nearly every prosecution case: "Instructions for the Organisation and Activity of Organs of the Serbian People in Bosnia and Herzegovina in Extraordinary Circumstances" ("Variant A and B Instructions"), issued by the Srpska Demokratska Stranka, or Serbian

Democratic Party (SDS) in 1991, and "Six Strategic Goals," proclaimed by Radovan Karadžić on 12 May 1992 in Banja Luka.[14]

Why would prosecutors want to interpose an expert between themselves and the judges on a matter seemingly as straightforward as tendering a document at the bar? First, as time went on, more government archives became available and prosecutors had recourse to a treasure trove of documents. Second, ICTY trials came to rely more on documents, in part because more high-ranking officials were being charged and senior leadership cases are, for the most part (though not exclusively), based on documentary evidence. Here, prosecutors must connect individuals to specific crimes that they usually did not commit themselves and for which there were few eyewitnesses willing to testify against the accused. Political leaders were typically far removed from criminal acts of murder or torture or forced removal, and the prosecution sought to demonstrate how their powers and authority (both *de facto* and *de jure*) conferred superior responsibility. Again, we see how legal imperatives can impel legal actors to call expert witnesses.

Yet there is still another rationale, often overlooked in international criminal law textbooks. Namely, documents do not entirely speak for themselves, as much as prosecutors hope that judges would grasp their meaning and implications. Legal argument seldom relies on the presentation of disparate facts but typically expresses those facts in a story line, that is, a chronological and narrative form.[15] The "narrative coherence" of a legal argument – defined as "a test of truth or probability in questions of fact and evidence upon which direct proof by immediate observation is unavailable"[16] – is an essential, if often unacknowledged, feature of a party's attempt to persuade the court. Ronald Dworkin (1986:228–38) has made constructionist and narrative theories of law widely accepted, and for Dworkin (1977:58, 78), "facts of narrative consistency" are forged in the synthesis of social norms and conventional material facts.

We can apply this to the subject at hand: what are often lacking in the prosecution case are the narrative coherence and higher-order unity of the

---

[14] See *Brđanin* Trial Judgment, §69, on the Variant A/B document. This was issued on 19 December 1991 by the main board of the SDS and provided instructions for specified activities in all municipalities in which Serbs lived. It mapped out the takeover of power by Bosnian Serbs in municipalities where they constituted a majority of the population (Variant A) and where they were in a minority (Variant B). Karadžić's "Six Strategic Goals" speech was given at the sixteenth session of the Assembly of the Serbian People in Bosnia and Herzegovina (*Brđanin* §75).

[15] On narrative and law, see Anderson et al. (2005:148, 262–70); Brooks and Gewirtz (1996); Conley and O'Barr (1998); Cover (1983); Danet (1980:445); Dworkin (1986); Ewick and Silbey (1995); Fleury-Steiner (2002); Jackson (1994); Nielsen (2000); Papke (1991); Phillips and Grattet (2000:567).

[16] Jackson (1994:27).

facts. As the historian and ICTY expert witness Dr. Robert Donia explained: "Most prosecutors don't really want to do anything with history per se. They just want to bring forward the facts, the eyewitness accounts and the forensic evidence to build their case. But even they realize this is not enough. They need a complex explanatory framework. In the [General Stanislav] Galić trial I was brought in to weave the web of context. There was an evolution in the prosecution's thinking."[17]

To be intelligible, each document calls out for a "web of context" that situates it and lays bare its significance, disclosing what it contains, who was involved in creating the document, an assessment of the authority and official position of the authors, and an explanation of who was excluded. Leaders' public statements contain a range of meanings for the local population, and parsing them requires immersion in a specific history and context. Ideally, the expert will spin a narrative thread that sutures together disjointed documents that have been produced in diverse sites and at distinctive moments to create the web of context that Donia alluded to. When asked to comment on what historical experts do when contextualizing documents, Predrag Dojcinović of the LRT replied, "They are little storytellers and big academic pipelines for various types of documentary evidence."[18]

Although prosecutors in international criminal trials do not appear before an impressionable jury that might be swayed by an emotive narrative, they still have to order the evidence in a way that sequences events and demonstrates a coherent pattern and policy of criminal activity. Our survey confirms the value prosecutors attach to having an expert in the Trial Chamber to compose a chronology that aligns the documents and connects them to one another. Prosecutors valued the presence of an expert testifying orally in the courtroom by a wide margin over the practice of simply tendering an expert report. When asked, "Which has greater significance for the outcome of a trial?" 61 percent of prosecutors responded, "Expert testimony led in the trial," and only 6 percent replied, "Expert reports tendered in the trial."[19] These data offer some confirmation of the relevance of narrative theories of law in international criminal trials.

Prosecutors called a range of expert witnesses to assist them in admitting documents. Dr. Stefano Bianchini, professor of East European politics and history at the University of Bologna, was one expert who reviewed, contextualized, and drew the connections between documents in the Krajišnik and Plavšić and Aleksovski trials. However, the historian Robert Donia has been

---

[17] Author interview, April 2003.
[18] Author interview, June 2006.
[19] Thirty-two percent of prosecutors expressed no opinion.

called repeatedly by the prosecution to testify, to write an expert report, or to do both – he has participated in fifteen trials to date. As far as I know, he has appeared in more international criminal trials than any other historian. Donia's changing role at the Tribunal exemplifies the general shift from grand to specific history. Donia first participated in 1997 in the trial of the Bosnian Croat General Tihomir Blaškić, and his early reports and testimony were expansive summaries of the history of the Balkans over the centuries. Donia's expert report "Bosanski Šamac and the History of Bosnia and Herzegovina," submitted in 2001 during the trial of Blagoje Simić, painted a broad canvas, from the medieval kingdoms to the nationalist movements of the nineteenth century, through the two world wars of the twentieth century, and into the period of socialist Yugoslavia. One of the overarching themes that stands out in the reports is Donia's rejection of the ancient-tribal-hatred view that claimed that ethnic, religious, and national groups in the Balkans had been at one another's throats for centuries and that, therefore, the war crimes committed between 1991 and 1995 erupted spontaneously out of adamantine antipathies.[20] By advancing an alternative view of Balkan history, Donia helped prosecutors attribute criminal responsibility to the senior political and military leaders who had orchestrated violence through their control of state institutions and the media.

After several years of experience as a witness, Donia moved away from an expansive and determinative view of history and criminal responsibility. He was one of the few prosecution historical expert witnesses interviewed for this book who was unwilling to accept that historical evidence is relevant to *mens rea*: "It became so in the Slobodan Milošević trial, but the problem is this: the Bosnian Serb project evolved rapidly from a general ideological premise about the Serb state to specifics, to being created through violence if needed, and then violence as required. There's no *Mein Kampf* wherein Serbs sat down and said let's exterminate all Muslims or Croats, but they did opt for decidedly violent means in late 1991."[21] Perhaps it is his rejection of a deterministic model of history that accounts for Donia's ease in transitioning from the early phase of the Tribunal's work right through to its finale and the trial of Radovan Karadžić.

In reviewing his performance on the stand over two days of the *Brđanin* trial (30–31 January 2002), it becomes evident why Donia became the favored prosecution expert witness, called back to testify time and time again. After reviewing Donia's professional credentials, the prosecuting attorney Andrew Cayley immediately set about admitting documents that pertained to the defendant:

---

[20] See Donia 2001, 2002.
[21] Author interview, May 2007.

the minutes of SDS meetings in 1992, decisions of local Serb assemblies, and speeches by Radovan Karadžić and Dragan Kalinić. In each instance, Cayley asked Donia, "What is the significance of this document?" Donia's answers embedded the documents into broader political events in the run-up to the armed conflict and, in so doing, elucidated an overarching pattern of regionalization. Regionalization described the way in which Serb-dominated municipalities joined together in regional agglomerations that ran parallel to, and thereby destabilized, the state of Bosnia and Herzegovina. According to Donia, regionalization "[i]nvolved splitting up, redefining, restructuring municipalities, as well as . . . forming regional associations of municipalities such as the ARK. . . . [T]he political foundation for a Serbian state was laid, in a sense, from the ground up" (T1177).

Regionalization by the new Bosnian Serb authorities entailed progressively taking over all governmental functions, from providing electricity and water supply to pursuing police and military campaigns to ensure ethnically homogenous areas (T1156–62, 1178). As for the array of new structures, such as assemblies, crisis staffs, and autonomous regions, Donia did not attach great significance to the variety of names and titles, "for they all shared the single purpose of creating a Serbian-dominated state on Serbian-dominated territory" (T1177–8). The assembly of the Autonomous Region of the Krajina, which Radoslav Brđanin presided over as president, coordinated government functions; therefore, the accused was in a position of superior responsibility for the crimes committed by his subordinates: "Regionalization of the conflict, beginning with the Serb Autonomous regions in September 1991, this was the essence of the Brđanin case." Donia told me: "It was a public movement and the discussion of regionalization was played out in the press and there was a coming together of the public and private documentary records."[22] By constructing the narrative scaffolding on which individual facts could be attached, the expert thus contributed substantially to the prosecution's theory of the case.

Donia's success as an expert witness was in part borne of his prior courtroom experience as a witness in civil cases and arbitration panels during his career with Merrill Lynch. Donia avoided convoluted responses and gave straightforward answers. His discussion of regionalization, although it dealt with an abstract concept, was delivered in lay terms. Robert Donia carefully avoided exceeding his expertise, and he resisted the temptation to speculate, surmise, or otherwise improvise on a subject extraneous to his report. In the *Brđanin* trial, when asked by the defense counsel John Ackerman whether international law favors the dissolution of a country into subnations, Donia answered:

---

[22] Author interview, May 2007.

"I can't make a judgment on international law. I don't feel I'm qualified to answer that question" (T1225).

Donia reflected on the process of cross-examination: "When taking the stand as an expert witness, the three words 'I don't know' are your best friends. This is not part of academic expectation. I had seen others on the stand try to talk themselves out of situations where they did not know the answers and it did not go well for them."[23] Most academics are unaccustomed to giving yes or no answers to complex historical questions, and many academic expert witnesses answered questions at such great length that judges felt it necessary to intercede. More often than one might hope, the expert witness tested the slender patience of the judges or used a colorful metaphor that gave the defense only more grounds for quarreling with their testimony.

Because expert witnesses tend to be much more interpretative and explanatory than fact witnesses or eyewitnesses, there are intermittent moments of overreach in the direct examination. In the *Brđanin* trial, the prosecuting attorney asked Donia to comment on the statement of the executive council of the Autonomous Region of the Krajina (on which Brđanin served) that guaranteed rights to citizens as long as they expressed their "patriotic inclination." Donia replied that "one must assume this refers to patriotic inclination in support of the Serbian people" (T1157). Ackerman objected, and his objection was sustained. Presiding Judge Agius, though appearing to agree with Donia's deductions, nonetheless asked him to allow judges to draw their own conclusions.

In general, however, Donia's performances on the stand are a case study in how to be an effective expert witness, especially when facing an able and tough cross-examiner such as Ackerman. During the *Brđanin* trial, Ackerman did his utmost to allege that Donia's expert report was marred by bias and selectivity, and to contend that the accused was merely responding as any rational individual would to unreasonable provocation. Ackerman made extensive reference to Croatian atrocities during World War II (T1202) and maintained that Bosnian Serbs were under attack from "especially vicious" mujahedeen fighters from Afghanistan (T1210). Donia acknowledged these points with equanimity and the proper degree of disinterest that judges admire, conceding that violations against Serbs have occurred at various points in history. At no point did he exhibit discomfort or seek to diminish Serb suffering, as expert witness Zwaan had in the *Milošević* trial. This studied neutrality has definite and positive consequences, as Donia notes: "I have been brought back because I'm not grinding the axe for any one ethnic group... in the clash of expert witnesses,

[23] Author interview, May 2007.

the vote goes to the prosecution if they retain someone who is impartial and the defense trots out an expert who is providing exculpatory justifications and it's not clear whether the defense witness is defending the accused or the cause of, say, Greater Croatia."[24]

Whereas some other prosecution witnesses reacted angrily to defense efforts to justify their client's crimes, Donia diffused defense rhetoric with understated humor. At one point during the defense cross-examination, John Ackerman furnished a long list of historical crimes that Croats had committed against Serbs in World War II. He then pointed out how the breakaway Croatian state made use in the 1990s of the red-and-white checkerboard symbol on its flag, with its "threatening and frightening" echoes of the pro-Nazi Ustaše state (T1205). At the end of this historical treatise, Ackerman delivered his rhetorical punch line: "In that context, it would not be difficult to understand why people might want to arm themselves for protection, if for no other reason." Donia replied plainly, "I don't share that conclusion, no" (T1206). Ackerman persisted, portraying Bosnian Serbs as reacting reasonably in the face of unwarranted provocation from Croats. Ackerman, a U.S. attorney based in San Antonio, Texas, said, "I think you would agree that it's not unusual in times of, say, a crime spree or something like that in the United States that people maybe without justification, but out of fear, will go to the gun stores and start buying guns. That happens, doesn't it?" Donia countered drily, "That happens a great deal in Texas, yes" (T1206).

Each time Robert Donia began his testimony in the courtroom, the defense sought to undercut his professional standing and credibility before the court. Defense lawyers cross-examining Donia inevitably point out that he has not held a tenured position at a university and suggest that his expertise is limited to only Bosnian Muslims. It is a question worth asking why the most eminent of historians at prestigious North American or European universities have usually not been selected by the prosecution, or why the most valuable prosecution historian has been a widely respected but nonetheless modest retired finance executive. The short answer is that distinguished scholars enjoying high status and great deference in their own world are by and large unsuited to the rough-and-tumble exchanges of the courtroom, where their reputation will be questioned and perhaps tarnished. A number of foremost scholars have deemed this a risk not worth taking. Prosecutors are aware of this, and at both the ICTY and the ICTR, they have preferred to work with scholars who are less garnished in laurels in the media and academic world but therefore are

---

[24] Author interview, April 2003.

less likely to make errors of judgment in the courtroom while defending their personal pride and professional reputation.

5.5. INTERNAL EXPERT WITNESSES AND HISTORY AS LINKAGE EVIDENCE

Now a leadership case is essentially a documents case.
– ICTY Senior Trial Attorney[25]

Over time, the Office of the Prosecutor (OTP) adjusted its strategy and began to commission more internal expert witnesses from the Military Analysis and Leadership Research teams to present expert reports and give oral testimony in the ICTY Trial Chamber.[26] When the ICTY first commenced its investigations, prosecutors had only one filing cabinet of documents, but after time, a pipeline of documents began to flow from Bosnia. Archives of municipalities and regional assemblies of Bosnian Croats, Bosnian Serbs, and Bosniaks were handed over by the parties themselves or by an opposing party whose military forces had previously overrun a police station or municipality. With the change in governments in Croatia and Serbia in 2000, ICTY staff obtained greater access to vital government archives in Belgrade and Zagreb. As time went on, ICTY investigators also became aware of remaining hidden document caches, and they aggressively pursued them with search warrants. As accession to the European Union loomed for states such as Croatia and Macedonia, sympathetic European diplomats became more empowered to lobby on behalf of the Tribunal for state cooperation.

Whatever methods were used, the end result was an avalanche of documentary evidence that was put to extensive use in senior political leadership cases. The situation became one of rolling historical documentation, of constant reformulation of history in the light of the new documents that appeared. Internal OTP staff from the LRT had more or less full access to the documents, and it was their full-time job to sift through them and catalog them. They became the experts on these special collections, which were ring fenced with byzantine confidentiality arrangements. External historians were permitted to review only ICTY archival material if they were commissioned by an STA and granted written approval. Access limitations created a number of obstacles. External experts would be given a commission and a collection of selected documents, not knowing whether other relevant documents existed.

---

[25] Author interview, June 2006.
[26] Senior Trial Attorneys have called, for instance, the military expert Philip Coo; the demographer Ewa Tabeau; and the historians Andrew Corin, Patrick Treanor, and William Tomljanovich.

During cross-examination, defense teams always probed in this area to suggest that the expert had been furnished only with incriminating evidence in support of the prosecution case. Furthermore, external experts reported incidents in which they had been given certain documents along with their original commission and then lost them to a computer glitch. On requesting the documents again, they were refused, as prosecuting attorneys cited more restrictive policies. Given the restrictions on access to the documentary collections, it increasingly made sense for internal LRT staff to serve as experts introducing documents in the Trial Chamber. The LRT leader Dr. Patrick Treanor explained: "We got to the point that there was so much information in-house that it became impossible to get anyone outside with the time or energy to analyze all the material. I discussed it with Michael Johnson[,] who was chief of prosecutions at the time[,] and convinced him that realistically we were the experts in this material and so internal experts started to appear more in the trials. It seemed to work well."[27]

Internal LRT staff drew upon the archival record to write expert reports that countered the stock defense deployed in trials of political leaders. For instance, in the trial of Radoslav Brđanin, the defense maintained that the accused did not hold a position of superior responsibility and that real authority for decision making lay elsewhere. On the surface, the defense theory was lent credibility by the fact that the governmental structures in Bosnia in 1991–5 had just come into being and their functions were constantly changing. Judges required an orientation in the transitional political universe of Bosnia during the conflict, as LRT member Andrew Corin explained: "It is very hard to deal with these issues through fact witnesses, as states are collapsing and new entities such as Republika Srpska are coming into being."[28]

The LRT's senior historian Dr. Patrick Treanor served as expert witness in the trial of Radoslav Brđanin and wrote the report "The Bosnian Serb Leadership 1990–1992 – Addendum: Governing Structures in the Autonomous Region of the Krajina 1991–2."[29] Treanor's expert report detailed the immediate context before and during the breakup of the Socialist Federal Republic of Yugoslavia. His report was far removed from conventional historical expert-witness reports insofar as it eschewed conceptual abstraction and all reflection on the macrohistory of the Balkans. It was certainly not the monumental history of *Milošević*, nor the background of *Tadić*, and it did not correspond exactly to the tightly targeted history of Robert Donia that was heard in the

---

[27] Author interview, June 2006.
[28] Author interview, May 2006.
[29] Expert report submitted on 4 June 2003. The report drew from an earlier report tendered on 30 July 2002 in the trial of Momčilo Krajišnik.

same trial. Instead, the internal expert's report operated at a tangibly concrete level, sharply delineating the specific microhistory of a region and telling that history primarily through the available documentary record. As Treanor himself described his function as an expert, "What I do is read documents and draw out the story."[30]

Treanor's microhistory took a magnifying glass to the new political structures that emerged in Bosnia during the disintegration of Yugoslavia and the spiral into war. It outlined the political arrangements of the Socialist Federal Republic of Yugoslavia; reviewed constitutional reforms in the 1980s and 1990s; and explained the transformation of the relationship among the assembly, presidency, and 109 municipalities of the Republic of Bosnia and Herzegovina. Then it turned to the emergency governance structures and described how they developed out of that prior set of arrangements. Reinforcing Donia's conceptual framework of regionalization, but without using that term, Treanor meticulously recounted how, in 1991–2, the SDS established municipal, regional, and republic crisis staffs and grouped municipal authorities into the Serb Autonomous Region of the Krajina (ARK).[31] Treanor's report also covered the period of the armed conflict and charted the creation and operation of war presidencies and war commissions.

Faced with a dizzying array of governance institutions, the report assiduously mapped the formal organization and powers of emergency authorities, both *de facto* and *de jure*, with due attention given to the lines of reporting between subordinates and leaders. Treanor's report and testimony had one central aim: to show the degree of control that political leaders exercised. Staff in the Office of the Prosecutor referred to this as "linkage evidence," or documentary evidence that connected leaders to crimes. Such connections were usually quite indirect and were several degrees removed from the crime scene itself. The prosecution might use the documentary record to outline, say, the large-scale goals of a political organization to establish a state on a particular territory, list the actions the leaders took on a political level to implement their higher goals, and then finally attempt to show how that led to the crimes being tried.

The *Brđanin* Trial Chamber was receptive to Treanor's comparatively narrow expert evidence, reliant as it was on documentation. Along with othei evidence presented by the prosecution, Treanor's evidence convinced the judges that a coherent and organized Bosnian Serb political structure had functioned during the armed conflict in Bosnia. The scenario was not one of

---

[30] Author interview, November 2009.
[31] Declared on 16 September 1991.

anarchy, in which mass crimes were committed by random or disorganized paramilitary or criminal gangs. Instead, there was a pattern to the crimes, and that pattern resulted from a plan formulated by senior political leaders and put into operation by organized political and military structures. The *Brđanin* Trial Judgment states:

> The Trial Chamber is satisfied beyond reasonable doubt that during the implementation of this policy, effective control over the Bosnian Serb military, police and civilian structures was exercised variously by political leaders from the Bosnian Serb Supreme Command and other governmental authorities of the SerBiH [Bosnian Serb state]. The impact of so-called uncontrolled elements was marginal. It is also satisfied beyond reasonable doubt that it was impossible to implement a systematic policy of this magnitude, just by spontaneous action or by criminal actions by isolated radical groups. (§119)

Calling internal OTP staff as background witnesses seemed to represent a successful adaptive strategy on the part of the prosecution, and defense lawyers such as Michael G. Karnavas took exception to the practice:

> I have objected to calling expert witnesses from the OTP. They are not independent, but have been part of the prosecution team for years. They are not going to jeopardize their position by going against the case an STA is trying to build. These prosecution analysts-turned-experts are usually engaged in the stages of drafting the indictment, gathering the evidence, and presenting evidence. Their reports mirror the prosecution theory as reflected in the indictment, and one can hardly claim these reports to be objective. There is a vast difference between hiring an expert to conduct a study and produce a report, and having a member of the prosecution team anointed as an expert whose mission, essentially, is to self-validate his own theory and the theory upon which the indictment was based.[32]

Undoubtedly, defense lawyers resented this development, and they meted out an especially unfavorable and antagonistic treatment to internal expert witnesses put forward by the prosecution. During the trial of the Bosnian Croat leader Jadranko Prlić, the LRT staff member William Tomljanovich replied repeatedly that the questions being asked by the defense were not topics included in his instructions from the prosecution. Alluding to the defense given by German soldiers after World War II, Karnavas repeatedly characterized the defense as a "Third Reich defense," which triggered a reprimand from the Swiss judge Stephen Trechsel.[33] The arguments of Karnavas and

---

[32] Author interview, June 2007.
[33] "Three Americans Argue about Herceg Bosna," *Sense Tribunal*, 18 September 2006, http://www.sense-agency.com/en/stream.php?sta=3&pid=8511&kat=3.

other defense lawyers convinced some ICTY judges to disallow internal expert reports and oral testimony.[34] Judges have also prevented prosecutors from calling an internal OTP staff member as an expert witness, permitting them to appear only as fact witnesses speaking on the provenance of documents and only after they removed all interpretative conclusions from their reports.[35] The former ICTY Senior Trial Attorney Susan Somers, however, disagrees with this policy:

> There was some resistance from judges to in-house experts. This is not universally shared. In the U.S. criminal justice system, for example, prosecutors regularly call police experts from police [and] law enforcement agencies with respect to a number of areas of expertise, including ballistics, questioned documents, blood, traffic accident investigation, sexual assaults, spectography, et cetera. In general the evidence should be admissible and challenges may go to the weight which judges give it.[36]

Senior Trial Attorneys continue to introduce internal experts into international trials, and this makes sense given their privileged access to documents and because the prosecution benefits from the professionalization of its experts. As law-and-society scholar Marc Galanter (1974) noted many years ago, repeat players in the courtroom became more proficient over time.[37] Although they may not be informed of the exact details of the case in which they are called, internal experts know, in principle, how prosecution cases are constructed, and they have been socialized into the legal culture and the reigning legal epistemology. Prosecution staff from the LRT or the Military Analysis Team are aware that the courtroom can be an inhospitable environment that is most unlike the academic seminar room, in that ruminating on peripheral issues is not welcomed. They avoid being drawn into diversionary debates. Crucially, as professional court staff, they are imbued with the ethic of maintaining an emotional distance from the subject. Perhaps most important, internal OTP experts, having worked in close proximity to STAs and having written extensive briefs for indictments and trials, are attuned to the precise information that the

---

[34] As, for example, in the trial of Sefer Halilović.
[35] This occurred during the trial of Milan Milutinović with the report and testimony of Philip Coo, of the ICTY Military Analysis Team.
[36] Author interview, April 2009.
[37] Thanks are due to Robert M. Hayden for drawing my attention to Galanter's point during a panel at the 2009 annual conference of the American Association for the Advancement of Slavic Studies.

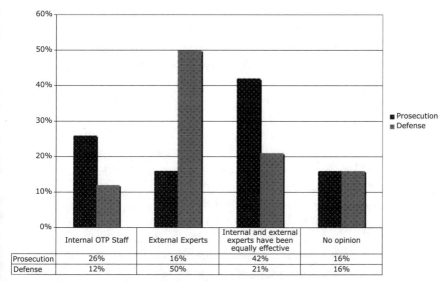

	Internal OTP Staff	External Experts	Internal and external experts have been equally effective	No opinion
Prosecution	26%	16%	42%	16%
Defense	12%	50%	21%	16%

FIGURE 5.2. Which have been more effective as expert witnesses in the Trial Chamber?

court values. They are aware of legal proofs and the types of sources that lawyers and judges find credible. When quoting numbers, especially with respect to civilian casualties in armed conflict, they scrupulously cite their sources, admit the margin of error, and use the most conservative figures in any numerical range. In their reports, they are cautious not to exceed their expertise, their brief, or the available documentary record. In their testimony, they generally refrain from interpreting the material and making ambitious inferences, instead deferring to the judges' desire to reach their own conclusions.

Our survey gauged prosecutors' and defense lawyers' opinions of the value of internal versus external expert witnesses, asking, "Which have been more effective as expert witnesses in the Trial Chamber?" As Figure 5.2 shows, prosecutors chose internal OTP staff over external experts, but a majority said that internal and external experts had been equally effective. Defense lawyers, as might be expected, seldom preferred internal OTP experts, and they favored external experts over internal and external experts combined.

The prevailing view of prosecutors that internal and external experts have been equally effective at the Tribunal requires further reflection. Despite the occasional incident of judicial resistance, internal expert reports and testimony often feature prominently in trial judgments. Crucially, prosecutors have found a way to use both together, and evidence from internal witnesses has complemented that of external witnesses. Treanor and Donia are both cited liberally in the *Brđanin* Trial Judgment, which drew on Donia's evidence up until the armed conflict and Treanor's evidence from the conflict onward, with substantial overlap in 1990–2.[38] Although there was some overlap, it seems the trial judges found the redundancy convincing, and even reassuring.

The *Brđanin* trial spelled the end of monumental history as a regular feature of prosecution cases, but it also consolidated a new formula that has been highly effective and is still widely in use at the time of writing. The formula brought together internal and external expert witnesses to contextualize documents and draw a thread through the ever-expanding archival record. Its specific micro-history possessed more causal force and explanatory power than that found in *Tadić* but less than in *Milošević*. Historical evidence in *Brđanin* gave little insight in the defendant's alleged criminal intentions, but it had major implications for political authority and individual criminal responsibility. It is probably less likely to satisfy academic historians than the narratives found in *Tadić* and *Milošević*, as history in the *Brđanin* mold did not constitute history for history's sake. It was history as told through documents, in the fashion that reflects the law's penchant for (an outsider might say "obsession with") backing each claim with a corresponding authenticated document. History in *Brđanin* was decidedly history for law's sake, and that is why it was so readily embraced by judges.

History for law's sake was also embraced by other legal actors, and our survey found widespread appreciation for the microhistorical approach adopted in *Brđanin* and afterward. Of respondents, 69 percent thought that ICTY historians had provided important information on "the authority structures of political parties," and 66 percent valued the information provided on "regional or municipal histories." These areas of historical discussion received higher approval than those indicating intent. For instance, when asked whether historians had provided important information on "the hidden meanings of political leader's speeches and statements" at the ICTY, the approval rating dropped to 41 percent. Figure 5.3 shows that respondents from the prosecution awarded the highest ratings to microhistories of political parties (77 percent) and regional or municipal histories (73 percent), but a sizable majority of defense lawyers (63 percent and 58 percent, respectively) and expert witnesses (58 percent and 58 percent) also saw merit in them.

5.6. JUDICIAL EFFICIENCY AND EXPERT WITNESSES

With internal and external expert witnesses working in tandem, a new template for prosecution history was forged in the *Brđanin* trial. Although prosecutors still faced objections from defense lawyers, and the courtroom reception of

---

[38] *Brđanin* Trial Judgment, §53 *passim.*

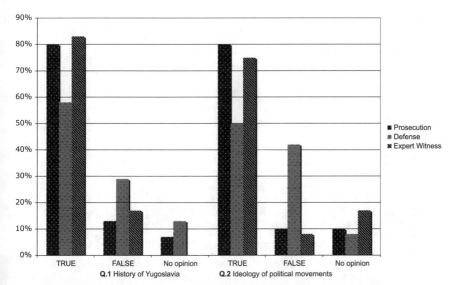

FIGURE 5.3(A). "In their reports and testimony to the ICTY, historians have provided important information on ..." 1. History of Yugoslavia; 2. Ideology of Political Movements.

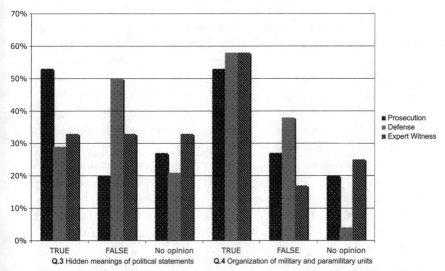

FIGURE 5.3(B). "In their reports and testimony to the ICTY, historians have provided important information on ..." 3. Hidden meanings of political statements; 4. Organization of military and paramilitary units.

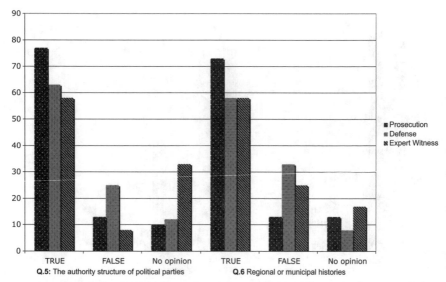

FIGURE 5.3(C). "In their reports and testimony to the ICTY, historians have provided important information on . . . " 5. The authority structure of political parties; 6. Regional or municipal histories.

their internal witnesses did not always go to plan, they had arrived at an arrangement that was effective in convincing the judges. And yet, as with every prosecution and defense strategy at the Tribunal, the arrangement did not remain intact forever – in recent years judges have dismantled the scaffolding of expert-witness testimony even further. Indeed, this is one of the main conclusions of this book: the relationship between law and history is in constant motion and fluctuates widely over the life of the same Tribunal.

As the end date envisaged in the completion strategy loomed, judges became ever more interventionist in their cases, under the guise of "judicial efficiency," which constitutes an intensification of the managerial judging model presented in the previous chapter.[39] This doctrine, closely associated with Scottish Lord Iain Bonomy, among others,[40] sanctioned broad judicial discretion to reduce the scope of the indictments; to slash the hours allocated for the prosecution's case; to trim down the list of witnesses; to exclude documents,

[39] The principle of judicial efficiency can also be indentified in national jurisdictions. See Kareem Fahim, "Amid Drama of Police Trial, a Judge Unfazed," *New York Times*, 1 February 2010. This article describes Judge Alan Marrus of the State Supreme Court in Brooklyn, a judge with experience in more than 550 trials who impatiently eschews sidebars, warns lawyers not to show up late, and threatens to seat jurors without them if they do.

[40] Judge Iain Bonomy served as a judge at the ICTY from 2004 to 2009.

reports, and exhibits in whole or in part; and to undertake further measures to expedite the trials. From 2008 onward, the prosecution strategy of using experts to weave a web of context while admitting documents came under intense judicial scrutiny. Under the regime of judicial efficiency, chambers imposed ever more rigorous standards of relevance and coherence on expert reports and testimony. Judges frequently rejected sections of reports or entire reports in which the content consisted of summaries or compilations of documents and the methodology was not spelled out precisely.

In the *Perišić* trial, the judges initially declined several expert reports of Donia and Treanor that contained excerpts of minutes of the SDC of the Federal Republic of Yugoslavia and the assembly of Republika Srpska. In a break with convention, the bench deferred deciding on whether to admit the reports until after the witness's oral testimony, during which there was an extensive debate on the proper function of the expert witness in a trial.[41] One tense exchange conveys the tenor of the courtroom discussion, as Judge Moloto asked Treanor pointedly:

JUDGE MOLOTO: It may very well be that you left certain documents that are relevant and brought in documents that are not relevant if you don't have a system of doing things, and this is the problem. . . . Then the question becomes: How do we take this report as an expert report? Because if you say you're a historian, anybody can write history, is that what you're saying, and pick up facts that he wants to pick up, based on his personal judgment?

THE WITNESS: Well, training for a historian involves doing research and producing an analytical product, an extensive analytical product, usually referred to as a thesis or a dissertation on a particular topic. And that product of thesis or dissertation is reviewed by usually senior people in the field, and they pass judgment on it. There is, as I said, there is no mathematical key to how you select documents. It's a judgmental question, and one develops one's judgment in this field by (a) reading history and (b) doing research.[42]

The Trial Chamber eventually ruled to admit Treanor's expert report, but Presiding Judge Bakone Moloto was unconvinced and issued a separate opinion, citing a "lack of objective and systematic criteria in selecting documents."[43]

---

[41] *Prosecutor v. Momčilo Perišić*, Case IT-04-81, Decision on the Defense Motion to Exclude the Expert Reports of Robert Donia, 27 October 2008; Decision on the Defense Motion to Exclude the Expert Reports of Patrick Treanor, 27 October 2008.

[42] *Perišić* Transcripts, 3 November 2008, T. 916–917.

[43] *Prosecutor v. Momčilo Perišić*, Case IT-04-81-T, Decision on Admissibility of Expert Report of Patrick Treanor, Separate Opinion of Judge Moloto, 27 November 2008, §1. Donia's reports and addendum were also admitted after his testimony on 18 November 2008. T. 1879.

What is remarkable is that seventeen years after the Tribunal was founded, judges were still wrangling with experts in the courtroom over first principles, trying to ascertain what it is exactly that historians do, what the place of historical evidence might be in an international criminal trial, and what criteria ought to govern the admissibility of expert-witness reports. The fact that such fundamental matters remain unsettled this late in the life of the Tribunal says something important about international legal institutions. More precisely, the fact that they function outside of supervisory state institutions and a mature legal tradition can contribute to inconsistent courtroom procedures.

Continuing in this vein, using the pretrial case-management framework established under Rule 65 *ter*, judges adopted a highly selective policy in admitting expert-witness reports. Until 2008, when the prosecution tendered an expert report, it was admitted in full, granted an exhibit number, and became a public document available through the ICTY registry. In the *Stanišić-Župljanin* and *Perišić* trials in 2008–9, judges initiated a practice of admitting only those pages or even paragraphs of the report that had been cross-examined in oral testimony. Other pages of the expert reports were excluded, including the opening page with the name of the author and title of the report. This exceedingly restrictive procedure extracted sections out of their context and jeopardized the coherence and integrity of expert reports.

Even defense lawyers expressed uneasiness about the impact of the completion strategy on established Tribunal procedures, and at times they joined with the prosecution to resist judicial encroachment. One defense counsel stated: "The completion strategy has created procedural disarray at the ICTY. To have a fair trial you have to have predictability and uniformity, so what is happening in Trial Chamber 1 is the same as Trial Chamber 2, but now each is different. Judges are intervening in the middle of a trial and changing the rules of the game to shorten a trial. In the *Prlić* trial, the prosecution case has been cut from 450 hours to less than 300 hours. How is anyone supposed to plan their case?"[44]

Despite the fact that the managerial judging model has at times diminished historical discussions at the ICTY, it has also ushered in some constructive developments. Enhanced judicial management during the pretrial process crystallizes the areas of agreement and disagreement between the parties and can establish a baseline of accepted history before the trial even starts. Some trials now begin with a set of historical and political questions already agreed to by both parties. The prosecution, perhaps as a result of greater judicial case management, is tending more toward disclosing its historical assertions up

[44] Author interview, June 2007.

front, in advance of the trial. One can see this, for example, in the indictment of the Serbian nationalist leader Vojislav Šešelj. Annex 1 of the indictment lists chronologically forty-five "additional historical and political facts" covering events in Croatia and Bosnia from the elections of 1990 to the start of the armed conflict.[45]

In summary, as judges subordinated the courtroom process to the necessities of the Tribunal's completion strategy, they regulated expert-witness testimony more and more after *Milošević*. Historical inquiry at the ICTY became less a complex historical overview assignment and more of a chronological list of agreed-on facts and a narrative that orders and elaborates on the documentary record. The edge of relevant history moved ever closer to the armed conflict, and the Tribunal's attention narrowed to specific locales. Although the prosecutorial formula put in place in the *Brđanin* trial has not been overturned, it is less elaborate than before. In all of this, the unique aspects of international law that made it potentially more inclusive of expert historical evidence have been altered, and if anything, prosecution cases at the ICTY have come to resemble more closely standard criminal trials in domestic jurisdictions. This should not be read as a straightforward reduction or diminution of history in trials, however, and historical evidence is poised to occupy as prominent a position in the final ICTY trials as ever before.

---

[45] *Prosecutor v. Vojislav Šešelj*, Case IT-03-67-T, Third Amended Indictment, 7 December 2007.

6

Exoneration and Mitigation in Defense Histories

I don't think you can get a grasp of what happened in Bosnia in this war in 1992 if you don't grasp some background, some history, because what happened – you know, people act out of their past. They act out of what they know from the past. They act out of history.

– ICTY Defense Counsel John Ackerman[1]

6.1. A SENSE OF GRIEVANCE

Many defense lawyers in international criminal trials have had recourse to historical arguments, believing that they provide the key to understanding the motivations for violations of international humanitarian law. As with prosecutors, however, a variety of views exist on the topic, and some defense attorneys recoil from using historical evidence in their cases. One prominent defense lawyer, Michael G. Karnavas, president of the Association of Defense Counsel of the ICTY, has maintained that it is "false and erroneous to assume that a court is there to find historical truth."[2]

As with previous chapters on the prosecution, this chapter explores the legal incentives for including historical arguments in defense cases. And yet one needs to acknowledge at the outset that there are compelling nonlegal reasons at play as well, because generally speaking, history matters more to the accused as an end in itself. It also carries weight with the audience back at home and with a majority of defense lawyers from the region. As observers note, international criminal tribunals have increasingly become venues in which the parties to an armed conflict seek to represent themselves as historical victims

---

[1] *Brđanin* Trial Transcript, 4 February 2004, T24275.
[2] Caroline Tosh, "Does Krajisnik Sentence Set Dangerous Precedent?" IWPR Tribunal Update No. 479, 1 December 2006.

and their opponents as serial perpetrators.[3] All communities of the former Yugoslavia have made structurally identical defense arguments based on past suffering. These debates constitute an extension into a new legal setting of historical disputes that have fueled violence in the region, and they influence the tenor of courtroom history as much as the internal dynamic of the legal proceedings.

Additionally, any evenhanded account must mention the profound sense of disadvantage and grievance that defense lawyers frequently voice. Prosecutors have much to say about aspects of the legal proceedings, but they seldom phrase it in such stark and sweeping terms as defense lawyers, who are much more likely to level charges of bias against international criminal tribunals. Some have even filed formal submissions to the Trial Chamber to this effect. In the *Brđanin* trial, defense counsel filed a final brief claiming that the Tribunal may have been informed by an "unintentional bias against Serbs" drawn from the international press and as a result, Bosnian Serbs could not expect a fair hearing in The Hague.[4] In addition, some defense lawyers find bias in the selection of cases coming to trial, seeing them as politically motivated. One defense lawyer stated:

> The most important thing about the historical record before the ICTY lies in what was excluded, or presented and ignored. Of course, none of this excuses the crimes that clearly were committed, but it diminishes the legitimacy of the judgments ultimately rendered. There will always be a lingering, valid criticism that certain prosecutions were selected for reasons other than the facts, the law, or history.[5]

Defense lawyers frequently insist that judges are negatively predisposed against the defense and favor prosecutors in the courtroom. Prosecutors often claim the reverse and say that the judges bend over backward to accommodate the other party, but complaints by the defense tend to be more vehement. As one survey respondent wrote: "Important information has been provided, but that information was not necessarily helpful, complete, or even accurate. The wider narrative was never really told in the ICTY because the chamber gave the prosecution considerable leeway in presenting its evidence, while being harder on the defense when it sought to meet the prosecution's evidence."[6]

---

3 See Saxon (2005:563).
4 *Brđanin* Trial Judgment, §§37–43. Trial Chamber judges dismissed this assertion as "misconceived and unfortunate" (§42).
5 ICTY survey response, 2009.
6 ICTY survey response, 2009.

TABLE 6.1. *Comparing judges' receptivity to prosecution and defense expert witnesses*

		Prosecution %	Defense %	Witness %
A) How receptive are ICTY	Highly Receptive	0	0	15
judges to the testimony of	Somewhat Receptive	61	50	46
historians serving as	Unreceptive	6	21	8
expert witnesses called by	Highly Unreceptive	0	21	0
the Defense?	No opinion	32	8	31
B) How receptive are ICTY	Highly Receptive	10	33	23
judges to the testimony of	Somewhat Receptive	71	50	54
historians serving as	Unreceptive	0	8	0
expert witnesses called by	Highly Unreceptive	0	0	0
the Prosecution?	No opinion	19	8	23

Defense teams also perceive bias in the evidence that judges are willing to admit. For example, judges are in the main disinterested in the international dimensions of the conflicts in the former Yugoslavia and in Rwanda. According to defense counsel interviewed for this book, when they apply to introduce expert evidence on the financial, material, and military support given to their opponents by powerful nations, judges have ruled that such information is irrelevant to trying the specific alleged crimes before them.[7] Even when judges permit discussion of the international dimensions of the conflict, the evidence is seldom, if ever, included in Trial Chamber judgments.[8] Our survey sought to ascertain whether a defense perception of bias extends to the topics examined in this book. In the results presented here, there is a variation in how prosecutors and defense counsel perceive judges' receptiveness to historians serving as expert witnesses for the defense. Judges were considered more receptive to prosecution expert witness by a substantial margin among all three groups surveyed (Table 6.1).

In interviews with defense counsel, one of the most common refrains is that there is an "inequality of arms" between the defense and the prosecution. As expressed by one defense attorney: "The defense generally was not given

---

[7] There are some obvious exceptions, such as during the trial of Slobodan Milošević, when the accused was given ample opportunity to discuss the international dimensions of the conflict.

[8] See the discussion of the Badinter Commission in the *Tadić* Trial Judgment in Chapter 4. Note that the Badinter Commission was discussed in subsequent trials such as that of Radoslav Brđanin, where the prosecution witness Robert Donia and the defense witness Paul Shoup presented evidence on the commission in their expert reports and oral testimony (*Brđanin* Trial Judgment, §§63–4).

TABLE 6.2. *Comparing preparation of defense and prosecution expert witnesses*

		Prosecution %	Defense %	Witness %
A) The degree to which contextual expert witnesses called by the Defense have been appropriately prepared for testimony in the courtroom.	Appropriately prepared	6	17	23
	Somewhat prepared	35	50	46
	Not appropriately prepared	26	8	8
	No opinion	32	25	23
B) The degree to which contextual expert witnesses called by the Prosecution have been appropriately prepared for testimony in the courtroom.	Appropriately prepared	55	13	38
	Somewhat prepared	29	54	38
	Not appropriately prepared	6	8	15
	No opinion	10	25	8

the resources needed to appropriately respond to the prosecution factually, legally, or historically."[9] Another respondent tied all the preceding prejudicial elements together: "Proceedings at the Tribunal are one sided. The Defense *de facto* has the burden of proof. There is no equality of arms or due process. The trials are patently unfair to the accused."[10] Defense lawyers are quick to observe that the financial and personnel resources of the OTP dwarf their own. Although a defense team may incorporate fewer than a dozen individuals, there were 1,135 staff members at the ICTY in 2006, and the Office of the Prosecutor accounted for a substantial percentage of that figure.[11] As a consequence, the defense regularly maintains that it is less well positioned to prepare its cases, and the survey revealed substantial disagreement on whether prosecution or defense expert witnesses were better prepared, as Table 6.2 indicates.

We need to be aware of the disadvantaged position in which many defense counsel see themselves, but the ensuing discussion does not adjudicate on whether or not their grievances are well founded. Instead, this chapter, like the previous chapters on the prosecution, concentrates on the legal relevance of history for the defense; that is, how historical arguments are deployed to

---

9 ICTY survey response, 2009.
10 ICTY survey response, 2009.
11 ICTY Communication Service, "General Information," 2006, p. 3. This figure remained stable and the ICTY Web site in 2010 referred to "over one thousand staff from more than 80 countries." http://www.icty.org/sid/325.

further certain legal objectives at the Tribunal. Historical evidence has been a cornerstone of two defense strategies; namely the chaos defense and the *tu quoque* defense.

In pursuit of recognizable legal goals, defense teams have expounded monumental histories of their own that encompass the grand sweep of Balkan history. These imposing histories across the ages run in parallel to prosecution histories of the sort advanced in the *Milošević* trial and are quite unlike the prosecution's specific microhistories of towns or regions. Over time, defense histories became even broader and more ambitious in scope, whereas prosecution histories, as we saw in the previous chapter, became narrower and focused on more prosaic tasks such as introducing documents.[12] This reflected the defense's desire to articulate a nationalist position in the courtroom and to score legal points in the process.

6.2. FIGHTING TO A DRAW

When I became Prosecutor at the ICTY, I went to the region to meet with the governments. I didn't want to meet with Milošević, Tuđman or Izetbegović since they were already under investigation for possible war crimes. So I met with the Ministers of Justice and Foreign Affairs. In Serbia, the Minister of Justice regaled me with a 45-minute lecture on the history of the region, starting with 1389 and the Battle of Kosovo. Like the Afrikaner nationalism I was familiar with, he started with a humiliating defeat. In Croatia, I was given another lecture on history. The two histories had similarities but they did not meet up.

– Richard J. Goldstone, former Prosecutor of the ICTY and ICTR[13]

In the introduction to their book *How Law Knows* (2007:2–9), Austin Sarat et al. interrogate legal epistemology, noting that law's ways of knowing can be radically unique and diverge from science and what passes for common sense

---

[12] Defense counsel use historian expert witnesses to contextualize documents just as prosecutors do. However, they seem less committed to this aspect and more concerned with wide-ranging historical narrative. For instance, on 12 November 2002 in the *Simić* trial, during the testimony of the expert witness Nenad Kecmanović, judges refused to allow the defense to introduce documents because they had not been previously attached to the expert report. This was a simple procedural error perhaps, but one that indicated that Kecmanović's overarching narrative was of greater consequence to the defense team than the documents he was meant to introduce.

[13] Author interview, June 2007.

in any given society.[14] Law's distinctiveness when compared to any other form of human knowledge is in part explained by the genealogy of common law fact-finding, which Barbara Shapiro (2007:28–31) traces from the Roman rhetorical tradition through Judeo-Christian scriptural witness rules and medieval approaches to proof of facts. The legal axiom "consensus equals fact" illustrates the way in which law's way of knowing can be utterly unique, and this applies to both national courts and international criminal trials. In his study of the French Conseil d'État, Bruno Latour (2004:75) found that an "incontrovertible" legal fact is really not a fact at all; it is merely a statement lodged in a file that has not been challenged by any party to the proceedings. Furthermore, for French administrative law, it does not matter whether there is a link between the unchallenged statement in the file and any reality outside the court.

When asked to define a legal fact during interviews for this book, STAs at the ICTY regularly replied, "That which is not contested by the defense." Rule 69 of the International Criminal Court's Rules of Procedure and Evidence explicitly endorses and codifies this principle: "The Prosecutor and the defense may agree that an alleged fact . . . is not contested and accordingly, a Chamber may consider such alleged fact as being proven."[15] To give one concrete instance in the international courtroom, prosecutor Geoffrey Nice affirmed this principle during the trial of Slobodan Milošević. With one hour left in his cross-examination of historian Dr. Audrey Budding, Milošević was still debating issues in the eighteenth and nineteenth centuries and had not arrived at the main body of Budding's expert report. Nice stood up to remind the Trial Chamber, "I make it clear that if the parts of this report . . . aren't challenged in cross-examination, it will be open to the Prosecution in its closing address to this court to say that they stand unchallenged, and that will be what we will be obliged, and indeed happy, to do."[16] What this means in daily courtroom practice is that where there is broad agreement between two background experts, the judges will normally accept the information contained in their testimony as fact. This occurs more often than might be expected given the adversarial nature of criminal proceedings. For instance, in the *Tadić* trial, the prosecution witness Dr. James Gow and the defense witness Dr. Robert Hayden agreed that the rise of nationalism in Yugoslavia was closely linked to the country's economic crisis in the 1980s. In the *Brđanin* trial, sizable

---

[14] They also acknowledge the converse: "law's ways of knowing are insufficiently removed from prevailing assumptions" (2).

[15] Rules of Procedure and Evidence. International Criminal Court. Adopted by the Assembly of States Parties, 1st sess., New York, 3–10 September 2002, ICC-ASP/1/3.

[16] 24 July 2003, T24915.

portions of the testimonies of Dr. Paul Shoup (defense) and Dr. Robert Donia (prosecution) overlapped and were incorporated into the final trial judgment.

In contrast, when expert witnesses disagree and a "war of experts" develops, and when each expert is more or less credible, then neither side usually wins outright, and the dispute ends in stalemate. When asked how judges decide between two more or less equally competent experts with diverging views, one prosecutor replied acidly, "They don't."[17] Where there is conceptual or factual uncertainty on a matter and there is not an imperative to resolve the matter so as to try the crimes, then judges oftentimes simply steer clear of taking a view. In the words of one expert witness: "Judges go to great pains to avoid ambiguity. They throw up their hands and say, 'We don't want to address those questions. Let's not figure out why Bosnian Muslims sought national minority status in the 1960s and not before.'"[18] Given the judges' aversion to contested matters not directly related to the alleged crimes, contextual and background expert witnesses of equal credibility tend to nullify one another.

Our survey participants were asked the following question on this issue: "When the historian expert witnesses of the Prosecution and Defense contradict one another, how do judges decide between their competing historical accounts?" The question elicited a conspicuous disparity between prosecution and expert respondents on the one hand and defense respondents on the other hand (Figure 6.1). By a wide margin, both prosecution and expert witness respondents felt that the judges' decisions depended on the case. Half of the defense respondents (i.e., a majority of those who offered an opinion) believed that judges generally give the benefit of the doubt to the prosecution.

Even if we accept that the disgruntled defense opinions documented previously are strongly held, they are not exactly borne out in a reading of trial transcripts and judgments. One could just as easily make the contrary argument that, over time, arriving at a stalemate favors the accused. After all, the defense has to unravel and invalidate only as many parts of the prosecution case as it can rather than build an entirely independent case of its own. In pretrial conferences that include prosecutors, judges, and defense lawyers, prosecutors protest indignantly when the defense disputes each and every aspect of the prosecution's case. Yet this is what any defense lawyer worth his or her salt ought to do, that is, thwart the prosecution's case whenever possible, from the critical issues right down to the mundane and seemingly irrelevant ones. In an adversarial legal setting, stalemate is a kind of victory for the defense.

[17] Author interview, May 2006.
[18] Author interview, prosecution expert witness, May 2007.

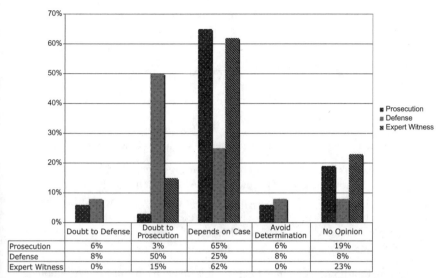

	Doubt to Defense	Doubt to Prosecution	Depends on Case	Avoid Determination	No Opinion
Prosecution	6%	3%	65%	6%	19%
Defense	8%	50%	25%	8%	8%
Expert Witness	0%	15%	62%	0%	23%

FIGURE 6.1. How do judges decide between competing historical accounts?

That a clash of experts may end in stalemate is not peculiar to international criminal trials but is commonly found in domestic jurisdictions, and indeed wherever experts appear in legal settings. In one recent high-profile case in the United States, *District of Columbia v. Heller* (2008), the U.S. Supreme Court struck down parts of a District of Columbia gun-control law on the grounds that the Second Amendment protects the individual right to possess firearms. Both sides in *Heller* called historians as expert witnesses and gave them the task of defining the "original" meaning of the Second Amendment's defense of "the right of the people to keep and bear arms" in the light of historical materials from the eighteenth century. Perhaps unsurprisingly, each side produced accounts of the historical backdrop to the Second Amendment that vindicated its reading of the text. Judge Harvie Wilkinson III (2009:267) writing in the *Virginia Law Review* noted that the upshot of all the historical argumentation in *Heller* was that "both sides fought into overtime to a draw." Professional historians did not find the historical debate before the Supreme Court particularly illuminating, and Stanford University historian Jack Rakove pronounced, "Neither of the two main opinions in Heller would pass muster as serious historical writing."[19] As we can see, one of the main purposes of defense historical witnesses is to pull one plank out from under the prosecution case,

[19] Adam Liptak, "Ruling on Guns Elicits Rebuke from the Right," *New York Times*, 21 October 2008, A1.

and in that way, international criminal trials are no different from domestic trials.

6.3. THE CHAOS DEFENSE

From the trial of Jadranko Prlić, 15 September 2008:

> DEFENSE COUNSEL MICHAEL KARNAVAS: What was it like in Mostar at or around that time that led the Assembly members to set up the Crisis Staff?
>
> DEFENSE WITNESS BORISLAV PULJIĆ: By that time, there had been a lot of shooting around the town. The town was also being shelled and all the public utilities had trouble operating. There was poor supply of running water and electricity. The cleaning services hardly did their job. The undertakers could not carry out the burials. Many residents fled the town, and at the same time there was a large inflow of refugees. In a word, chaos reigned in the town.
>
> DEFENSE COUNSEL: For how long did this chaos reign until the Assembly decided to set up the Crisis Staff?
>
> WITNESS: Chaos started as soon as the reservists of the Yugoslav People's Army came over from Serbia. These troops appeared in the streets of the town, chaos emerged, and this situation prevailed through to the time when the last session of the Assembly was held.[20]

Where there is compelling evidence that a crime has been committed, attorneys have only so many options available in constructing a viable defense case. One of the most common is the capacity defense, which is based on the defendant's inability to be held accountable for an illegal act.[21] In layperson's terms, the defense declares that "indeed horrible crimes were committed, but my client cannot be held responsible for them." The chaos defense is a subcategory of the time-honored capacity defense in criminal law. At the ICTY and other international tribunals, a chaos defense conventionally claims that owing to a general situation of confusion and uncertainty, the accused did not plan, instigate, order or command, or otherwise participate in the planning and executing of a crime and was not in a position of *de jure* or *de facto* authority, effective control, or substantial influence over those subordinates committing the crimes. Moreover, it is often contended that the accused was not even aware of the crimes being committed. Awareness is crucial when considering whether a political official or commanding officer is guilty of a crime of omission, as Article 7(3) of the ICTY Statute makes clear that "[t]he

---

[20] Exchange in the trial of Jadranko Prlić and others, Trial transcript, 15 September 2008, T32091.
[21] For an excellent legal-philosophical discussion of capacity in English criminal law, see Lacey (2007).

fact that any of the acts referred to in articles 2 to 5 of the present Statute was committed by a subordinate does not relieve his superior of criminal responsibility if he knew or had reason to know that the subordinate was about to commit such acts or had done so and the superior failed to take the necessary and reasonable measures to prevent such acts or to punish the perpetrators thereof."

A chaos defense has been an integral part of the cases of senior and middle-ranking political leaders such as Radoslav Brđanin; Momčilo Krajišnik; and as we just saw, the Bosnian Croat leader Jadranko Prlić. It has been especially prevalent where the accused is a middle-class professional – a university professor or medical doctor such as Blagoje Simić, who held an official position in the crisis staffs and regional and municipal assemblies of Bosnia in 1991–2. Leadership cases invariably hinge on elements of the chain of command and the degree of responsibility held by each individual in a political or military structure. Prosecutors seek to hold the accused criminally responsible on the grounds that she or he occupied a position of *de facto* or *de jure* power, or both, and substantial influence in an organization that orchestrated widespread and systematic crimes. Leaders created the policies and plans for war and exercised effective control over subordinates in a functional institutional or organizational apparatus such as a political party or regional assembly.

The chaos defense aims to disrupt a key element of the prosecution case by advancing a thesis of the "missing middle." That is, during the 1991–5 conflict in Bosnia, a yawning chasm opened up between national political leaders such as Franjo Tuđman and Slobodan Milošević and senior Bosnian leaders such as Mate Boban and Radovan Karadžić on the one hand and local armies, paramilitaries, and the civilian military mobilization on the other hand. The missing-middle thesis disconnects regional authorities from their erstwhile bases and constituencies. As evidence, the defense points to the anarchic political situation on the ground in the early 1990s, characterized by mass movements of refugees and a hodgepodge of disorganized municipal and regional bodies.

The chaos defense seeks to distance regional political leaders such as Simić and Prlić from the official and informal militias operating in their areas. Defense lawyers note that relations between political parties and their armies were strained at various points; thus, there was no clear chain of command that reached from political and military authorities down to the official militaries and informal paramilitaries.[22] As the defense expert witness in the Brđanin trial

---

[22] Paul Shoup stated in his testimony, for instance, that by the end of the war, SDS leader Karadžić and Bosnian Serb Army General Mladić had split and Mladić was "operating on his own." *Brđanin* trial transcripts, 5 February 2004, T24394.

Dr. Paul Shoup (2004:29) wrote in his expert report: "Placing all the blame on the VRS [Bosnian Serb Army] for the ethnic cleansing in the late spring and summer of 1992 nevertheless seems to overlook the general confusion in the region at the time." Political party leaders did not control their own ragtag armies or even know what they were doing. Defense teams have quoted military top brass, such as Yugoslav National Army (JNA) General Slavko Lisica, to characterize the belligerent parties in the Bosnian conflict thus: "not fighters but adventurers and the usual dregs that every war brings to the surface . . . [T]hey are disorganized, irresponsible."[23] According to Brđanin's defense counsel in his closing arguments, only those individuals holding the guns were in charge, as "weapons defined power and authority, calling into question the very existence of accountable government."[24] Former Bosnian Serb President Radovan Karadžić adopted similar tactics to undermine charges of superior responsibility for the Bosnian Serb army's forty-four-month siege of Sarajevo that left about twelve thousand people dead. While cross-examining the prosecution's expert witness British Army Lieutenant Colonel Richard Philips, Karadžić presented documents outlining problems of drunkenness, inadequate training, and lack of discipline and claiming "ineffective command control at almost all levels."[25]

The chaos defense emphasizes the grassroots nature of the armed conflict by highlighting the extensive popular mobilization and portraying civilian participation as spontaneous, self-motivated, and directed. Rather than instigating and coordinating the conflict, the accused was faced with a violent popular uprising he could not control, as much as he would have liked to. Such views were expressed at the ICTY on the day I wrote this sentence, when a former official of the Ministry of Internal Affairs (MUP) in Bosnia stated how the barricades "came about spontaneously" in Sarajevo in 1992 after a Serb bridegroom was shot: "It is hard to control reactions of ordinary people when something that big happens."[26] Because the violence was organized from below and there was no structured and methodical policy or plan, culpability is not concentrated in a linear chain of command but is fragmented and diffused. Such an argument unmistakably counteracts the prosecution's case for superior or command responsibility.

---

[23] Quoted in Shoup (2004:29).
[24] Defense closing arguments, *Brđanin* Trial Judgment, §44.
[25] Rachel Irwin, "Karadzic Speaks of Army Problems," IWPR ICTY Tribunal Update No. 650, 25 June 2010.
[26] Velma Sarić, "Trial Hears Sarajevo Barricades Were Spontaneous," IWPR ICTY Tribunal Update No. 635, 21 February 2010. The testimony of Nedjo Vlaski was heard in the *Stanišić* and *Župljanin* trials.

Certain historical arguments typify the chaos defense outlined here. To understand them more fully, it is instructive to scrutinize the report and testimony of one defense expert witness, Dr. Paul Shoup. Shoup is a retired professor of political science at the University of Virginia and a former president of the American Association for East European Studies, whose coauthored book *The War in Bosnia-Herzegovina* (1999) won the prestigious Ralph J. Bunche award of the American Political Science Association. Shoup testified over four days in February 2004 as a background expert witness in the trial of Radoslav Brđanin.[27] Shoup explained to me what he wished to convey to the judges in his courtroom testimony:

> The break up of Yugoslavia was bound to unleash problems in Bosnia – it's very nature and existence was at stake. I wanted to inform the judges that it was complicated and there was a different atmosphere in the Balkans where people settle things by fighting. All sides did this. It doesn't exonerate anyone who committed an atrocity. The other camp thought that if Serbs hadn't engaged in aggression then everything would be fine, but the court must look at the evidence very carefully. All sides were engaging in violence and committing excesses.[28]

Two elements from Shoup's expert report and testimony were germane to the defense's theory of the case: the historical lack of control of Bosnian authorities over their own destiny and a deeply entrenched Balkans culture of vengeance and feuding.

The chaos defense is premised on a lack of effective control on the part of political authorities, with all the complications that proving a negative implies. It benefits from being able to show that authorities have not been able to govern Bosnia over a long historical period. In Shoup's report and testimony, Yugoslav history became a kind of Russian-doll tragedy, where each individual or political level was controlled by the one immediately outside or inside it. At the outermost level, Shoup's (2004:3) report described how Yugoslavia was buffeted by overpowering external forces: "In both Yugoslavia (and Bosnia), the delicate balance between accommodation and conflict from 1918 to the present was at the mercy of the evolving international situation over which Yugoslavs themselves had little control." Bosnians themselves were unable to shape the country's destiny, as "the key to the fate of Bosnia lay with Yugoslavia" (ibid.:5), an external power over which Bosnians themselves exercised little control. Without Yugoslavia's authoritarian rule, Bosnia would have been torn apart much earlier by its ethnic, national, and religious differences – divisions

[27] Shoup testified on 4–6 February and 9 February 2004, T24271–24645.
[28] Author interview, May 2009.

it had surmounted only by "submitting to foreign rule" (7). For those reasons, Yugoslavia's dominion over Bosnia brought tangible benefits to the republic, as "the cohesiveness of Bosnia was a consequence of external pressures and constraints" (44).

An inexorable narrative ran through Shoup's history of Bosnia, as modern-day events were overdetermined by their historical precursors, weighed down by a heavy chain of causality. As Shoup testified on the stand, "When Titoism collapsed, when communism collapsed ... the past captured the present."[29] The disintegration of Bosnia was the inevitable corollary of the lifting of authoritarian constraints and "Bosnia was overwhelmed by events for which she herself was not responsible" (44). That conflict would erupt out of the disintegrating Yugoslav state was a "grim inevitability" (44). Nationalism in the Balkans was a phenomenon that was "deeply rooted in the cultures, history and politics of the country" (3). Bosnian leaders themselves had little control over the nationalist fervor of their population, and as a historical parallel, Shoup cited accounts of eastern Bosnia in the 1940s, when civilian paramilitary irregulars were accompanied by peasants – including women and children – who pillaged the villages of their enemies. During World War II, "commanders ... were not always able to stop this slaughter," and Shoup notes identical modern-day complaints from JNA officers regarding Bosnian paramilitaries. For Shoup, the history of the region carried a bitter taste of fate and destiny.

The second historical dimension of Brđanin's chaos defense portrayed a deeply ingrained culture of vengeance in the "Balkan character." This could be seen as the defense counterpart of the Serbian "national mind-set" central to the prosecution's monumental history during the Milošević trial. In its closing arguments, Brđanin's defense counsel invoked the "need to view events from a historical and cultural perspective" and to understand how modern events were shaped by "historical events and the individual and collective memories of World War II."[30] Shoup's expert report documents how the majority of Yugoslavs were deeply (if at times unconsciously) bound to their respective ethnic, national and religious communities. This applied especially in Bosnia, which had exhibited an incapacity to function as a viable state in modern times and was fundamentally unsuited to independent statehood. Serbs and Croats had a more "highly developed" national awareness, but in Bosnia a "more primitive" (5) ethnic identity prevailed that was fueled by vivid historical memories of the horrors of World War II.

---

[29] 5 February 2004, T24370.
[30] *Brđanin* Trial Judgment, §§44–5.

Driving home these points, Defense Counsel Ackerman read aloud the following section of Shoup's expert report in the courtroom: "The notion that the peoples of Bosnia were prisoners of their violent past enrages the critics of the 'ancient hatreds' theory. Yet the fact of the matter was that families remembered who had engaged in atrocities during World War II, and vengeance became the order of the day as regime collapse gathered speed" (44). Ackerman then asked Shoup a follow-up question: "What role does vengeance play in the Balkan character?" Shoup replied that it played a vital role in rural areas: "these are mountain men, you know."[31] In detailing a culture of revenge in the Balkans, the expert witness proceeded to mention an anthropological account of a murderous feud between two Croat clans in Međugorje, Western Herzegovina, a Catholic pilgrimage site.

Shoup's expert report did not only portray Bosnians as aggressive and cruel peasants; it also recognized a distinctly Bosnian tradition of coexistence. However, Shoup made clear that he thought Bosnian coexistence was precarious, "over-glamorized in the West," and achieved only through authoritarian means (13).[32] Shoup expanded on this aspect in our interview:

> They co-existed with deep apprehension, a fear of Muslims. If a polarization begins then the natural tendency is for people to gather in their own communities for protection. The old animosities were incited by irresponsible people, this was true even on the Muslim side. When the national question erupted in Bosnia people coalesced with their own people. When you hear about violence, you want to get even. This is part of a deeply rooted sense of who you are. You can never tell me there's another way.[33]

What impact did the defense counsel's historical line of argument, and Shoup's testimony and report in particular, have on the outcome of the *Brđanin* trial? At first glance, it seemed that Shoup had undermined his own case in certain ways during the Trial Chamber. As did a number of other background expert witnesses, including, as the reader will recall, some from the prosecution side, he let his emotions get away from him. He appeared offended by the forceful manner of Senior Trial Attorney Joanna Korner's cross-examination, and at one point he indignantly banged the table.[34] On the final tempestuous day

---

[31] 5 February 2004, T24387.
[32] It is important to recognize in summarizing Shoup's report and testimony that he is careful to give different accounts of each topic, and for each assertion, there is reasonable consideration of an alternative view. However, in my reading, the weight of Shoup's evidence leans in the direction indicated in the text.
[33] Author interview, May 2009.
[34] See testimony at the end of the day on Thursday, 5 February 2004, and Friday, 6 February 2004.

of his courtroom testimony, Shoup and Korner exchanged barbed comments
as the prosecutor disputed the statements contained in Shoup's expert report,
claiming that the filming of inmates at the Trnopolje camp was "staged" by
British Independent Television News (ITN) journalists and that the camp
was a "transit, not concentration camp" (52). A formidable presence in the
courtroom, Joanna Korner seized on Shoup's construal and referred to a prior
British libel trial in which the court rejected the allegation that the ITN crew
misrepresented the images of emaciated Bosnian Muslim men behind barbed
wire at Trnopolje.[35] Pointing out that this matter had been resolved in a court
of law, Korner badgered the expert to change his evidence while on the stand,
but Shoup would not budge. Korner charged him with bias, challenged his
entire methodology, and suggested that "this whole report is full of errors
because you have done . . . insufficient checking."[36]

These heated exchanges notwithstanding, the defense succeeded in obtaining an acquittal on the genocide charge, and Shoup's testimony strengthened
the defense position on the central legal issue at stake in the trial. The defense
had portrayed the Bosnian conflict as a dispute over territory between various
groups rather than a program of extermination of any group in whole or in
part. Shoup's expert report fortified the defense's theory by offering a comparison of ethnic cleansing in the 1940s and the 1990s. Ustaše Croat attacks on
Serbs in the 1940s were "genocidal in intent" in that they had extermination
of a group as their goal. In contrast, the ethnic cleansing and the massacres
of 1990s committed by Serbs (including at Srebrenica) were not genocidal
in intent according to Shoup, because their aim was to consolidate territory
rather than physically liquidate Croats and Bosnian Muslims as groups. Judges
were seemingly convinced by this interpretation, and in acquitting Radoslav
Brđanin of genocide, the trial judgment endorsed the view that ethnic cleansing was part of an overall plan of Bosnian Serbs to secure territory rather than
to exterminate a population group (§§76–7).

Although the full exculpatory potential of the past was tapped in the *Brđanin*
trial, other defense teams have not replayed the score exactly, as it contains
an inherently hazardous element of foreseeability. *Foreseeability* is defined
in law as "the quality of being reasonably anticipatable" and as a type of
actual causation.[37] For international crimes to be justiciable, certain acts
must be a foreseeable consequence of other acts. As the trial of Radovan
Karadžić illustrates, foreseeability is increasingly a feature of prosecution cases

[35] Trial Transcript 24614 *passim*.
[36] 9 February 2004, T24625.
[37] Garner (2006).

of political leaders in international criminal trials. As has been often noted, political leaders such as Karadžić seldom committed actual criminal acts such as murder or torture themselves. Instead, they drew up plans, proposed policies in assemblies and political party meetings, issued public statements and direct orders, and made public speeches to their constituencies. Drawing on the available documentary evidence, the prosecution usually alleges that the leader instigated and incited others to commit criminal acts in furtherance of an overall criminal policy or plan.

Some historical elements of the chaos defense might provide additional fodder for the prosecution in this way: if indeed there were simmering ancient hatreds and a culture of revenge, then it could be argued that criminal acts were a foreseeable consequence of an inflammatory speech or political statement. If there is overwhelming evidence of a history of interethnic hostility, then everyone, including the accused, should have reasonably anticipated the harmful consequences of a provocative, inciting, or instigating statement, order, or speech. If the prosecution can prove that the additional crimes were foreseeable to the accused, then according to the ICTY's jurisprudence, this establishes *mens rea* under Article 7(1) of the ICTY Statute ("individual criminal responsibility"), as well as under the third "extended" type of joint criminal responsibility.[38] Clearly, it is not in the interest of defense counsel or the accused to hand the prosecution grounds for intent, and this is what historical elements in the chaos defense can do. Because of this potential weakness, many defense lawyers have pulled back from calling expert witnesses to make ancient-hatreds background arguments.

6.4. *TU QUOQUE*, THE IMPERFECT DEFENSE

> If Doenitz and Rader deserved to hang for sinking ships without warning, so did [U.S. Admiral] Nimitz.
> – Nuremberg Chief Prosecutor Telford Taylor (1992:409)

In international criminal trials, the defense has often contended that the accused is charged of crimes also committed by his adversaries. Because the opposing side initiated the conflict, it bears the burden of responsibility for any crimes that ensued. This is known as a *tu quoque* defense, defined at the ICTY thus: "The defense of *tu quoque* concerns the allegation that the opposing party to the conflict committed similar atrocities" or "the allegation that that

---

[38] *Kvocka et al.*, Appeals Judgment, §83: "The third, 'extended' form of joint criminal enterprise entails responsibility for crimes committed beyond the common purpose, but which are nevertheless a natural and foreseeable consequence of the common purpose."

party was responsible for the commencement of the said conflict," or both.[39] The *Kupreškić* Trial Judgment notes that "Defense counsel have indirectly or implicitly relied upon the *tu quoque* principle, i.e. the argument whereby the fact that the adversary has also committed similar crimes offers a valid defense to the individuals accused" (§515).[40]

Since its appearance in the Nuremberg trials, international criminal law has formally rejected the principle of *tu quoque*, declaring it an illegitimate defense against an indictment for war crimes or crimes against humanity.[41] The ICTY has also categorically rejected *tu quoque* as a legitimate defense:

> This is an argument resting on the allegedly reciprocal nature of obligations created by the humanitarian law of armed conflict. This argument may amount to saying that breaches of international humanitarian law, being committed by the enemy, justify similar breaches by a belligerent. Or it may amount to saying that such breaches, having been perpetrated by the adversary, legitimize similar breaches by a belligerent in response to, or in retaliation for, such violations by the enemy. Clearly, this second approach to a large extent coincides with the doctrine of reprisals. . . . [T]he *tu quoque* argument is flawed in principle. It envisages humanitarian law as based upon a narrow bilateral exchange of rights and obligations. Instead, the bulk of this body of law lays down absolute obligations, namely obligations that are unconditional or in other words not based on reciprocity.[42]

International criminal law textbooks give short shrift to the subject of *tu quoque*, and William Schabas's (2009:397) definitive *Genocide in International Law* summarily dispatches the topic in less than half a page. International lawyers approach the *tu quoque* defense as international lawyers are wont to do: by citing the 1949 Geneva Conventions and the obligations *erga omnes*

---

[39] Decision on Evidence of the Good Character of the Accused and the Defence of *Tu Quoque*, *Prosecutor v. Zoran Kupreškić* et al., IT-95-16-T, 17 February 1999.

[40] This also shares some elements of a justifiable-provocation defense, whereby even a reasonable person might commit a crime when prior offenses have been committed against him or her.

[41] See Chief Prosecutor Telford Taylor (1992:409) on the issue of *tu quoque* in the Nuremberg trials. German naval judge advocate Otto Kranzbueler, representing Admiral Doenitz, extracted from U.S. Admiral Nimitz the admission that the U.S. Navy followed the same rules of engagement as the Germans for submarine attacks against merchant vessels.

[42] *Prosecutor v. Zoran Kupreškić* et al., IT-95-16-T, Trial Chamber judgment, 14 January 2000. §515 and §517). The Trial Chamber had earlier ruled: "The *tu quoque* principle does not apply to international humanitarian law," § (iii) in Decision on Evidence of the Good Character of the Accused and the Defence of *Tu Quoque, Prosecutor v. Zoran Kupreškić* et al., IT-95-16-T, 17 February 1999. The judgment then goes on to describe how international law constitutes the translation into legal rules of the "categorical imperative" and the moral philosophy of Immanuel Kant (§518) that insists on fulfilling obligations regardless of whether others comply with them. Mark Osiel (2009a) recently challenged the place of Kantian ethics in national and international law in *The End of Reciprocity*.

to punish violations of international humanitarian law and then moving on. For their part, defense attorneys in our survey rejected by a margin of two to one the statement: "The Defense calls historians as expert witnesses in order to mount a *tu quoque* defense." Prosecutors, in contrast, thought the statement was true by a margin of over three to one.[43] And yet despite the cursory dismissals by international lawyers and defense denials, the principle of *tu quoque* remains a chief defense strategy in the living law, and as such, it deserves our full attention. Even a cursory exposure to actual trials at the ICTY and ICTR conveys how defense teams seldom resist the allure of *tu quoque*. These arguments appear time and again in international criminal trials, to the extent that one could fill the rest of this book documenting their many manifestations. *Tu quoque* assertions are even more pronounced in genocide trials and were a prominent feature of the *Milošević* trial,[44] and they made yet another appearance in the opening stages of the trial of Radovan Karadžić. In his comments on the Srebrenica massacre, confirmed as genocide in the earlier *Krstić* trial and appeal judgments, Karadžić stated that prior attacks on Serbs had been "very[,] very violent." He claimed to possess evidence that Bosniak Muslim "fighters from the enclave returned with chains of Serb ears around their necks." Presiding Judge Kwon interrupted him to remark: "It's one thing to have a legitimate cause in waging war, but totally a separate matter on how it is waged."[45]

One of the most common manifestations of the *tu quoque* principle occurs during the defense's cross-examination of prosecution expert witnesses, as we saw in Chapter 5, when John Ackerman sparred with Robert Donia in the *Brđanin* trial.[46] Only a few months later, Donia faced a similar interrogation by the defense counsel John Ostojić in the trial of Milomir Stakić regarding the "reactive measures" taken by the Serbs of Prejidor against prior attacks by Muslim fighters.[47] After having already asked the defense not to "to touch upon the issue of *tu quoque*,"[48] Judge Wolfgang Schomburg confronted Ostojić robustly: "Counsel, do you really want to make the point that the accused in this case,

---

[43] The full range of responses to the statement "The Defense calls historians as expert witnesses in order to mount a *tu quoque* defense" were as follows: prosecution – true, 48 percent; false, 13 percent; no opinion, 39 percent; defense – true, 17 percent; false, 42 percent; no opinion, 42 percent; expert witnesses – true, 23 percent; false, 23 percent; no opinion, 54 percent.

[44] There were *tu quoque* qualities in much of the accused's questioning of prosecution witnesses, but *amicus curiae* Tapušković also rehearsed *tu quoque* arguments (e.g., during cross-examination of prosecution expert witness Dr. Renaud de La Brosse) (T21277–8).

[45] Rachel Irwin, "International Community Smuggled Arms, Claims Karadzic," Institute for War and Peace Reporting, 19 February 2010.

[46] 31 January 2002.

[47] 24 April 2002, T2131.

[48] T2121.

Dr. Milomir Stakić, acted in defense against fighters from Afghanistan at that point in time?"[49] Defense counsel backed down in the encounter but returned to the theme of *tu quoque* time and time again in the *Stakić* trial. For instance, Ostojić's questioning of prosecution expert witness James Mayhew focused not on the site of the accused's alleged crimes in Prejidor but on massacres of Serbs by Muslim and Croat militias in other, often distant locales.[50]

What does the defense hope to achieve when it cross-examines prosecution experts in this way? It wishes to demonstrate that the opposing side attacked first, thus creating a state of emergency. All subsequent actions by the accused's party therefore constituted justifiable reprisals. It also pursues a more ordinary legal objective, to undermine the credibility of the expert witness by suggesting that his or her report is bowdlerized and has omitted major events in the armed conflict. *Tu quoque* is central to the defense's contention that the prosecution expert witness is not neutral, and the expert report is tainted by an underlying prejudice and should be set aside. In suggesting partiality, often combined with the insinuation that the expert has been improperly steered by the prosecution, the defense hopes to provoke an emotional response from the witness or lure him or her into a prejudicial statement that will exhibit antipathy toward the accused and his or her ethnic, religious, or national group.

Some expressions of *tu quoque* sentiment in international criminal trials are simplistic, finger-pointing, "but you did it too" accusations that can be heard on any elementary school playground.[51] However, more sophisticated versions also exist. At the ICTY, these formulate the defense theory of the case by constructing an argument for reprisals that combines the enemies' extreme provocations in the early 1990s with a historical explanation for why certain acts or statements held special meaning. Insofar as *tu quoque* is a doctrine of justifiable reprisals, historical chronology is crucial. Political historians are one of the most effective kinds of expert witness for expounding on chronology and narrative, and defense attorneys have relied on them frequently in mounting a *tu quoque* defense.

We can learn more about how the *tu quoque* principle functions in practice at the ICTY by examining the trial of Blagoje Simić, president of the Serbian Democratic Party (SDS) in Bosanski Šamac in 1991–2 and president of the

---

[49] T2131.

[50] *Stakić* trial transcripts, 18 July 2002, T6106–6114.

[51] See, for example, the testimony of defense expert witness historian Dr. Srdja Trifković in the 2003 trial of Milomir Stakić. After a day of Trifković's testimony, Judge Schomburg commented that the expert witness had demonstrated a "clear lack of tolerance" and that his assertions relied on a "poor basis of facts," making Schomburg "absolutely hesitant from the beginning of this case to go too much into details of so-called history" (19 March 2003, T13820).

Crisis Staff and War Presidency in 1992. The prosecution had previously called Dr. Robert Donia of the University of Michigan to produce an expert report and testify on the collapse of the former Yugoslavia and the nationalist policies of the SDS. Defense counsel countered by calling their own background expert witness, Dr. Nenad Kecmanović, a political scientist from Belgrade University who had been rector of the University of Sarajevo and had served as a Serb representative in the Bosnian presidency in July 1992 before moving to Belgrade.

In his testimony on November 12, 2002, Kecmanović gave classic *tu quoque* testimony designed to shape the judges' views on the proportionality of Bosnian Serb actions. Leaders of the SDS responded in a manner commensurate with the level of threat they faced from Croatian political parties, and especially from the Bosniak Party of Democratic Action (SDA). In his expert-witness report, Kecmanović (2002:7, 16) stressed how the "cunning" and "manipulating" SDA leader Alija Izetbegović wanted to impose an Islamic society and Islamic state at odds with "general western values." Kecmanović omits entirely from his report and testimony the role in the conflict of Serb parties such as the SDS and armies such as the JNA and Bosnian Serb Army (VRS). Instead, SDS-instigated crimes were spontaneous reactions to unwarranted SDA provocations; a view, if accepted by the judges, that would have considerably weakened the prosecution charge that Simić and his coaccused were acting in a joint criminal enterprise to commit crimes against humanity. Given the magnitude and immediacy of the threat, the actions of the accused were hasty responses to acute circumstances rather than premeditated crimes coordinated through a concerted policy or plan.

Kecmanović laid the blame for starting the conflict squarely at the door of Bosnian Croat and Muslim political leaders. Defense Counsel Igor Pantelić asked the expert witness about the withdrawal of Serb deputies from the Bosnian assembly on 14–15 October 1991, a protest seen by many observers as bringing Bosnia closer to the precipice of war. Kecmanović replied:

> The constitutional status of people was violated. At that time, Bosnia and Herzegovina was defined as a republic which was neither Croat nor Serb nor Muslim, but all of these three together. This was a political principle that was very important for the functioning of all three peoples in Bosnia Herzegovina. And up until that moment, this principle was upheld, even in that assembly, regardless of numerous conflicts that existed between political parties . . . and it held the entire Bosnia-Herzegovina together. . . . [T]his caused a break up and the Serb part, upon facing the fact that it was ignored by the other two sides, left the joint administration and organs of Bosnia and Herzegovina.[52]

---

[52] *Simić* trial transcript, T12072.

The expert witness then described how Croats began unilaterally establishing their own autonomous regions in Western Herzegovina. An armed conflict broke out between Croatian military units and the predominantly Muslim Bosnian Army, and this precipitated the breakup of Bosnia and Herzegovina. At this historical juncture, the three ethno-national groups set up their own state administrations "and naturally, they waged war against each other."[53] Meanwhile, Serb parties kept negotiating and seeking compromise, but in March 1992, the Muslim leader Izetbegović withdrew his signature from the Carrington–Cutileiro peace plan and plunged the region irrevocably into war.[54]

Kecmanović's account of the conflict is widely held among Serbs from a variety of political affiliations in the former Yugoslavia. In this view, Bosnia had been founded on a long-standing consociational compact among the three ethno-national groups, in which a "national key" distributed political offices among members of the three groups. By consistently voting against Serbs en bloc, Croats and Muslims had broken the contract and violated the minority rights of Serbs. This left Serbs with no choice but to withdraw from the political framework, at which point Croats and Muslims began fighting among themselves, with Serbs as the innocent and injured third party. Serbs were spurred on not by an ideology of Greater Serbia and aggressive territorial expansion but by "the preservation of Great Yugoslavia," the political system and principles that had historically secured peaceful coexistence in Bosnia and Herzegovina.[55]

Prosecutor Philip Weiner's cross-examination of the defense expert witness was among the most uncompromising seen at the ICTY. He objected to Kecmanović's statements that Serb atrocities were "exaggerated" and that Serbs were "demonized" in the Western media.[56] The expert witness's report had cited an article in the London *Times* newspaper alleging that Muslims themselves had shelled the Markale marketplace in central Sarajevo in 1994 to gain international sympathy. The *Times* article cited as its source a UN investigation into the massacre but mistakenly attributed to the UN report the finding that a Muslim artillery position had fired the shells. Weiner pulled up the UN report on the courtroom monitors and demonstrated that the UN investigation had made no such finding, and he referred to the earlier ICTY trial that convicted Serb General Galić of the shelling.[57]

53 T12073.
54 A point reinforced in the expert witness report by Kecmanović (2002:27).
55 Testimony by Kecmanović, T12108.
56 Statements reiterated in the courtroom testimony, T12094.
57 T12085–9.

Prosecutor Weiner also picked up on Kecmanović's assertion that the Western media had "flimsy evidence" on Serb camps at Omarska, Keraterm, and Trnopolje.[58] Weiner cited ICTY cases in which camp guards had been convicted of committing atrocities in the three concentration camps. In one dramatic courtroom moment, Weiner, clearly bristling with enmity, showed a grisly photograph of an execution by camp guard Goran Jelisić and asked whether Kecmanović would change his testimony in relation to his remarks about "alleged atrocities" and "flimsy evidence."[59] Kecmanović refused to change his testimony and instead replied in an unadulterated *tu quoque* vein: "I lived in Sarajevo during a portion of the war. There were crimes committed against Serb civilians there, and I did not need photographs to learn of this. I was there and I saw that directly. Those were crimes committed against Serb civilians."[60] Weiner invited the expert witness another four times to amend his report in the light of the evidence presented. Kecmanović refused: "I cannot give you a yes or no answer. The question is much too complex for that."[61] For outside observers, this was gripping courtroom drama, but judges watched the passionate exchanges with palpable boredom, displaying minimal interest in the expert witness's testimony. The bench limited the defense counsel Pantelić's redirect examination, with Presiding Judge Florence Mumba uttering, "I don't think there is any more reason[] why we should spend more time with this witness."[62]

The *Simić* trial was one in which the prosecution and defense historical witnesses talked past one another and there did not exist any areas of intersecting testimony or evidence. Robert Donia focused almost exclusively on the actions of the SDS, and Kecmanović made no mention of the prewar preparations of Bosnian Serbs. Although Donia is cited extensively in the final *Simić* judgment, the Trial Chamber did not cite either historical defense expert witness (Nenad Kecmanović or Pavle Nikolić) anywhere in the Trial Judgment. The exonerating political history proposed by the defense seemed to be entirely rejected by the Trial Chamber judges, at least as factual information about the alleged crimes. Nevertheless, prosecution staff interviewed for this book confirmed that, at the time, they felt that Kecmanović had damaged aspects

---

[58] T12090–4.
[59] T12095.
[60] T12096.
[61] T12096. Redirect by defense counsel Pantelić reinforced the theme that Bosnia's very existence was based on the political principle of "consensus among the three constituent peoples" and referred to the massacre of Serbs at Sijekovac, returning again to the default *tu quoque* position (T12173).
[62] T12170.

of the prosecution case. Blagoje Simić was eventually convicted by the Trial Chamber of persecutions on the basis of the unlawful detention of Bosnian Muslim and Bosnian Croat civilians, beatings, torture, forced labor, deportation, and forcible transfer. On appeal, the torture and beating charges were overturned and the conviction for persecutions was reduced to "aiding and abetting."[63] Simić was sentenced to fifteen years, which he presently is serving in a prison in the United Kingdom.

6.5. *TU QUOQUE*, MITIGATION, AND THE DEFENSE EXPERT-WITNESS EFFECT

The *tu quoque* defense contributes nothing to the question of individual criminal responsibility, and no accused has been acquitted of a crime on the basis of a *tu quoque* defense. Why, then, does the *tu quoque* defense strategy endure in international criminal tribunals, even after the tribunals confirmed its long-standing rejection by international criminal law and even when judges explicitly discourage it in the courtroom? The most obvious answer is that the accused (and, potentially, the accused's defense team) may actually believe that moral and legal obligations are reciprocal and that the actions were legitimate because they were rational reactions to extreme provocation. For nationalists (i.e., for a substantial proportion of the Balkans' population), *tu quoque* arguments provide the ideological and historical justification for their participation in the armed conflict. The reprisals, therefore, have moral legitimacy for the defense because they believe that victims of violent acts are not bound to exercise restraint.

Other reasons are related to lawyers' courtroom strategies. The *tu quoque* principle has become the defense's preferred rhetorical framing device, wherein background and contextual evidence lay a mantle of legitimacy across the defense theory of the case. This applies directly to the *Simić* trial we have just considered, and the accused Blagoje Simić testified the very next day after Kecmanović appeared. It is easy to understand why the defense would want to pause the procession of factual elements of the alleged crimes and introduce an expert witness. In the place of squalid acts and widespread criminality, the court was treated to a refined and elevated discourse on the constitutional law elements of historic Yugoslavia, furnished by a respected academician and former rector of the University of Sarajevo. The appearance of Kecmanović

---

[63] The Appeals Chamber found that Simić had not been properly informed by the prosecution that he was being accused of a joint criminal enterprise until the end of the trial, rendering aspects of the trial unfair.

interrupted the grim procession of fact witnesses speaking about crimes and lent a veneer of respectability to the accused.

While such explanations make sense, the main reason the *tu quoque* defense is entrenched in international criminal trials is the role it plays in mitigation. To be clear, the strategy does not acquit or absolve the accused of the crimes, but that is not its objective. It is an imperfect defense that patently fails to meet the legal requirements of the trial, but that does not mean that it is a sham or frivolous defense, insofar as it is dedicated to a reduction in the sentence. Moreover, international trials are not especially unique in this aspect, and the role of expert witnesses in international criminal trials shares attributes with their role in domestic jurisdictions. Explaining the context in which crimes occurred does seem to favor the defense case for mitigation.

In Anglo-American domestic criminal trials, defense teams are more likely to adopt this tactic when the perpetrator's responsibility for a crime is not being questioned. Perhaps the best recent example of this is in trials of battered women who have killed their abuser. A number of studies have examined the impact of defense expert-witness testimony in battered wife cases in Europe and North America, especially with regard to sentencing.[64] One study by the Canadian psychologists Schuller and Hastings (1996:170) noted how expert witnesses in Canadian courts have developed a standard portrayal of battered-woman syndrome in which the behavior of the "reasonable battered woman" is not pathologized but represented in the overall social context and "a normal response to a traumatic situation."

The research the authors presented to respondents was a model version of an actual Canadian homicide trial (*Lavallee v. Regina*) in which a woman killed her abusive husband. In the psychological experiment conducted by the authors, a control group of participants was presented with twenty-three pages of trial testimony. A second group received the same trial transcripts but also received extensive expert testimony about battered-woman syndrome. Participants gave more lenient sentences where expert witness testimony was introduced and where such testimony focused on the woman's social context and reality rather than on her psychological state. Respondents also tended toward more lenient sentences where the conceptual terminology of battered-woman syndrome was used. The more educated the respondent, the more susceptible he or she was to the conceptual arguments of expert witnesses speaking abstractly and conceptually about domestic violence as a social phenomenon.

In assessing whether such experiments in a domestic legal setting are applicable to the international criminal context, it needs to be acknowledged that

---

[64] See Romkens (2000) and Schuller and Hastings (1996).

there are two elements of international tribunals that are quite dissimilar. First, the respondents in the experiments were lay people, not professional judges, and international crimes are brought before a panel of judges, not juries of peers who are potentially unfamiliar with the law. This raises the question of whether judges are like other persons in their emotional and intellectual responses to narratives of crimes. The official response from the legal profession is that lawyers are trained to know and apply legal rules of procedure and evidence and to disregard emotive appeals and other forms of argumentation. This would seemingly militate against the influence of a *tu quoque* defense in international trials. However, there is a wealth of data from domestic justice systems indicating that "judicial decision-making conforms to the same social and cognitive mechanisms that govern ordinary citizens."[65] Furthermore, judges in international criminal courts might well be less like domestic criminal trial judges and more like the educated respondents of the behavioral studies cited previously, as only a minority of the first group of ICTY judges arrived with experience as a judge in a criminal courtroom before their appointment to the Tribunal.[66] Perhaps, then, they are more vulnerable than their domestic counterparts to the defense's overtures to understand how irrational actions might seem rational in extreme circumstances. To determine this conclusively either way would require further research on the nature of judicial decision making in the international setting.

Second, at the two *ad hoc* international criminal tribunals, judges simultaneously deliver the verdict and the sentence.[67] Further, ICTY and ICTR Rule 86(C) obliges both the prosecution and the defense to "address matters of sentencing in their closing arguments." The simultaneous rendering of trial and sentencing judgments represents the single most convincing explanation for the prevalence of the *tu quoque* defense in international criminal trials. In common law jurisdictions, the criminal trial verdict is conventionally made first – only if the defendant is found guilty are further arguments heard to

---

[65] Braman and Kahan (2007:108). These authors particularly cite the work of Richard L. Revesz on judicial decision making and political party affiliation.

[66] ICTY Deputy Prosecutor Graham Blewitt famously stated on 7 March 2001, "Of the candidates for election [as ICTY judges], none is experienced as a criminal trial judge." He apologized for commenting on the competence of judges in an official ICTY press release of 9 March 2001 (http://www.icty.org/sid/8009). A 2003 review by Lawyers Committee for Human Rights of the background of judges nominated to serve at the International Criminal Court indicated that eight of eighteen did not have "established competence in criminal law and procedure" (2). Lawyers Committee for Human Rights, "International Criminal Court: Election of Judges. Chart Summarizing the Qualifications of Elected Judges," 3–7 February 2003, http://www.humanrightsfirst.org/international_justice/icc/election/chart_el_judges.pdf. This figure is probably lower than initially found at the ICTY and ICTR.

[67] Rule 87 of the ICTY and ICTR Rules of Procedure and Evidence.

determine the sentence. Sentencing hearings can be extensive and almost constitute a second trial in which the prosecution brings new witnesses to give victim impact testimony, with the objective being to assess the gravity of the crimes. Because in international criminal trials at the ICTY and ICTR the trial verdict and sentencing judgment are coterminous, judges have no choice but to tolerate *tu quoque* statements from defense lawyers and their expert witnesses. It is not a coincidence that Rule 92 *bis* of the ICTY and ICTR Rules of Procedure and Evidence governing the evidence of expert witnesses includes a clause admitting expert-witness evidence that "relates to factors to be taken into account in determining sentence."[68]

In international trials, then, defense teams are placed in the tenuous position of having to argue in mitigation before knowing what factual findings the Trial Chamber will make. Defense counsel must argue for the innocence of the accused while concurrently explaining the extenuating circumstances in which he or she acted, should the accused be found to have committed the alleged crimes. Cassese (2003:421) remarks (without much sympathy) that defense arguments can sound like "the old schoolboy plea, when charged with breaking the window in the headmaster's study: (i) first, there is no witness in the headmaster's study, (ii) if there is a window, it is not broken, (iii) if it is broken I did not do it, (iv) if I did it, it was an accident." Not a very convincing defense to be sure, but the present system makes certain that *tu quoque* will remain a prominent feature of defense arguments in future international criminal trials. Cassese (2003:421) observes that, at the International Criminal Court, Article 76 and Rule 143 compel the ICC Trial Chamber to consider matters related to sentencing before the end of the trial.

Having established how mitigating arguments are folded into the process of judgment, the next question is, What impact have *tu quoque* arguments had on sentencing at international criminal trials? No clear data exist to show that sentences are lesser in trials in which a *tu quoque* defense was used. Further, the *tu quoque* defense is but one factor of many that influence sentencing. Yet overall, sentences at the ICTR and ICTY are significantly smaller than prosecutors have requested, and less than one might reasonably expect given the crimes that individuals have been convicted of. The next question then becomes, Compared to what? First, we must recognize that no guidelines exist for judges carrying out sentencing in international criminal cases. Cryer et al. (2007:396) observe that "the ICTY Appeals Chamber has repeatedly refused to set down a definite list of sentencing guidelines." Justice ministries in many countries monitor and supervise criminal sentencing as a matter of course, and

---

[68] ICTY and ICTR Rules of Procedure and Evidence Rule 92 *bis* (A)(i)(f).

in the United States, the U.S. Sentencing Commission issues a manual incorporating guidelines and statutory provisions regulating sentencing. Any U.S. judge passing sentence on a conviction for, say, first-degree murder would be greatly constrained by the existing guidelines and the sentencing range would be fairly predictable (at the time of writing, forty-three years or more).[69] The lack of an oversight body and clear guidelines makes it hard to assess sentencing in international tribunals. A comparison of sentencing with historical trials for mass atrocities is also problematic, as they invariably took place in a variety of international or national settings that were quite unlike modern international criminal tribunals. The International Military Tribunal at Nuremberg and the Israeli court sentencing Adolf Eichmann were able to issue the death penalty, but that sentence is unavailable to international tribunals.

Still, if we compare cases that are relatively similar, we might have some indication of how sentencing in international criminal tribunals compares with sentencing in a national court. In 1996, a South African court convicted the security policeman Eugene de Kock on eighty-nine charges, including six charges of murder and two of conspiracy to commit murder, and sentenced him to 212 years in prison.[70] De Kock also had recourse to a *tu quoque* defense, explaining that his actions were part of an all-out war against communism and complaining that former police offers "who were just as guilty as him" were going free.[71] At the ICTY, the camp guard Goran Jelisić was convicted of fifteen counts of crimes against humanity and sixteen counts of violations of laws of war and the murder of thirteen people.[72] He was sentenced to forty years in prison (which he is presently serving in the United Kingdom), one of the longest sentences handed down at an international criminal tribunal thus far. In Jelisić we have a case in which multiple counts of crimes against humanity and murder carried a sentence that was a fraction of that in a comparable case in South Africa and markedly less than the minimum in the U.S. federal guidelines.

It might be objected that I have simply selected criminal cases to fit my argument, but many other commentators both inside and outside the two *ad hoc* tribunals agree that sentencing at the ICTR and ICTY has been arbitrary and erratic.[73] Cryer et al. (2007:397) note that "the sentencing practice of the

[69] U.S. Sentencing Commission, Guidelines Manual, §3E1.1 (November 2009).
[70] In South Africa, the death penalty had been abolished the year before in 1995.
[71] South African Press Association (SAPA), 29 October 1996, http://www.doj.gov.za/trc/media/1996/9610/s961029m.htm.
[72] The Appeals Chamber later found he had not committed two of the murders, but it did not reduce the sentence.
[73] See Drumbl (2007:55–66, 154–166) for a thorough discussion of the various legal and ethnical aspects of sentencing at the ICTY and ICTR.

ICTY and ICTR has not been consistent, neither within the same Tribunal nor between them." A number of former ICTY judges, such as Judge Patricia Wald, have also raised doubts about the unpredictability of sentencing for international crimes: "I am no fan of our federal sentencing guidelines, but I do think some form of presumptive range for certain categories of crimes would give a more uniform face to the process."[74] The enduring nature of the *tu quoque* defense in international criminal trials can therefore be explained primarily by reference to its mitigating effect on sentencing and this goes a long way to clarifying why defense attorneys have continued to find historical experts useful in their cases.

6.6. "COOKED HISTORY" IN THE ADVERSARIAL COURTROOM

> There is a serious danger that the record of the ICTY will be seen as a history of the Balkan conflicts. It is not. The conflicts continued in the courtrooms with each side to those conflicts fighting with words rather than weapons. False testimony is rampant and impossible to control. . . . Historians need to look for the truth about the Balkan conflicts in places other than the ICTY records. It did not need to be that way.
>
> – ICTY Defense Counsel[75]

At the beginning of the ICTY's work, the prosecution was the party most invested in expert witnesses, but as time went on, defense teams became more and more committed to historical and political experts. We might have arrived at the point at which prosecutors are trying to anticipate and defuse what they expect defense expert witnesses will say rather than vice versa. Defense lawyers may be motivated by an ideological commitment to a history of victimhood and, in addition, may perceive compelling legal incentives to use historical evidence in a trial. The defense uses historical evidence to frame the crimes in a way that portrays the accused in the best possible light. History is used to cut the link with culpability in the chaos defense and to mitigate the sentence in the *tu quoque* defense. The utility of these defense strategies means that historical arguments will continue to feature in international criminal trials for some time to come. The *tu quoque* principle has featured prominently and will continue to feature as long as the procedural arrangements that practically mandate it are still in place.

---

[74] *Penn Law Journal*, Fall 2004, http://www.law.upenn.edu/alumni/alumnijournal/Fall2004/the_brief/index.html.

[75] ICTY survey response, 2009.

However, it is not clear that the more partisan versions of history we have seen thus far at international tribunals are that illuminating, whether exculpatory or inculpatory. Overall, historical evidence led by the defense receives a fairly low rating when compared with that of the prosecution. When asked whether historical evidence led by the defense has provided important insights into violations of international humanitarian law in the former Yugoslavia, 50 percent of defense lawyers agreed or strongly agreed, whereas only 32 percent of prosecutors agreed and 31 percent of expert witnesses did so.[76] This does not compare favorably with the responses regarding whether historical evidence led by the prosecution has provided important insights; there the combined "agree or strongly agree" figure rises to 61 percent for prosecutors, 62 percent for defense, and 77 percent for expert witnesses. The divergence in these figures might be interpreted in various ways. Defense lawyers could simply be more generous in their assessment than their prosecutorial counterparts. However, my inclination is to say that historical evidence led by the defense is less valued because it is used in a more tactical and therefore partial way, and because it is corrupted by elements of *tu quoque*.

The adversarial process of the courtroom has many benefits: one side exists to champion the rights of the accused at each step of the way, and any witness, document, or other item of evidence is subjected to rigorous testing by the parties. A capable defense is absolutely necessary for any semblance of due process and a fair trial. However, when it comes to considering how the past shaped the armed conflict, the picture is less rosy and may constitute an argument for a more civil law set of procedures. Instead, what we see are legally motivated strategies from both prosecution and defense that distort the record and that result, as vividly conveyed in the quote earlier in this chapter (p. 144) from Richard Goldstone, in polarized historical narratives that do not meet up. In extreme instances, this reproduces the sense of victimhood that, in part, fueled the conflict in the first place. One ICTY defense attorney acknowledged this in a final survey comment:

> Testimony by "historians" in many, if not all, of these trials, has been used itself to manipulate and mold the view of which ethnic group is bad, according to which ethnic group has been the victim. There is no consistency. If the Muslims are the victims, then the history is manipulated to show that either the Serbs or the Croats are the bad guys from an historical perspective,

---

[76] Thirty-eight percent of defense participants were neutral, and 13 percent disagreed or strongly disagreed. Twenty-nine percent of prosecutors were neutral, 23 percent disagreed or strongly disagreed, and 16 percent expressed no opinion. Fifteen percent of expert witnesses were neutral, 23 percent disagreed or strongly disagreed, and 31 percent expressed no opinion.

and vice versa. This has especially been appalling when one sees how the prosecution has argued one thing in cases against Serbs, for example, for crimes against Croatians which occurred in Croatia, and then argue the *exact opposite*, with a straight ethical face, in cases against Croats, for crimes which occurred in Croatia. (Emphasis in original)[77]

Prosecution respondents generally expressed their reservations less resolutely, but they still recognized that the adversarial process could degrade the quality of historical evidence introduced by the parties. One prosecution respondent wrote: "Under the adversarial system, trial lawyers prefer a version of history that supports their case (they are not looking for objective (?) truth). . . . There is a tendency to produce 'cooked history.'"[78]

On a more optimistic note, there is also the sense in which the international tribunals are one of the few places in which opposing historical arguments actually interact and are tested rigorously, and in which a new generation seeking to make sense of the past might turn for information that has been tested in the courtroom, should they be so inclined. True, at times, the parties present extremely polarized versions of history in international criminal trials, but the patently unsatisfactory nature of revisionist accounts may engender a more measured and balanced reading of the historical record in the future. The historical points of view are all aired openly and are all challenged robustly, thus illustrating their strengths and weaknesses and leading the court to search for new material to make sense of the past. In the words of one expert witness for the prosecution, the road is a long one, and the Tribunal's work is only the beginning:

> The process of international criminal justice at the ICTY, and the testimony and evidence that it has produced has added significantly to the available historical evidence concerning events in the former Yugoslavia during the final decades of the 20th century. The use made of this body of evidence by future historians may eventually lead to a fuller understanding of the critical questions about these events than one could reasonably expect from the expert presentations prepared within the context (and limitations) of specific cases before the court.[79]

[77] ICTY Survey response, 2009.
[78] ICTY Survey response, 2009.
[79] ICTY Survey response, 2009.

7

Misjudging Rwandan Society and History at the International Criminal Tribunal for Rwanda

7.1. LEGAL EXCEPTIONALISM

The previous three chapters have primarily addressed the strategies and dispositions of legal actors at the ICTY, with a view to understanding the process leading up to the Tribunal's judgments and legal decisions. The present chapter turns to the International Criminal Tribunal for Rwanda (ICTR) and evaluates the Tribunal's reasoning on one fundamental and highly contested topic: whether Rwandan social groups constituted protected groups under the UN Genocide Convention of 1948. Resolving this issue was essential to the viability of the Tribunal, because if the social categories "Hutu" and "Tutsi" were not protected groups, then the Tribunal would not be able to find that genocide occurred in Rwanda in 1994. This would have been a disastrous result for the Tribunal, because the charge of genocide had been the single most important reason for the UN Security Council to establish the ICTR in the first place. When UN Resolution 955 founded "an international tribunal for the prosecution of persons responsible for genocide," it could be said that the Security Council prejudged the question of whether the crime of genocide had occurred in Rwanda and allowed little room for maneuver on the part of the ICTR Trial Chamber.[1]

Despite these external pressures, actually fulfilling the legal criteria for genocide was more arduous than expected at the ICTR, although this was true to an even greater extent at the ICTY. Whereas prosecutors at the ICTY struggled to convince judges that the accused held the requisite special intent to commit genocide, at the ICTR one of the thorniest legal issues was the definition of Rwandan social groups. Even when ICTR judges found that the accused committed genocide, they repeatedly wrestled with the question of

---

[1] UN Security Council Resolution 955 (1994). Adopted by the Security Council at its 3453rd meeting, 8 November 1994, U.N. Doc. S/RES/955 (1994).

whether Tutsis, the main victims in the 1994 conflict, constituted an ethnic or racial group or some other kind of stable and permanent group. In their pursuit of fixed categories of identity that corresponded to the Genocide Convention, ICTR judges embraced a flawed and inaccurate picture of Rwandan history. To comprehend why the Tribunal's account of Rwandan society and history has been so erroneous, we must return to the critiques of law's knowledge system laid out in Chapter 1. The ICTR's reasoning on ethnic and racial categories illustrates law's epistemological exceptionalism or, less generously phrased, Charles Dickens's "law is a ass" view. In particular, an unusual requirement contained in the founding statute of the Tribunal distorted the Tribunal's view of Rwandan society and history. A comparison of similar issues at the ICTY reveals that this is not an inevitable feature of international criminal law or all international justice institutions but instead is specific to the ICTR.

7.2. THE *AKAYESU* TRIAL JUDGMENT

To understand how some Rwandans could carry out a genocide and how the
rest of the world could turn away from it, we must begin with history.
                                        – Alison Des Forges (1999:31)

After a fourteen-month trial, the ICTR's first Trial Chamber Judgment was handed down in 1998, setting a number of legal precedents.[2] It was the first time an international criminal tribunal had convicted an individual for genocide and had determined that rape was a crime against humanity. The panel of three judges (Kama, Aspegren, and Pillay), found that Jean-Paul Akayesu, the mayor of Taba municipality in the prefecture of Gitarama, had ordered and organized the murder and rape of Tutsis in his town.[3] The Trial Chamber found Akayesu guilty of one count each of genocide and incitement to commit genocide and of seven counts of crimes against humanity. Akayesu was sentenced to three life sentences plus eighty years in prison. In 2001, the Appeals Chamber dismissed the grounds of Akayesu's appeal, and at the time of writing, he is serving his sentence in a prison in Mali.

To convict Jean-Paul Akayesu on two counts of genocide, the prosecution had to show that there was special intent to destroy, in whole or in part, one of the four groups listed in Article 2 of the Genocide Convention, that is,

[2] *Prosecutor v. Jean Paul Akayesu*, Case No. ICTR-96-4-T, Trial Chamber Judgment, 2 September 1998.
[3] Akayesu's culpability for murder is stated at §268 and his responsibility for sexual violence at §452.

"a national, ethnical, racial or religious group, as such." Even before this, the prosecution first had to define *racial group* and *ethnic group*, as these terms had not been previously defined in the Genocide Convention or in the International Convention on the Elimination of All Forms of Racial Discrimination. Defining complex social categories was a considerable undertaking that involved the translation of historical and social science knowledge into formal legal concepts, and yet the Office of the Prosecutor at the ICTR did not count with the same research capacity as the ICTY. In particular, there was no specialist team of analysts such as the Leadership Research Team (LRT). Furthermore, the position of research analysts in the Office of the Prosecutor (OTP) was tightly monitored and constrained. While LRT staff at the ICTY were able to interact frequently and informally with Senior Trial Attorneys (STAs), ICTR investigation team members were rigidly controlled. Through much of the Tribunal's work, investigators could not exchange ideas with attorneys without prior permission from their supervisor.

In the absence of a team of in-house research analysts, the ICTR's OTP relied a great deal on the Human Rights Watch activist and historian Dr. Alison Des Forges as their historical and contextual expert witness.[4] In effect, she was the ICTR's equivalent of the ICTY's LRT. Until her untimely death in an airplane crash in February 2009, Des Forges gave background testimony for the prosecution in more than a dozen ICTR trials. The prosecution adopted the account of Rwandan history contained in her 1999 book *Leave None to Tell the Story: Genocide in Rwanda*, published by Human Rights Watch, to articulate its case theory in trial after trial. Defense teams were unsuccessful in challenging its premises and in advancing the thesis that the mass killings were not planned in advance but were part of a counterinsurgency war against the Rwandan Patriotic Front (RPF) instead of a premeditated genocidal campaign to exterminate Tutsis as a group. For that reason, defense counsel avoided historical inquiry to a greater degree than their ICTY defense counterparts and hewed more closely to a straightforward crime-based approach.

The prosecution's version of history, based as it was on Des Forges's writings and testimony, prevailed at the Tribunal and was incorporated, more or less in its entirety, by judges into ICTR decisions and judgments. It is not an overstatement to say that Des Forges's *Leave None to Tell the Story* became the official version of Rwandan history at the Tribunal. It remained authoritative in part because, as noted in Chapter 2, only individuals from the losing side (Hutu

---

[4] Human Rights Watch staff members Fred Abrahams, Peter Bouckaert, and Jeri Laber also testified in a number of ICTY trials.

Power) were prosecuted at the ICTR. The fact that no individual representing the ruling RPF has been prosecuted at the ICTR thus far, despite *prima facie* evidence of RPF war crimes in 1994, means that other historical versions were never fully taken into account.[5] The RPF's ability to hold the Tribunal to ransom has unfortunately meant that the process has produced victor's justice and victor's history.

In defining Rwandan social groups for the purpose of substantiating the genocide charge, the Akayesu prosecution team, led by Pierre-Richard Prosper,[6] argued that the Tutsis are an ethnic group in Rwandan society, and it called Des Forges to explain to the judges the development of ethnicity in the twentieth century. Unfortunately, the expert testimony was contradictory, or at least highly ambivalent. The *Akayesu* Trial Judgment (hereafter, *Akayesu*) quoted Des Forges's definition of ethnic group: "The primary criterion for [defining] an ethnic group is the sense of belonging to that ethnic group. It is a sense which can shift over time. In other words, the group, the definition of the group to which one feels allied may change over time.... [R]eality is an interplay between the actual conditions and peoples' subjective perception of those conditions" (§172). In emphasizing "peoples' subjective perception," Des Forges was restating the accepted wisdom in history, sociocultural anthropology, and other social sciences: there are no objective criteria for determining social identities, which vary across historical periods and are based on self-perceptions and the perceptions of others.

In addition to a subjective view of identity, the prosecution also advanced an alternative position that accorded greater weight to the role of colonialism in entrenching ethnic categories. The prosecution's historical narrative began with the German and Belgian colonial authorities who formally institutionalized a system of ethnic classification in the 1930s. The colonial hierarchy in turn laid the groundwork for the identity-based policies of the postcolonial state (§80 *et passim*). For the prosecution, historical (though not legal) blame for the 1994 genocide lay more with colonial regimes than with their successors, a view echoed by scholars such as Mamdani (2001:9) who claim that the Rwandan genocide resulted from the "logic of colonialism." In her discussion of the colonial era, Des Forges advanced a more categorical position on ethnicity than she had earlier in *Akayesu*:

In Rwanda, the reality was shaped by the colonial experience which imposed a categorisation which was probably more fixed.... The categorisation

[5] To her credit, Des Forges (1999:540–58) did not shy away from documenting evidence of RPF crimes.
[6] Prosper later became ambassador-at-large for war crimes issues in the U.S. State Department.

imposed at that time is what people of the current generation have grown up with. They have always thought in terms of these categories.... This practice was continued after independence by the First Republic and the Second Republic in Rwanda to such an extent that this division into three ethnic groups became an absolute reality. (§172)[7]

These two versions of Rwandan history set up an unresolved tension in the prosecution's case that would persist in subsequent ICTR trials: does ethnic identity result from a fluid "interplay" of conditions and perceptions, or is it a hard-and-fast "absolute reality," institutionalized by colonial rule? The prosecutor did not resolve this tension in the closing arguments because he did not submit them in time. According to Judge Navanethem Pillay, one of the three judges during the trial: "The Office of the Prosecutor never came up with a satisfactory argument or definition of ethnic group. Pierre-Richard Prosper for the Prosecutor was late with his closing brief. The deadline had passed and we said we would not read it after the deadline and we really did not read it. Maybe we would have had the benefit of the Office of the Prosecutor's definition of ethnicity in their submission."[8]

In the absence of a prosecution final brief explaining how exactly Rwandan Tutsis corresponded to one of the four protected groups in the UN Genocide Convention, the matter was left to the judges to decide. They passed it to a Danish senior legal adviser, Frederik Harhoff, who crafted the relevant section on race and ethnicity designating the Tutsi as a protected group under the Genocide Convention. This was the first time an international tribunal judgment had defined two of the Convention's four protected groups, framing ethnicity in cultural terms and race according to physical and biological criteria:

> An ethnic group is generally defined as a group whose members share a common language or culture. (§513)

> The conventional definition of a racial group is based upon the hereditary physical traits often identified with a geographical region, irrespective of linguistic, cultural, national or religious factors. (§514)

These definitions are virtually identical to those in the 1987 U.S. Genocide Convention Implementation Act ("Proxmire Act").[9] However, when I asked

---

[7] This position on ethnicity was also more categorically stated than anything contained in Des Forges's 1999 book.

[8] Author interview, May 2006.

[9] 18 U.S.C. 1093. The Genocide Convention Implementation Act is contained in Chapter 50A of the U.S. Code, Title 18 (Crimes and Criminal Procedure), Part I (Crimes). Section 1091 deals specifically with genocide, and the terms are defined in Section 1093 as follows: an

Judge Pillay where the definitions originated, she replied: "The definitions of race and ethnicity in *Akayesu* came from Rwandan witnesses, there was an accepted social structure for these things. In the Judgment, we cited the UN treaties and articles but we said that they didn't fit the Rwandan situation. We had very little help so we relied on the evidence and views of the people of Rwanda."[10] Applying these definitions to the Rwandan case, the Trial Chamber observed that separate ethnic groups do not exist in Rwanda, as all Rwandans speak the same language and share the same cultural and religious traditions: "The Chamber notes that the Tutsi population does not have its own language or a distinct culture from the rest of the Rwandan population" (§170). Are Hutus and Tutsis therefore distinguished by race, as claimed by the Hutu Power extremists who set up the roadblocks and carried out the mass killings? Apart from the formal definition, *Akayesu* was largely silent on the question of race.

At this point, *Akayesu* concluded that the Tutsi did not meet any of the four categories named in the Genocide Convention and noted that this placed the Tribunal in something of a quandary (§516). It stated its predicament as follows: "the question that arises is whether it would be impossible to punish the physical destruction of a group as such under the Genocide Convention, if the said group, although stable and membership is by birth, does not meet the definition of any one of the four groups expressly protected by the Genocide Convention" (§516). In any conventional interpretation, the answer would have to be in the affirmative: punishment under the Genocide Convention is impossible if the group does not conform to the requirements of the Genocide Convention. Had *Akayesu* stopped there, the Trial Chamber would have had to conclude that genocide had not occurred in Rwanda, thereby contradicting UN Security Council Resolution 955 that established the Tribunal.

Recoiling from this potentially disastrous decision, *Akayesu* forged ahead, keeping alive the idea that the Tutsi are a protected group by taking an unexpected and innovative, though ultimately hazardous, tack. The judges went back to 1947–8 and the Genocide Convention's *travaux préparatoires* (preparatory work) of committee writing to maintain that the intention of the

ethnic group is "a set of individuals whose identity is distinctive in terms of common cultural traditions or heritage," and a racial group is "a set of individuals whose identity as such is distinctive in terms of physical characteristics or biological descent." To my knowledge, no charges have been brought in the United States under this statute.

[10] Author interview, May 2006. Pillay described how, at the beginning of the ICTR's work, Tribunal staff had very few resources and no library – all they had was the case law of the European Court of Human Rights and the U.S. Supreme Court. She noted that at the outset, none of the judges had been an international judge before, and some individuals, herself included, had not been a judge at all. Before coming to the ICTR, Pillay practiced law as a widely respected defense attorney in South Africa.

drafters was "patently to ensure the protection of any stable and permanent group" (§511–16). The drafters of the Genocide Convention wished to protect not only national, ethnical, racial, and religious groups from genocide but also "any group which is stable and permanent like the said 4 groups" (§516). In clarifying what it meant by "stable and permanent," *Akayesu* referred to groups "constituted in a permanent fashion and membership of which is determined by birth," where membership in the group is "not normally challengeable by its members, who belong to it automatically by birth in a continuous and often irremediable manner" (§511).

The question then became, Did this new set of criteria apply to the Tutsi? The Trial Chamber answered in the affirmative, finding "that there are a number of objective indicators of the group as a group with a distinctive identity" (§170). What were these objective indicators of group status? *Akayesu* referred to the forms of classification used by the Rwandan state to distinguish identity, and in particular the identity cards carried by all Rwandans that indicated ethnic classification as Hutu, Tutsi, or Twa (formerly, "Pygmy"). *Akayesu* emphasized the evidence that Tutsis were selected for murder at roadblocks on the basis of ID cards (§123). *Akayesu* cited Article 57 of the Rwandan Civil Code of 1988, which provided that all persons would be identified by their membership in an ethnic group, and it noted the existence of "customary rules exist[ing] in Rwanda governing the determination of ethnic group which followed patrilineal lines of heredity" (§171). For the Trial Chamber, this was conclusive proof that although the Tutsi did not qualify straightforwardly as an ethnic or racial group under the terms of the Genocide Convention, permanent membership in the group was conferred both by the Rwandan state (in the form of ID cards and birth certificates) and Rwandan society (through conventions of patrilineal descent).

7.3. A TRIBUNAL VEXED

In order to target a social group for social and physical destruction, perpetrators must fundamentally depart from reality. They must see masses of individuals and families living in disparate communities through the distorting lens of pseudo-classification, in order to convert them into a collective "enemy" of a kind whose ways of life and physical existence must be brutally crushed.

– Martin Shaw (2007:105)

Since 1998, *Akayesu* has become a cornerstone of the jurisprudence of genocide in international criminal law. Its definitions of racial and ethnic groups have influenced subsequent cases at the ICTR[11] and the ICTY[12] and are frequently cited in international criminal law textbooks.[13] Yet its legal reasoning has also been found wanting, and two main critiques of *Akayesu* have emerged – one legal and the other anthropological.

The international law expert William Schabas (2009:152) remarks that the "categorization of Rwanda's Tutsi population clearly vexed the Tribunal," and he works through the issues surrounding the legal definitions of protected groups. Schabas expresses skepticism regarding the Tribunal's interpretation of the Genocide Committee's *travaux préparatoires* and its extension of the concept of genocide to include any "stable and permanent" group, warning that this move flouts the Genocide Convention's definitions and terms. He observes that the UN Declaration on Human Rights grants the right to change nationality and religion, which means that these terms are neither stable nor permanent. Schabas acknowledges that the concepts of racial, ethnic, and national group are imprecise and contentious, but he pulls back from the logical implications of this imprecision, citing the ICTY Appeals Chamber ruling in *Stakić*, that a subjective approach to target groups is "not acceptable" (ibid.:124–8).

Seeking a way through the impasse, Schabas considers Raphael Lemkin's (1944) original intention when he coined the term *genocide* in *Axis Rule in Occupied Europe, Analysis of Government, Proposals for Redress* to mean "the protection of what were then called 'national minorities' (119–121)." Schabas claims, "Use of terms such as 'ethnic,' 'racial' or 'religious' merely fleshed out the idea, without at all changing its essential content" (20). The terms define one another, in a "dynamic and synergistic relationship" (130), and jurists should not get too caught up in the irreducible differences they convey. He asserts that "the 1948 meaning of "racial group" encompassed national, ethnic and religious groups as well as those defined by physical characteristics, [and this meaning] ought to be favoured over some more contemporary, and more restrictive, gloss" (143). Schabas's solution is to apply the four terms in a holistic manner, with the intention of protecting national minorities, more or less understood as they were in 1947–8 by Lemkin and the drafters of the Genocide Convention. Schabas notes that this interpretation has by and large been the dominant view in European human rights law since the 1950s, which continues to prefer the term *national minorities* to racial, religious, or ethnic categories.

---

[11] For example, *Rutuganda*, §48.
[12] For example, *Jelisić*, §61.
[13] Cassese (2003:49, 50, 100–3), Kittichaisaree (2001:69 *passim*), Schabas (2009:131, 140, 151–3).

Schabas's discussion accurately diagnoses international law's recent tribulations with defining protected groups, but his holistic approach does not
adequately resolve them. Instead, it just shifts the imprecision to another
level and term, namely *national minority*. Ultimately, Schabas's notion of a
dynamic and synergistic relationship among the four categories is just as vague
and inexact as the social categories themselves. What exactly might a synergy
between race and ethnicity and nationality mean in practice, when presented
as prosecution or defense evidence in the courtroom? It could well mean that
if one group term becomes too difficult for the prosecution to pin down, then
it can always turn to another, and another, which clarifies very little and will
likely confuse a panel of judges further. Our experience thus far might warn
us that such imprecision could leave the door open to misleading social and
historical arguments on the part of both the prosecution and the defense.

A trenchant social science critique of *Akayesu* comes from the social anthropologist Nigel Eltringham in his book *Accounting for Horror* (2004). Eltringham (2004:30) contends that, in *Akayesu*, the Trial Chamber ignored the
génocidaires' primary justification of the genocide, namely race: "The Tribunal failed to deal with how Tutsi were targeted: the perception of indelible,
racial distinction. The Tribunal missed the opportunity to reveal the wholly
ideational nature of the genocidal mentality." As noted earlier, *Akayesu* elided
racial beliefs in Rwanda, but as numerous commentators have observed, the
ideology of the Hutu Power activists who committed the genocide drew from a
long-standing "Hamitic myth" that portrayed Tutsis as foreigners who invaded
from Ethiopia in the North and Hutus as "indigenous Bantus," with each
group being distinguished by its conformity to physical stereotypes.[14] Racial
ideology was exploited by extremist politicians in the months and years before
the 1994 genocide, and it served as the main justification for genocide by
advocates of Hutu Power. *Akayesu* refers to Hutu Power leaders, such as the
university professor Léon Mugesera, exhorting Hutus to throw the corpses
of Tutsis into tributaries leading north into the Nile so they could "return
to where they came from" but does not adequately explain the social and
historical significance of this statement (§100).[15]

When Judge Pillay was asked why there was no meaningful discussion in
Akayesu of race or racism, she replied that the majority of Rwandan witnesses

[14] On colonial racial ideology and the Hamitic myth, see Des Forges (1999); Magnarella (2000);
Prunier (1995); Taylor (1999).
[15] In *Akayesu* (§100), Mugesera's statement is cited and sourced in Prunier (1995:171–2). For a
full discussion of the context and consequence of Mugesera's speech, see Taylor (1999:80–1).
The ICTR Defense Counsel Diana Ellis disputes such claims, saying that the Mugesera quote
has been improperly used at the Tribunal. Author interview, July 2006.

coming before the Trial Chamber had rejected concepts of racial categorization. This may be so, but more likely the judges at the Rwanda Tribunal were
wary of even broaching the question of race, given its incendiary properties
in Rwandan politics and its unsound conception of race based on hereditary
physical traits. The ICTR judges may have felt pressured by the Rwandan
government's suppression of any discussion of race in Rwanda, which led to
a vaguely defined statute making "genocide ideology" a criminal offense in
2008.[16] Eltringham asks, "Did it fear that by defining the Tutsi as a race (in
accordance with how they were defined by perpetrators) they would be accused
of endorsing this view?" (ibid.:30). Perhaps international criminal judges were
deterred from using the idea of racial differentiation by international legal
instruments, for instance, the preamble to the 1966 International Convention on the Elimination of All Forms of Racial Discrimination, denounced as
"scientifically false, morally condemnable, socially unjust and dangerous."[17]

    Whatever their reasons for rejecting racial distinctions, Eltringham finds
fault in international criminal jurists' attempts to construct ethnic groups
according to objective criteria. Eltringham's recommendation is that the Tribunal adopt a subjective view of either ethnicity or race; that is, it should
have relied either on the victims' self-identification in an ethnic group or
on a perpetrator-based definition of race. He prefers the latter, noting the
perpetrators' intent is the primary consideration in a court of law. This position finds support among legal commentators such as Verdirame (2000:594):
"The perception of the perpetrator of the crime is after all more important
for establishing individual criminal responsibility than the putative 'authentic'
ethnicity of the victim."

    Eltringham's recommendations are, in my view, highly persuasive. For
about the past hundred years in sociology (i.e., since Max Weber), ethnicity
has been understood as a subjective social category. It appealed to social
scientists in the 1960s precisely because it offered a sociological alternative to
pseudoscientific and *faux*-objective theories of race. Contemporary research
in sociology and sociocultural anthropology either disputes existing concepts
of race or ethnicity or treats them as unstable, contextual, fluid, changing, and
subjective states of mind.[18] As a leading anthropological textbook concludes:

[16] Human Rights Watch, *World Report 2010: Rwanda*, 20 January 2010.
[17] Preamble to International Convention on the Elimination of All Forms of Racial Discrimi-
    nation. Adopted and opened for signature and ratification by General Assembly Resolution
    2106 (XX) of 21 December 1965, Entry into force 4 January 1969, in accordance with Article
    19. In contrast, the Race Convention can be seen as substantiating the existence of races when
    it encourages "understanding between races" (Preamble) and "eliminating barriers between
    races" (Article 2.1.e).
[18] See Brace (2005); Eriksen (1993); Montagu (1997).

"the social world can rarely be neatly divided into fixed groups with clear boundaries, unambiguous criteria for membership and an all-encompassing social relevance."[19] If the Tribunal were to focus primarily on the perpetrator's intent to destroy a protected group, then it does not matter whether or not the group in question is an "objectively real" group, so long as the idea of group identification is firmly established in the mind of the perpetrator who demonstrates the requisite special intent to destroy a group in whole or in part, through words and deeds. It is the act and intention of stigmatization that matters, not the object of stigmatization.[20] As we will see, ICTR judgments did shift in this direction, but judges continued to yearn for solid and immutable categories when trying crimes involving inter-group animus.

7.4. REFORMULATING RWANDAN SOCIAL CATEGORIES

In ensuing judgments and decisions, other ICTR judges expressed their profound reservations about the legal reasoning in *Akayesu* that invoked the idea of "stable and permanent groups." Instead of clarifying the categories of "Hutu" and "Tutsi," however, Trial Chamber judges vacillated between objective and subjective definitions, and their formulations were characterized by confusion regarding race and ethnicity in Rwanda.

In the May 1999 *Kayishema* Trial Judgment (hereafter, *Kayishema*), a new Trial Chamber composed of three different judges threw out the formulation in *Akayesu* that the Tutsi are not an ethnic or racial group but nonetheless constitute a stable and permanent group protected by the Genocide Convention.[21] The judges rehabilitated the notion that the Tutsi are an ethnic group, and *Kayishema* declared categorically, "Tutsis were killed, based on their ethnicity" (§312). Ethnicity was conceived as a synthesis of victims' subjective self-identification and the categorizations of perpetrators: "An ethnic group is one whose members share a common language and culture; or, a group which distinguishes itself, as such (self-identification); or, a group identified as such by others, including perpetrators of the crimes (identification by others)" (§98). *Kayishema* took note of the prosecution's position that a perpetrator's intent is the central question at stake in the trial, regardless of whether or not the *génocidaires'* perceptions were correct: "The Prosecution submit that it is the

---

[19] Eriksen (1993:156).
[20] Similar and additional ideas on genocide and conceptions of group identity are developed further by Martin Shaw in chapter 7 of his 2007 book *What Is Genocide?*
[21] *Prosecutor v. Clément Kayishema and Obed Ruzindana*, Case No. ICTR-95-1-T, Trial Chamber Judgment, 21 May 1999.

intent of the perpetrator to discriminate against a group that is important, rather than whether the victim was, in fact, a member of that targeted group" (§131).

So far, so good. But then the *Kayishema* Trial Chamber judges lost confidence and began to question the prosecution's subjective theory of ethnic identity: "The Trial Chamber opines that the Prosecution must show that the perpetrator's belief was objectively reasonable – based upon real facts – rather than being mere speculation or perverted deduction" (§132). This has to be one of the more perplexing statements in international legal reasoning, and not only because of its tortured grammar but also because it obligates the prosecution to show the eminent reasonableness of the beliefs of mass murderers. During widespread and systematic political violence, there is seldom much in the way of "objectively reasonable – based upon real facts" behavior. Requiring the prosecution to show the "real facts" motivating mass murder is rather like asking for solid evidence of witchcraft to explain the burning at the stake of women in early-modern Europe. It takes the view that, "well, there must have been *something* there to motivate this kind of behavior," when no such assumption is warranted. History is full of delusional and violent mass movements motivated by ideas with no basis in "real facts." Genocide itself is characterized by a fundamental irrationality, and Martin Shaw (2007:105) observes that, although genocidal thought constructs its mental fabrications from real elements, what is striking is the "deeply fantastical character of all genocidal thought." In Rwanda in 1994, the killing was often random and unpredictable, and it lacked the kind of systematic nature that prosecutors represented before the Tribunal. In the aftermath of violence, researchers collected numerous reports from survivors that some individuals holding Hutu identification cards were still killed because they "looked Tutsi" and that other individuals with Tutsi identification cards walked free because they "looked Hutu."[22]

After pulling back from a subjective view of identity, *Kayishema* then proceeded to decisively endorse an objective theory of racial and ethnic groups: "the Tutsis were an ethnic group. . . . [S]ince 1931, Rwandans were required to carry identification cards which indicated the ethnicity of the bearer . . . in accordance with Rwandan custom, the ethnicity of a Rwandan child is derived from that of his or her father" (§523). Moreover, *Kayishema* brazenly rewrites the conclusions of *Akayesu*, stating, "In *Akayesu*, Trial Chamber 1 found that Tutsis are an ethnic group, as such" (§526). Yet we just saw earlier how *Akayesu* did nothing of the sort. Having established the precedent in *Kayishema* that Tutsis are an ethnic group, objectively defined, the Trial Chamber revisited

[22] Des Forges (1999:33) cites the case in which Hutu relatives of Colonel Renhazo were killed at a barrier after having been mistaken for Tutsis. See also Eltringham (2004:25–6).

the question yet again in the December 1999 *Rutuganda* Trial Judgment (hereafter, *Rutuganda*).[23] *Rutuganda* was heard by the same panel of three judges as in the *Akayesu* case: Judges Kama (Presiding), Aspegren, and Pillay. In *Rutuganda*, the bench showed an appreciation for a subjective view of ethnic group membership:

> [T]here are no generally and internationally accepted precise definitions' of the concepts of national, ethnical, racial or religious groups . . . [M]embership of a group is, in essence, a subjective rather than an objective concept. The victim is perceived by the perpetrator of genocide as belonging to a group slated for destruction. In some cases, the victim may perceive himself/herself as belonging to the said group. (§56)

The implication here could be that the Trial Chamber had reconsidered its prior preference for objective definitions, but the next paragraph rejected, once and for all, a subjective definition of the four groups protected by the Genocide Convention: "Nevertheless, the Chamber is of the view that a subjective definition alone is not sufficient to determine victim groups, as provided for in the Genocide Convention" (§57). *Rutuganda* does not rest here though, and the judges then took an unexpected tack. They decided that the task of defining racial and ethnic group is so impossible that the Tribunal would adopt no formal policy on the matter. A paragraph later, the judges of Trial Chamber 1 threw in the towel and conceded defeat: "Therefore . . . in assessing whether a particular group may be considered protected from the crime of genocide, it [the Trial Chamber] will proceed on a case-by-case basis, taking into account both the relevant evidence proffered and the specific political, social and cultural context" (§58). For the following seven years, this was the official statement of the Rwanda Tribunal's thinking on race and ethnicity, and it was repeated verbatim in succeeding genocide judgments.[24]

In the space of a little more than a year, the ICTR Trial Chamber had reversed its position four times on an essential matter in the determination of the crime of genocide. First, it maintained that Tutsis did not constitute an racial or ethnic group but were nonetheless an objectively "stable and permanent group." Then it came to regard them as an ethnic group, subjectively defined. Then it rejected a subjective formulation of identity and defined Tutsis as an objectively constituted ethnic group. Finally, it arrived at the position that Tutsis must be defined objectively but in an *ad hoc* fashion rather than generally. This is an unsatisfying end result that advances two logically

---

[23] *Prosecutor v. Georges Anderson Rutuganda*, Case No. ICTR-96-3-T, Trial Chamber Judgment, 6 December 1999.

[24] For instance, *Prosecutor v. Alfred Musema*, Case No. ICTR-96-13-T, Trial Chamber Judgment, 27 January 2000, §§161-2.

self-contradictory views, namely (1) the concepts of racial and ethnic groups must be objectively defined and (2) the Tribunal cannot take a general or objective view of racial or ethnic groups during the killings in Rwanda in 1994. Immediate problems arose in evaluating statements in Tribunal judgments, such as "there was a widespread and systematic attack on the Tutsi ethnic group, on ethnic grounds" (*Rutuganda* §416). Given the inconsistencies in the ICTR's reasoning, one might reasonably ask, What exactly are these ethnic grounds based on? More practically, the Tribunal's case-by-case view of ethnicity had a concrete impact on trials insofar as it has placed a particular burden on the Office of the Prosecutor to prove the existence of the Tutsi as a group in each and every case in which an individual was accused of genocide. Between 1999 and 2006, every genocide trial began in more or less the same way: by reviewing the same historical development of Hutu and Tutsi identities all over again.[25]

The conclusion to this long-running story came at the start of the *Karemera* case, when Chief Prosecutor Hassan Jallow filed a motion under Rule 94 requesting that the Trial Chamber take judicial notice of six "facts of common knowledge" drawn from prior judgments such as *Akayesu, Kayishema, Rutuganda*, and *Musema*.[26] The most significant facts that the prosecutor sought judicial notice of were that the Hutu, Tutsi, and Twa are ethnic groups in Rwanda; that widespread and systematic attacks took place against Tutsi civilians in Rwanda; and perhaps most important, that genocide occurred in Rwanda in 1994. In its reply, the Trial Chamber took judicial notice of two of the lesser six facts of common knowledge proposed by the prosecution and dismissed the request to take notice of widespread and systematic attacks and genocide. It accepted the designation of Twa, Tutsi, and Hutu as protected groups but in modified form, retreating from using the term *ethnic*, on the grounds that "the jurisprudence has not clearly established that those three groups are ethnic groups *per se*."[27]

The prosecution appealed, and on 16 June 2006, the Appeals Chamber issued an authoritative decision instructing the Trial Chamber to take judicial notice of the three following facts: (1) the existence of the Twa, Tutsi, and Hutu

---

[25] And thereby taking up court time at a point when the Tribunal was ostensibly operating under acute pressures resulting from the 2003 Completion Strategy of the International Criminal Tribunal for Rwanda (U.N. Doc S/2003/946 (2003)).

[26] Motion for Judicial Notice of Facts of Common Knowledge and Adjudicated Facts, 30 June 2005, *Prosecutor v. Édouard Karemera, Mathieu Ngirumpatse, Joseph Nzirorera*, Case No. ICTR-98–44-AR73(C). Rule 94(A) of the ICTR Rules of Procedure and Evidence reads as follows: "A Trial Chamber shall not require proof of facts of common knowledge but shall take judicial notice thereof."

[27] *Prosecutor v. Édouard Karemera, Mathieu Ngirumpatse, Joseph Nzirorera*, Decision on the Prosecution Motion for Judicial Notice, ICTR-98–44-AR73(C), 9 November 2005, §8.

as protected groups falling under the Genocide Convention (§25); (2) the existence throughout Rwanda, between 6 April and 17 July 1994 of widespread and systematic attacks against a civilian population on the basis of Tutsi ethnic identification (§§26–32); and (3) the existence of genocide in Rwanda between 6 April and 17 July 1994 against the Tutsi ethnic group (§§33–8).[28] This was the most momentous legal decision of the ICTR thus far. Twelve years after the catastrophic events in Rwanda, the international criminal tribunal found that genocide had occurred throughout the country and placed the matter beyond all legal dispute. At the Tribunal, the decision's immediate practical consequence was to relieve the prosecution of the burden of proving widespread and systematic crimes, of proving genocide, and of demonstrating the existence of the Tutsi as a protected group under the Genocide Convention.

Having said all that, the Appeals Chamber's decision never did solve the enigma of Tutsi identity, and the reader will note that "fact 1" above made no reference to exactly how the Twa, Tutsi, and Hutu conformed to the list of four protected groups. In determining the status of the Twa, Tutsi, and Hutu, the Appeals Chamber harked back to the contentious conception of "stable and permanent groups" first proposed in *Akayesu*. It justified dismissing the prosecution's request to classify the Tutsi as an ethnic group on the grounds that its official designation as a protected group under the Genocide Convention meant the prosecution would be relieved of introducing further evidence, and so the basis of Tutsi identity was no longer an issue that required resolution. They were protected groups, and that was that, even if the basis for this determination remained opaque and ill-defined. In their final statement on the matter, ICTR judges continued the practice established at the outset, namely adjudicating crimes that occurred in Rwanda while failing to address adequately the matters of legal consequence in Rwanda's history. Ideally, the two ought to go together, and regrettably the *Karemera* Appeals Chamber missed an opportunity to combine law and social research thinking on one intractable problem in adjudicating genocide.

7.5. SOCIAL GROUPS AND LEGAL REIFICATION

What reasons might explain why the Rwanda Tribunal was so inconsistent in its formulations of race and ethnicity? Why was an issue that was so straightforward for Hutu Power activists as they embarked on their killing spree so

---

[28] *Prosecutor v. Édouard Karemera, Mathieu Ngirumpatse, Joseph Nzirorera*, Decision on Prosecutor's Interlocutory Appeal of Decision on Judicial Notice, ICTR-98-44-AR73(C), 16 June 2006.

difficult for international jurists to grasp? The fact that the problem existed without resolution for so long, and reproduced itself in so many successive trials with different judges, prosecutors, defense attorneys, and defendants points to underlying systemic factors deeply embedded in either international criminal law, the ICTR, or both.

The law-and-society literature on "how law knows" may provide insights here, and especially the critique developed by legal anthropologists. In their book *Culture and Rights*, Cowan, Dembour, and Wilson (2001:10) identify the "essentializing proclivities of law" with regard to cultural questions, noting that legal institutions tend to reify culture and social identity, that is, to convert a concept, idea, or the property of a relationship into a concrete thing or object. In reviewing a number of instances in which social groups have made cultural rights claims in national and international legal settings, these authors observe that such claims are subjected to a set of legal requirements of fixity, long-term duration, and intrinsic solidity of the type seen in the ICTR's quest for objectivity in the notion of ethnicity. For Anthony Good (2008:53–4), legal reification is particularly common in the cultural defense, a defense legal strategy used in U.S. courts when a criminal defendant has recently arrived in the country and, it is claimed, has acted according to the dictates of his or her original culture. In the national criminal courtroom, legal thinking often essentializes social groups by treating the immigrant's culture as a monolithic entity shared by all its members. The idea of a minority culture is taken for granted by courts of law and construed as an overbearing structure that eradicates individual agency and voluntary choice. Legal essentialism is intensified in cases involving native peoples or indigenous groups. In legal disputes over cultural artifacts, land rights, and intellectual property rights, claims are often premised on "pristine cultures 'out there'" (Good 2008:55).[29]

This analysis extends beyond ethnic groups and cultural minorities, and it can also be applied to how law deals with other social groups, such as people with disabilities. Jill Anderson (2008) has eloquently diagnosed the flaws in the implementation of the Americans with Disabilities Act (ADA) of 1990. Although the ADA was designed to protect people with disabilities from discrimination in employment, public services, transportation, and accommodation, it "has lost much of its expected force in the courts" (Anderson 2008:995–6). Eighty-six percent of court cases brought under the ADA were dismissed or dropped in 1998, a large proportion of them because the plaintiffs were not able to prove "impairment" to the satisfaction of the court and therefore to

[29] The anthropological literature on this is now vast, but one might start with Jackson (2007) and Stavenhagen (2008).

qualify for membership in the social group "people with disabilities."[30] As with the ICTR's formulation of ethnic group, the ADA statute defined impairment in both subjective (what Anderson calls the "regarded as" having an impairment prong) and objective ("the actual disability prong") terms. According to Anderson, the "structurally ambiguous" nature of the definition stymied courts, which failed to fully apprehend the "regarded as" prong of the ADA and instead opted for an overliteral interpretation. The failure of U.S. courts to apprehend the subjective dimensions of disability in the ADA is analogous to the failure of the ICTR to apprehend the subjective aspects of ethnic identity, and it points to a deeply ingrained incapacity of legal institutions to comprehend how social groups actually exist in the world outside of the courtroom.

Law's tendency to apply a literal-minded and rigid template to social categories is intensified in international tribunals trying the crime of genocide. This partly results from the mid-twentieth-century provenance of the concept of genocide, which combines universal legal prohibitions with romantic conceptions of peoples and social groups. Alexander Greenwalt (1999:2272) observes that the main intellectual author of the Genocide Convention, Raphael Lemkin, "offered a Romantic vision in the Herderian tradition." Greenwalt (ibid.) illustrates Lemkin's understanding of national groups by quoting from his 1944 tract *Axis Rule in Occupied Europe*: "The world represented only so much culture and intellectual vigor as are created by its component national groups. Essentially the idea of a nation signifies constructive cooperation and original contributions, based upon genuine traditions, genuine culture, and a well-developed national psychology." Lemkin's conception of nations as constituted by genuine culture and tradition and a shared national psychology unmistakably draws from the German romantic tradition, which perceived national groups as bounded wholes that were internally homogenous and had deep historical roots.[31] When these ideas were incorporated into the international humanitarian law of genocide, the collective social group assumed great prominence and became a juristic person, a status that is comparatively rare in international criminal law. A number of legal judgments at both the ICTR and ICTY confirm this principle, using the same wording: "The victim of the crime of genocide is the group itself and not the individual alone."[32]

---

[30] DeLeire (2000:23) analyzed 108,939 ADA discrimination cases filed with the Equal Employment Opportunity Commission in 1998.
[31] On J. G. Herder, the German romantic tradition, and ideas of *Kultur*, see Berlin (2001).
[32] At the ICTR, see *Musema* Trial Judgment, §165. At the ICTY, see *Prosecutor v. Duško Sikirica et al.*, Judgment on Defense Motions to Acquit, Case No. IT-95-8-T, 3 September 2001, §89. See also *Brđanin* Trial Judgment, §698.

If we take into account Lemkin's Herderian views on nation and culture, combined with the elevated status of collective categories in the international law of genocide, then we can come to appreciate the impetus behind the ICTR's tendency to objectify and essentialize Rwandan social groups. To convict for the crime of genocide, the requirement of special intent meant that the criminal acts had to be directed toward destroying a protected group as such, and the ICTR judges demanded categories of groups that met strict criteria of fixity and facticity. Under international criminal law, the facts of each case must be determined beyond reasonable doubt, and for ICTR judges, this applied equally to ethnic groups, which must be constituted as unimpeachable facts. Formulations of the group at the ICTR had to be ontologically secure and objectively demonstrable, and proof was required that group membership was the primary reason ("as such") the accused perpetrated prohibited acts. Group identity must refer to a permanent thing, and that "thingness" cannot be in doubt. Otherwise, the accused's intent would have been to destroy a group that counted with no real existence beyond the flawed misconceptions in the minds of perpetrators. The prosecution, as we have seen, did not flinch from this conclusion. Judges, however, wanted racial and ethnic groups to exist as durable and objective facts, as factual as the dead bodies in the ground. If a group's existence was not a hard fact but a soft fact dependent on a subjective state of mind (as most social facts are), then judges behaved as if this destabilized the entire edifice of the Tribunal's mandate to prosecute the crime of genocide.

7.6. THE PLACE OF DISCRIMINATORY INTENT AT THE ICTR AND ICTY

It would be misguided, however, to conclude that the inclination to reify social groups is an inherent predisposition of international criminal law and all international tribunals. What is surprising is the degree to which the two *ad hoc* Tribunals adopted utterly dissimilar reasoning when defining protected group status, even though they shared the same prosecutor until 2003. Whereas the Rwanda Tribunal sought "objective indicators" for racial and ethnic groups, the ICTY consistently used the local terms for ethnic groups in line with "accepted common usage."[33] The ICTY's 1999 *Jelisić* Trial Judgment cited

---

[33] *Tadić* Trial Judgment: "Since all three population groups are Slav it is, no doubt, inaccurate to speak of three different ethnic groups; however, this appears to be accepted common usage" (§56).

the ICTR's previous definitions of race and ethnicity[34] but rejected them in favor of a subjective reading of social groups that takes as its starting point the intention of the perpetrators of criminal acts:[35]

> Although the objective determination of a religious group still remains possible, to attempt to define a national, ethnical, or racial group using objective and scientifically irreproachable criteria would be a perilous exercise whose result would not necessarily correspond to the perception of the persons concerned by such a categorisation. Therefore, it is more appropriate to evaluate the status of a national, ethnical or racial group from the point of view of those persons who wish to single that group out from the rest of the community. The Trial Chamber consequently elects to evaluate membership in a national, ethnical, or racial group using subjective criterion [sic]. It is the stigmatization of a group as a distinct national, ethnical or racial unit by the community which allows it to be determined whether a targeted population constitutes a national, ethnical, or racial group in the eyes of the alleged perpetrators. (*Jelisić* §70)

Jelisić went on to distinguish between negative stigmatization, which identifies individuals as not part of the perpetrator group, and positive stigmatization, in which the perpetrators distinguish individuals by the characteristics that members of that group are thought to share. The Trial Chamber accepted the positive view of discriminatory intent advanced by the prosecution, on the basis of evidence that Jelisić called his Bosnian Muslim victims "Turks" and forced them to sing Serbian songs (§75). Subsequent judgments reinforced this reasoning. The 2001 *Krstić* Trial Judgment reiterated earlier jurisprudence on what constitutes a group and asserted that any attempt to differentiate "on the basis of scientifically objective criteria would thus be inconsistent with the object and purpose of the [Genocide] Convention. . . . A group's cultural, religious, ethnical or national characteristics must be identified within the socio-historical context in which it inhabits."[36] The 2004 *Brđanin* Trial Judgment acknowledged that ethnicity was not the perfect category for all social distinctions at work in Bosnia, yet it did not excessively belabor the point: "The Trial Chamber recognizes that the terms 'ethnic identity' or 'ethnicity' may not describe the distinguishing feature of Bosnian Muslims, Bosnian Croats and Bosnian Serbs in their entirety, since other factors, such as religion and nationality, are of importance" (§54n93).

---

[34] Citing *Kayishema* at 70n95.
[35] It should be noted that Goran Jelisić was convicted not of genocide but of persecution, a crime against humanity committed with discriminatory intent.
[36] *Krstić* Trial Judgment, §§556–7.

By adopting a subjective approach to group identity, the ICTY avoided many of the pitfalls that the ICTR fell into as it grasped for objective indicators of ethnicity. Why was it that the ICTY succeeded where the ICTR failed? Part of the answer lies in the ICTR's lack of an internal research unit similar to the LRT that could provide guidance on these matters and consult from a wider range of expertise outside the Tribunal. A lone scholar, even one as knowledgeable as Dr. Alison Des Forges, cannot be expected to serve as an expert on all facets of a country's history. International tribunal histories are enriched by behind-the-scenes discussions between experts holding varying interpretations and testing the prosecution's theory of the case. Lacking a critical mass of social and historical researchers in the Office of the Prosecutor, the ICTR's analysis had a thinner and brittler quality than that at the ICTY. The fact that the prosecution won the battle over the first paragraph in so outright a fashion, and on the basis of one external expert witness's view of Rwandan history, ironically undermined the ICTR judges' ability to engage with the complexities of that country's history.

Yet the most persuasive explanation so far for the ICTR's tribulations lay in an idiosyncratic requirement contained within the Tribunal's statute, which elevated discriminatory intent to a level not seen in other international criminal tribunals up to that point, or since. A unique clause in the Rwanda Tribunal Statute indicates that all crimes against humanity, not only genocide, require evidence of discriminatory grounds. "Crimes against Humanity" are defined in Article 3 of the Rwanda Statute thus:

> The International Criminal Tribunal for Rwanda shall have the power to prosecute persons responsible for the following crimes when committed as part of a widespread or systematic attack against any civilian population *on national, political, ethnic, racial or religious grounds*: (a) murder; (b) extermination; (c) enslavement; (d) deportation; (e) imprisonment; (f) torture; (g) rape; (h) persecutions on political, racial and religious grounds; (i) other inhumane acts. (My emphasis)

The burden of proving group membership is integral to all genocide cases, but Article 3 demanded racial, ethnic, national, political, or religious grounds for all crimes against humanity as well. The exact meaning of *grounds* is ambiguous here, as *grounds* can refer both to criminal intention and to ulterior motive. Whichever is the case, Article 3 meant that proof of discriminatory intent was required not only for genocide, as is always the case, but also for crimes against humanity, which do not usually require such grounds. The requirement that all crimes against humanity contain discriminatory intent raised the profile of intergroup animus at the Rwanda Tribunal. Diane Amman

(1999:196) remarked on the curious inclusion of this element in the ICTR Statute and she observed that group membership was not part of the definition of crimes against humanity in either the ICTY Statute or the 1998 Rome Statute of the International Criminal Court. Moreover, the ICTY explicitly rejected the necessity to prove discriminatory intent in the *Tadić* Appeals Judgment. After reviewing the jurisprudence, it concluded: "customary international law . . . does not presuppose a discriminatory or persecutory intent for all crimes against humanity" (§292).

Placing a burden of proof of discriminatory intent for genocide and all other crimes against humanity made the Rwanda Tribunal particularly susceptible to the inherent problems in defining racial and ethnic groups. With discriminatory intent occupying the place it did in the statute, the ICTR had much more to lose than the ICTY if social groups were not constituted as objective and real facts; namely, if the social groups were fictions, then grounds for finding discriminatory intent would be undermined if not completely impossible. The judges' logic seemed to be this: if there were no identifiable social groups, then there could be no discriminatory grounds on which civilians were attacked, and without discriminatory grounds, there could be no crimes against humanity as defined in the statute, and without any justiciable crimes, there could be no Tribunal. In this way, more was at stake in the discussion of protected social groups than "just" genocide convictions – adjudicating all crimes against humanity required solid proof of intent to attack civilians on the basis of their membership in the social groups listed in the statute. This helps explain why the Rwanda Tribunal, after a long and agonizing decision-making process, ultimately came to reject the ICTY's subjective approach to defining national and religious groups. The striking differences that emerged between the two Tribunals' approaches to social identity came down to the peculiarly burdensome mandate contained in the ICTR's founding statute, a statute that compelled the Rwanda Tribunal to identify discriminatory grounds for alleged crimes against humanity brought before it.

There are a few points we might draw from this discussion. First, a comprehensive analysis of international criminal trials implies close attention to the institutional framework of each court, as every one operates on a different statutory basis. Ultimately, each international tribunal requires its own special consideration, and the problems encountered by one may not be endemic to international criminal law more widely. The conundrum faced by the Rwanda Tribunal was avoidable, and one clear message is that the statute of any future international criminal tribunal should not require proof of discriminatory intent for crimes against humanity, with the exception of the crime of persecution. At the ICTR, emphasizing the animus between groups may have initially seemed the appropriate course of action given the nature of the massive violations that had occurred, but this had an unfortunate unintended consequence; namely, judges adopted a literal-minded reading of Rwandan social groups and were predisposed to deny the weight of historical and social science evidence to the contrary.

8

Permanent Justice: The International Criminal Court

8.1. THE POLITICS OF INTERNATIONAL JUSTICE REDUX

This chapter examines historical discussions in a new legal setting, that of the International Criminal Court (ICC), a permanent international justice body that will outlast the ICTY and ICTR and adjudicate international crimes for some time to come. The ICC is the premier court in a second generation of international criminal justice institutions established in the twenty-first century, along with the Special Court for Sierra Leone and the Extraordinary Chambers in the Courts of Cambodia. These newer courts have all been shaped by the experiences at the two *ad hoc* tribunals, and their designers have sought to avoid previous missteps while carrying forward the good practice developed. Because the ICC is such a relatively new court that has yet to complete its first trial, my comments must be fairly tentative and provisional.[1]

A brief history of the Court, including a description of its structure and mandate, is roughly as follows: on 17 July 1998 in Rome, 120 countries signed on to the Statute of the International Criminal Court. The ICC Statute entered into force on 1 July 2002 after ratification by sixty countries.[2] At the time of writing, 111 of 192 member nations of the United Nations had signed and ratified the treaty. Article 5 of the ICC Statute grants the Court jurisdiction over four crimes deemed to be "the most serious crimes of concern to the international community as a whole," namely genocide, crimes against humanity, war crimes, and the crime of aggression.[3] Not included are a number of other international crimes, such as international terrorism, piracy, narcotics trafficking, money laundering and financial criminality, and slave trading.

---

[1] For a review of the ICC, see Blattmann and Bowman (2008); Moghalu (2008); Peskin (2008).
[2] The ICC can investigate and prosecute crimes committed only after this date.
[3] For legal reviews of the elements of the crimes contained in the ICC Statute, see Dörmann (2003); Schabas (2001:21–53).

According to the ICC Statute, investigations can be initiated in three ways: on referral by the UN Security Council acting under Chapter VII of the UN Charter (Article 13), by a state party (Article 14), or by the Chief Prosecutor acting on his or her own accord (Article 15). If the Chief Prosecutor acts *proprio motu*, the investigation is subject to authorization by a pretrial panel of three judges. Under Article 16, the UN Security Council may also suspend an ongoing investigation temporarily for a twelve-month period by passing a resolution invoking Chapter VII of the UN Charter pertaining to threats to international peace and security.[4]

The ICC is different in a number of respects from the two *ad hoc* tribunals that preceded it. In the most general way, it was created by an international treaty rather than established by the UN Security Council. The fact that the Rome treaty was voluntarily negotiated and agreed to by sovereign states gives the ICC added legitimacy but also places it outside the protective umbrella of the Security Council, which makes it more vulnerable to the influence and interference of nation-states. The Security Council played a vital role in compelling recalcitrant states to cooperate with the *ad hoc* tribunals, and the provisions to clamp down on noncompliance with the ICC are much weaker. The Assembly of States Parties that oversees the ICC has nothing like the influence of the UN Security Council and has so far shown little willingness to pressure states to cooperate with ICC arrest warrants or requests for evidence.

Although it falls well short of commanding universal jurisdiction, the ICC enjoys a much broader jurisdiction than the *ad hoc* tribunals. However, this jurisdiction is heavily diluted by the state-consent provisions contained in the statute. According to Article 17(1), a case is inadmissible if it is being investigated or prosecuted by the state party with jurisdiction or when a case has already been investigated and the state has decided not to pursue legal proceedings. Under the complementarity principle, state parties have the right to try their citizens first, which makes the ICC a court of last resort that comes into play only when a state is unable or unwilling to try an individual accused of violations of international humanitarian law or when the state conducts sham legal proceedings designed to shield a person from criminal liability.[5] The state-consent provisions have prompted observers such as Victor Peskin (2008:247) to conclude that the legal authority of the ICC is "significantly curtailed" as compared with that of the ICTY and ICTR.

---

4 This potentially allows for a paradoxical situation to develop in which the UN Security Council could invoke Chapter VII to refer an investigation on grounds of international peace and security but then invoke Chapter VII again to suspend the investigation on grounds of international peace and security.

5 On complementarity at the ICC, see Cryer et al. (2007:127–33, 447–8); Schabas (2001:67–70).

The ICC is also exposed to pressure from powerful countries that refuse to accede to its treaty, including China, India, Russia, and the United States. Much has been written about the hostility of U.S. lawmakers to the Court. Recall the intemperate words of Tom DeLay, former Republican majority leader in the U.S. House of Representatives, who referred to the ICC as a "kangaroo court... a shady amalgam of every bad idea ever cooked up for world government."[6] Perhaps most damaging has been the U.S. policy of strong-arming weaker state parties to the ICC to sign impunity agreements and threatening to cut off military aid in some instances if they demurred.[7] The Bush administration concluded bilateral immunity agreements with approximately one hundred countries that pledged not to arrest U.S. citizens or to place them before the ICC. U.S. antipathy to the Court was not just confined to foreign relations, and the American Service-Members' Protection Act of 2002 prohibited local, state, and federal government agencies from assisting the ICC, such as by providing classified information to the Court or extraditing an individual to face charges before the Court. The Act authorized the U.S. president to "use all means necessary and appropriate" to obtain the release of U.S. military personnel detained by or on behalf of the ICC, thus conjuring up fantastical images of a U.S. amphibious assault on the Scheveningen seaside resort of The Hague.

Without a doubt, U.S. opposition to the Court has hampered its work in critical ways, but in other ways it has granted it a certain legitimacy. It is hard to argue that the ICC is a mere instrument of American global hegemony. Moreover, the ICC's cautious beginnings helped facilitate a softening of the U.S. position during the second term of President George W. Bush. The United States did not veto UN Security Council Resolution 1593, which referred the Darfur case to the ICC Chief Prosecutor Luis Moreno Ocampo, nor did it oppose the transfer of the trial of former Liberian president Charles Taylor to be tried by the Special Court for Sierra Leone on ICC premises in June 2006. These two events signaled a recognition by some U.S. opponents of the Court that its operations could potentially coincide with U.S. global security interests. The Obama administration has vowed to end U.S. hostility to the Court and to cooperate in the Darfur situation. It has begun to engage with the ICC on an official basis, and it sent a delegation of observers to the Assembly of State Parties meeting in The Hague in late 2009.[8] However, the bilateral immunity agreements have remained in place, and the U.S. political

---

[6] "Let the Child Live," *Economist*, 27 January 2007, 59.
[7] See Johansen (2006).
[8] BBC News, "US to Resume Engagement with ICC," 16 November 2009.

establishment is many years away from even contemplating ratification of the ICC Statute.

Even as U.S. foreign policy has become more amenable to the Court, some of the Court's most ardent early supporters in Africa have seemingly turned against it. Initially, Africa was the continent most deeply committed to the ICC, and several African states voluntarily referred cases to the ICC for investigation.[9] The turning point came on 4 March 2009, when the ICC's pretrial chamber issued a warrant of arrest for sitting Sudanese president Omar al-Bashir in relation to crimes committed in the Darfur region, where the United Nations has determined that three hundred thousand people have died and 2 million have become refugees since 2003.[10] The prosecutor had indicted President Bashir in July 2008 on three counts of genocide, but these charges were dismissed by the pretrial chamber for lack of evidence.[11] In the 2009 arrest warrant, President Bashir was charged with two counts of war crimes, including intentionally directing attacks against civilians and pillaging their villages, and five counts of crimes against humanity, including murder, rape, forcible transfer, torture, and extermination.

The fifty-three-nation African Union (AU), alarmed by the indictment of a sitting head of state, strenuously objected to the ICC's arrest warrant for President Bashir. The AU assembly meeting in Libya in July 2009 made a decision not to cooperate with the ICC in arresting and surrendering Bashir, citing concerns that the warrant of arrest would hamper peace negotiations and ongoing humanitarian relief efforts in Sudan, all the while affirming their "unflinching commitment . . . to combating impunity and promoting democracy, the rule of law and good governance on the continent."[12] The AU has campaigned vigorously against the ICC's arrest warrant in the media and in diplomatic circles, using nationalist and anticolonial rhetoric.[13] The AU has lobbied the UN Security Council, which referred the case to the ICC in the first place, requesting that it suspend the legal proceedings initiated against Bashir under its powers contained in Article 16 of the ICC Statute. Thus far, the AU campaign has not been successful, and tensions escalated

---

9 Democratic Republic of Congo (2004), Uganda (2004), and Central African Republic (2005).
10 BBC News, "African Union in Rift with Court," 3 July 2009.
11 For an illuminating discussion of the prosecutor's motivations and strategies in the Darfur and Ugandan cases, see Peskin (2008).
12 African Union Press Release, Decision on the Meeting of African States Parties to the Rome Statute of the International Criminal Court (ICC), Addis Ababa, 14 July 2009, §3.
13 See statements by the African Union's most senior diplomat Jean Ping, who has accused the ICC of unfairly targeting African countries: "We are not for a justice with two speeds, a double standard justice – one for the poor, one for the rich." BBC News, "Bashir May Face Genocide Charges," 3 February 2010.

further in February 2010 when the ICC Appeals Chamber found that the pretrial chamber had made an error of law and placed too high a threshold on the evidence required to include genocide in the arrest warrant. The Appeals Chamber ordered the pretrial chamber to revisit the genocide charges against President Bashir.[14]

By virtue of the international framework in which it was established, the ICC is more susceptible to malign state influence than the ICTY and ICTR. It cannot count on the fulsome cooperation and protection of either the UN Security Council or the world's most powerful states. Even states that have ratified the ICC Statute can campaign against ICC measures they dislike, seemingly without meaningful reproach from the Assembly of States Parties. It is unclear what impact this might have on historical discussions in cases brought before the ICC. We can expect, however, that the distance from state interference that has at times facilitated investigative autonomy at the *ad hoc* tribunals will be much attenuated at the ICC, at least in the near future.

8.2. REGULATING EXPERT WITNESSES AT THE ICC

Too much focus on the events themselves may be conducive to producing a history of a particular place, rather than on creating a strategy to pursue the most senior persons responsible for the crimes.

– Minna Schrag (2003:4), *Lessons Learned from the ICTY Experience: Notes for the ICC Prosecutor*[15]

The ICC's rules and regulations embrace a liberal and flexible approach to expert-witness evidence that is quite comparable to that of the ICTR and ICTY. Consistent with what we saw at the ICTY and ICTR, Rule 63(5) of the ICC Rules of Procedure and Evidence eschews national laws governing evidence.[16] There is no hearsay rule, and the evidentiary regime allows most evidence to be admitted and trusts professional judges to separate the pertinent from the extraneous and the reliable from the implausible. In determining the relevance and admissibility of evidence, Article 69(4) adopts similar language to that found in the jurisprudence of the *ad hoc* tribunals, stating that the Court may take into account "the probative value of the evidence and any

---

[14] Aaron Gray-Block (2003:4), "Court Ordered to Rule Again on Bashir Genocide Charge," Reuters News Agency, 3 February 2010.

[15] See Schrag (2003), contribution to an expert consultation process on general issues relevant to the ICC Office of the Prosecutor.

[16] International Criminal Court Rules of Procedure and Evidence. Adopted by the Assembly of States Parties, 1st sess., New York, 3–10 September 2002. Official Records ICC-ASP/1/3 at 10, and Corr. 1 (2002), U.N. Doc. PCNICC/2000/1/Add.1 (2000).

prejudice that such evidence may cause to a fair trial." Few exclusionary rules are set down in the ICC Statute, but Article 69(7) states that evidence may be ruled inadmissible if the methods used to obtain it are illegal or violate human rights. The ICC Statute allows an innovative approach to the forms of testimony permitted, allowing witnesses to testify via video or audio link, as well as via prior recorded testimony, as long as both the prosecution and defense had the opportunity to examine the witness during the recording.[17]

Beyond the most general level, however, it is apparent that the ICC is quite a distinctive institution as compared to its *ad hoc* predecessors. For starters, the ICC is an abundantly regulated legal body, possessing an operational blueprint that is remarkably comprehensive and even exhaustive. Whereas the ICTY began with a few brief UN resolutions, a statute of fewer than ten pages, and no rules of procedure and evidence, the ICC is presently under way with an immensely detailed statute of 128 articles and a set of rules of procedure and evidence containing 225 rules. If this were not enough, there are also three sets of internal regulations: for the Court (73 pages), the Office of the Prosecutor (OTP; 30 pages), and the Registry (110 pages). Contained in this intricate matrix of rules and regulations are extensive powers for judges to supervise, guide, and effectively control the legal process, from the first glimmers of an investigation to the final closure of the appeals stage. If they learned anything at all from the *ad hoc* tribunals, the architects of the ICC learned one lesson – an unvarnished adversarial process is inimical to trying cases of the size and magnitude that normally fall under the jurisdiction of an international criminal court or tribunal.

Looking more closely at the evidentiary and procedural framework of the ICC, we find a remarkable degree of judicial management of expert-witness participation in a trial. Expert-witness testimony is governed by Regulations 44 and 54 of the Regulations of the Court. Regulation 44 mandates the Registry to maintain an official list of experts, and it indicates a preference for joint instruction of experts by the parties, in an attempt to move away from the adversarial model of warring experts in the Trial Chamber. Judges are empowered to call their own expert witnesses. They may issue any orders regarding the subject of expert reports, the number of experts called, the instruction of experts, the manner in which expert evidence is presented, and the time allotted to experts to prepare their report (Regulation 44(5)). Regulation 54, "Status Conferences before the Trial Chamber," provides sweeping powers to judges to exercise control over not only the procedure of the courtroom but also the very content

---

[17] ICC Rules of Procedure and Evidence (RPE), Rules 67–8.

of the trial, thus permitting them to "issue any order in the interests of justice" on the length and content of opening and closing statements, the issues the parties propose to raise during the trial, the type of defenses advanced by the accused, the length of evidence and the time allowed for questioning of witnesses, the number of witnesses and documents, the identity of witnesses and the instruction of expert witnesses, and the conditions under which victims participate in the proceedings. In reaction to widespread criticism of the long and unwieldy trials of the ICTR and ICTY, the ICC has been designed as the apotheosis of the managerial judicial model. However, some international criminal law experts feel that the pendulum has swung too far and have expressed consternation at the Pretrial Chamber judges' assumption of the authority to, for instance, amend the charges against the accused in the first ICC trial.[18]

With respect to the internal structure of the OTP at the ICC, it appears that its research capacity and ability to engage with expert witnesses is significantly attenuated as compared to the *ad hoc* tribunals, and to the ICTY in particular. Former ICTY Senior Trial Attorney Minna Schrag (2003:6), in an official advisory document to the ICC prosecutor noted the importance of having "on staff persons with capacity to analyze data, and in particular to have analysts with military expertise." Yet the ICC Office of the Prosecutor contains no internal unit comparable to the Leadership Research Team (LRT) or the Military Analysis Team of the ICTY that can undertake some of their main functions, namely to analyze large archives of documents and data, to integrate internal historians and social scientists into the investigative and trial processes, and to liaise with external expert witnesses and consultants.

There are some understandable reasons why the OTP might lack such a separate team of research analysts. Unlike the ICTR, ICTY, or Special Tribunals for Lebanon or Sierra Leone, the ICC is not focused on violations of international humanitarian law in just one country or region. Its mandate presently encompasses 111 states in Africa, Asia, Europe, and the Americas. A permanent court with such a broad jurisdiction cannot afford to maintain on staff research specialists on all the areas of the world in which it might potentially conduct investigations. At the same time, its internal research capabilities do not seem sufficient to the task at hand, and presently the OTP has only one dedicated research analyst specializing in the Great Lakes region of Africa, where it is conducting a number of investigations and trials. The OTP staff interviewed for this book openly acknowledged this deficiency

---

[18]   War Crimes Research Office (2009:1).

while contending that they have sought out a wide range of expertise from outside consultants. Experienced staff who previously worked at the ICTY acknowledged that calling in outside expertise is no substitute for a cadre of research staff with formal and independent standing inside the OTP and that is fully integrated into the fabric of investigations and trials. The autonomous standing of such research and analysis units both facilitates an independent investigative culture and permits prosecuting attorneys to call internal experts as expert witnesses in their trials.

The OTP's diminished research capacity is cited by some critics as one reason the Pretrial Chamber rejected the three genocide charges in the indictment of Sudanese President Bashir on grounds of lack of evidence. Journalist Julie Flint and Alex de Waal (2009), a former expert consultant to the ICC on Africa, write that "there is much speculation, inside and outside the ICC, at how Moreno Ocampo arrives at his figures for death rates in Darfur. . . . The OTP itself possesses no specialist epidemiologists or demographers who might generate such figures, and no one working in Darfur proposes figures even remotely close to these. . . . Moreno Ocampo's arithmetic is simply fantastical." The Flint and De Waal article exudes personal antipathy toward ICC Chief Prosecutor Luis Moreno Ocampo, so its assertions ought to be approached with care, but there seems little doubt that a team of social science and historical experts would strengthen the analytical and investigative capacity of the OTP and provide more rigor to the Chief Prosecutor's claims of the number of dead in Darfur.

8.3. "EVERYTHING IS ELASTIC": THE PROSECUTION HISTORIAN EXPERT WITNESS IN THE TRIAL OF THOMAS LUBANGA DYILO

> Well, sir, we're dealing with Africa. Pity, please, a little common sense. This isn't how things work there.
> – Dr. Gérard Prunier, Prosecution Expert Witness (26 March 2009)

In 2009, two expert witnesses made courtroom appearances in the ICC's first trial, that of Thomas Lubanga Dyilo. Prosecution expert witness Gérard Prunier took the stand in March 2009 and court-appointed expert Roberto Garretón testified a few months later in June, each providing both extensive reflection on the historical origins and causes of the conflict in the Democratic Republic of the Congo (DRC) and information with implications for the parties' theories of the case. As for the weight and value accorded to their evidence by the bench of three judges, the trial judgment has not been rendered, so a final appraisal will have to wait. What can be said at this point is that there are some striking variations in how experts are handled in the Trial Chamber compared with the *ad hoc* tribunals and that there are some time-honored features of expert-witness cross-examination that seem to recur with great regularity in international criminal trials.

Thomas Lubanga Dyilo is a middle-ranking figure in the armed conflict in the Ituri region of the Democratic Republic of the Congo that has claimed more than sixty thousand deaths between 1999 and 2006.[19] He held the positions of president of the Union of Congolese Patriots (UPC) and commander in chief of its military wing, the Patriotic Force for the Liberation of the Congo (FPLC), and he led the UPC's militias against Congolese government forces and their local proxies in Ituri. He forged alliances at various points with both Uganda and Rwanda, international actors that at times maintained a stronger military presence in the region than the DRC government itself. Lubanga himself belongs to the Hema ethnic group and his supporters were mostly Hemas, although there is a general consensus that the armed conflict did not originate in the first instance in ethnic animosity. Instead, the Ituri conflict is viewed as a struggle that broke out over political and economic resources, and developed an ethnic character only as the conflict deepened.

The DRC government arrested Lubanga in 2005 and held him in the capital Kinshasa while it referred the case to the ICC Chief Prosecutor, who decided to take on the case. The ICC issued an arrest warrant, and Lubanga was transferred in 2006 to The Hague. He faces six charges of war crimes, involving acts of enlistment and conscription into the FPLC of children under the age of fifteen and the use of children under fifteen to participate actively in hostilities during internal and international armed conflicts in the eastern Ituri region of the DRC between July 2002 and December 2003.[20] Lubanga entered a plea of innocence, and although there is ample evidence that child soldiers were deployed by UPC militias as well as by most other parties to the Ituri conflict, Lubanga's distance from the front lines and the actual process of conscription means that the prosecution case is made more difficult.

The ICC's first trial got under way on 26 January 2009, almost three years after the accused was first transferred to The Hague and after prosecutorial procedural missteps in disclosing exculpatory evidence in a timely manner

---

[19] Agence France-Presse, "Probe into War Crimes in DRC," 3 April 2006, http://www.news24.com.

[20] *Prosecutor v. Thomas Lubanga Dyilo* (Case No. ICC-01/04-01/06), Warrant of Arrest, 10 February 2006; Decision on the Confirmation of Charges, 29 January 2007. Lubanga's trial opened with him facing charges both under Article 8(2)(b), relating to war crimes during an international armed conflict, and Article 8(2)(e), which refers to war crimes in noninternational armed conflicts, of the 1998 Rome Statute.

nearly led to the case's dismissal by exasperated trial judges. Immediately, the trial felt unlike any previous international criminal trial, and it bore all the hallmarks of the ICC's regulatory blueprint for judicial case management. Presiding Judge Sir Adrian Fulford is a highly experienced High Court Judge in the United Kingdom and a forceful personality who guides the trial with a deft touch, his every utterance a gem of wit and erudition. At the same time, there is no doubt that Judge Fulford is in charge of his courtroom in a way seldom seen at the *ad hoc* tribunals, and it would be imprudent to flout his authority. Although Judge Fulford's authoritative manner and disposition are beneficial in many ways for the proceedings, one negative consequence of them is that both the prosecution and the defense are reluctant to confront the bench with challenging in-courtroom applications, as is frequently seen at both the ICTY and the ICTR.

Even though it is easy to admire Judge Fulford, his commanding position does not simply result from his personal attributes. Compared with their ICTY and ICTR counterparts, ICC judges are in control in a deeper structural sense, as they have a more defined role in the proceedings. At the two *ad hoc* tribunals, the underlying philosophy of the courtroom is that the prosecution case is the engine of the trial. The defense case is constructed in reaction to whatever the prosecution brings. The judges are relatively passive observers of the contest between defense and prosecution, intervening only where necessary to guide the legal proceedings and keep them in the boundaries of fair procedure and due process of law. At the ICC, in contrast, judges appear as actors in the trial as significant as the defense and prosecution, and they have appreciably more scope to shape the actual content of the trial (i.e., what the parties argue, not just how they argue it).

As a consequence, the first ICC trial had a less adversarial quality than trials at the ICTY and ICTR. Thus far, the parties have been kept to a higher standard of courtroom behavior, and this applies equally to their treatment of expert witnesses. Gone is the familiar tearing down of an expert's credibility and personal standing in his or her field that characterized the ICTY, as the judges enforce the view that the expert witnesses are there at their behest and are therefore to be appreciated and respected. During an increasingly testy exchange between a defense lawyer and a prosecution expert witness, Judge Fulford issued a mild reprimand to the defense lawyer, making it "absolutely clear that the whole issue of background evidence was one that was raised by the Judges and this evidence has been called essentially at our request."[21] As Fulford noted, judicial oversight of the expert's participation had been

---

[21] Trial transcript 26 March, p. 57, ll. 9–12. Henceforth, I use the following format for citing ICC trial transcripts: date, page(s)/line(s).

exercised before the expert's courtroom testimony. Judges had requested background evidence, vetted the expert's credentials, supervised his instructions, and even pronounced on the level of interaction between the prosecution and expert in advance of his or her testimony.[22] This precise combination of constraints was seldom placed on prosecutors at the ICTY and ICTR, and they likely would have chafed at the bit of such extensive judicial participation. But the advantage of their involvement in all levels of the trial was that ICC judges exhibited a greater commitment to hearing expert witnesses and their evidence in the courtroom.

In the Lubanga trial, the prosecution team selected as its background expert Dr. Gérard Prunier, professor of African history at one of most eminent institutions of higher education in France, the Centre National de la Recherche Scientifique of the University of Paris. Prunier took the stand for two days, 26–27 March 2009. He was introduced very briefly by Prosecutor Nicole Samson, who went over his biographical details and tendered his three expert reports into evidence. The greater part of his questioning and examination was carried out by the panel of judges and the defense lawyer, Mr. Jean-Marie Biju-Duval. The lower profile of the prosecution was both a result of standard ICC courtroom procedure and a strategic decision taken by the prosecution team, as the relevance of Prunier's report and testimony to the charges against the accused was not immediately apparent. The expert presented a historical narrative with only a weak sense of causality and a slender connection to the crimes. Prunier's testimony was definitely not the taut and inexorable prosecution narrative of the *Milošević* trial, or even the more nuanced history and contextualization of documents of the *Brđanin* trial. Instead, the prosecution's historical evidence bore strongest resemblance to the ICTY's first trial, of Duško Tadić, in that it offered a general framing of the crimes that informed judges of a complex historical situation. Unlike some previous trials at the ICTR and ICTY, no part of the prosecution case drew legal sustenance from the historical arguments that Prunier put forward, and no part would stand or fall on its reception by judges.

Prunier located the origins of the Ituri conflict in the categories of race and ethnicity defined by "white anthropologists" from Belgium.[23] In 1910, ethnological categorizations were codified by Belgian administrators. The local population was divided into groups such as the Hema, the Lendu, and others, and the colonial regime fashioned a hierarchy based on each group's putative

---

[22] See oral decision from Trial Chamber 1 in the Lubanga case on whether a party can meet in advance with an expert witness; trial transcripts 16 January 2009, 28/18–29/9.

[23] 26 March 2009, 23/7.

racial proximity to Europeans. The Hema were considered a superior race and were granted favorable access to educational opportunities and official positions in the colonial administration.[24] Colonial-era inequalities engendered a long-standing land struggle within and between communities and ethnic groups. The trigger of the modern armed conflict in Ituri came in 1999, when a dispute over the property of a Hema farmer, a certain Singa Kodjo, escalated into a massacre of Hemas.[25] For Gérard Prunier, this incident and its aftermath constituted "the beginning of the armed ethnicisation."[26]

The conflict intensified as international actors – primarily Ugandans and Rwandans – become militarily active in the DRC. Hema leaders employed ideas of ethnic solidarity to win influence with outsiders. Although the Hema speak a sub-Saharan Bantu language, they sought to identify as a Nilotic group with a northern provenance. They used the Hema name to claim ethnic affiliations with Himas of Uganda and Tutsis of Rwanda, as Ugandan Himas and Rwandan Tutsis are said to share common origins: "The Hemas . . . told the Himas [of Uganda] . . . we are your cousins, we are like you, you should take sides with us because we are like you."[27] Prunier asserted that "the Hema after the Rwandan genocide tried to Tutsify themselves" to gain a political advantage by pretending they were "martyrs."[28] Despite the shaky historical grounds for their ethnic claims, Hema leaders' efforts to forge ethnic alliances with outsiders met with success. With the help of Ugandan soldiers, Hemas began illegally appropriating land and cattle from Lendus in the late 1990s. This ethnic solidarity strategy worked for a while, but then local Ituri militias began to rapidly shift their allegiances with outside parties, who were in turn unable to control their erstwhile proxies. The triangular war between Rwanda, Uganda, and the DRC government in Kinshasa disintegrated into a Hobbesian war of all against all.[29]

The prosecution's expert witness infused his chronology of the Ituri conflict with negative images of Thomas Lubanga and the UPC. The accused and his party, said Prunier, were opposed to Ugandan withdrawal, resisted pacification efforts, and promoted the succession of Ituri from the Democratic Republic of the Congo.[30] Prunier's (2009:69) views of Lubanga's malign role was particularly evident in his expert report, which quoted a local Catholic

---

[24] 26 March, 35/22.
[25] 26 March, 30/19.
[26] 26 March, 42/16.
[27] 27 March 44/4–7.
[28] 26 March, 22/8, 23/22.
[29] 26 March, 76/5.
[30] 26 March, 80/1–10, 90/9–10, 95/9–16.

bishop alleging that the UPC cannibalized Pygmies and that the Bunia population referred to Lubanga as "Al-Qaeda 2."[31]

The defense's cross-examination was led by the French lawyer Jean-Marie
Biju-Duval, a skilled cross-examiner with prior international legal experience
as defense counsel for Ferdinand Nahimana at the ICTR. Biju-Duval immediately set about undercutting the reliability of the information provided by
the prosecution's historical witness and pursuing a line of questioning that
plainly articulated one aspect of Lubanga's defense. He did not lay siege to the
expert's credentials, as was common at the ICTY and ICTR, but instead began
by querying his methods and sources. Able defense lawyers often prevail using
this line of attack against expert witnesses, as they possess a better understanding of the epistemological rules of the criminal courtroom, regardless of the
expert's better grasp of social research methods or the facts themselves. Biju-
Duval began by asking for the sources of Prunier's demographic information
and his claims about the ethnic composition of Hema and Lendu communities and the Kodjo land dispute that sparked the conflict.[32] Prunier fell back on
the same sources for most of his information, unnamed administrative officials
from Ituri whom he had interviewed in Ugandan refugee camps.[33]

In contrast, Biju-Duval brandished documents – tangible, concrete reports
of the UN Mission in the Democratic Republic of the Congo (MONUC), a
government census of 1995, reports of nongovernmental organizations such
as the International Crisis Group, and official declarations of the UPC and
written statements of the accused. Prunier's rejoinder to this flurry of official
documentation was that of an old Africa hand who relied more on fieldwork
than paperwork: "I tend to trust people in the field more than people who have
documents. Documents are a lot nicer and a lot more elegant. It's intellectually
a lot more satisfying, but people in the field tend to base themselves on practical
measurements."[34] Prunier might have scored a minor victory for ethnographic
fieldworkers everywhere had he stopped there, but he proceeded to deride
demographic data in Africa as "a black hole," to call the land register in
Bunia and Ituri a "joke," and to cast doubt on UN reports and investigations.[35]
However well founded his skepticism of these sources, Prunier rejected any
notion of the certitude of facts in the African context, where "everything
is elastic."[36] When Biju-Duval asked what reliable sources he would then

[31]   27 March, 30/14, 31/11.
[32]   26 March, 18/19–20, 20/18–19, 31/9–12.
[33]   26 March, 19/25–20/5.
[34]   26 March, 20/5–9.
[35]   26 March, 18/21–19/14, 38/18.
[36]   26 March, 41/16.

recommend to the Court, Prunier responded starkly, "Sir . . . you wouldn't find such sources anywhere."[37] These exchanges throw into relief some of the conspicuous disparities between legal and historical ways of creating and evaluating knowledge. The eminent French historian's manner of handling evidence may be based on decades of experience in Africa, but it holds little sway in the international criminal courtroom, where documents will trump an expert's oral evidence every time. To international jurists, documents seem a surer path to the truth, because they can be referenced and because they appear, at least superficially, to be more reliable. One former ICC prosecutor interviewed reflected that the judges' penchant for documents extended even to the kinds of documents: in a triumph of form over content, typed documents were held to be more objective and reliable than handwritten ones.

Relativism bordering on cynicism, though common among researchers of Africa (and not only among Europeans), has the effect of undermining the expert witnesses' own reliability in the eyes of international judges. As his testimony unfolded, Prunier became ever more trapped in a relativist conundrum of his own creation; that is, making claims while casting doubt on the very possibility of making claims. This exposed him further to defense skepticism regarding the credibility of his assertions about Ituri and the DRC. Biju-Duval could rightly ask how he could attribute attacks to one group or another with any degree of certainty, given his own position on the dearth of reliable knowledge of the situation.[38] Epistemological openness might be commendable in the seminar room, but radical uncertainty has little to no purchase in a court of law that applies universal standards of proof and facticity.

Prunier's testimony was also impaired by a lack of specificity, another common Achilles' heel of expert background witnesses. Prunier could not provide any concrete details of instances of Hemas taking land from Lendus with Ugandan help, and he could not speak in any detail about most the important land dispute in Ituri – that of the Kodjo farm that he had earlier identified as the trigger of the conflict. This illustrates a deeper structural issue regarding expert background witnesses in criminal trials. Experts are called to make general statements, to identify trends and patterns, but they are seldom able to muster the granular detail on specific cases that is required by a court of law to substantiate their larger analytical claims. Furthermore, the relationship between individual cases and social or historical patterns is a gray area in international criminal law more generally. How many individual instances are needed to constitute a widespread and systematic attack, for instance? A

---

[37] 27 March, 13/23.
[38] 27 March, 16/18.

background expert's evidence often requires an intuitive leap from specific cases to wider patterns, but that is a leap that most triers of fact in a criminal courtroom are loath to make, unless the extrapolation is backed by "hard" scientific and statistical data and methods.

Lacking a firm grasp of the minutiae of the examples he was presenting, Prunier fell back on grandiose generalizations about Africa and beyond, and he used distant events to bear out his statements about events in Ituri. In one example, when the defense disputed the expert's assertion of an alliance between Lubanga and the Ugandans, Prunier mentioned the rapidly changing alliances between groups: "It's all over Africa. I've seen it in Uganda, in Somalia, in Sudan. You know groups keep changing, they change alliances at lightning speed because really there is no ideology driving them, there are no fundamental beliefs."[39] The expert then carried on to ponder the unstable nature of the pact between Germany and the Soviet Union at the beginning of World War II. The expert's point about shifting military alliances in Ituri was entirely relevant to the trial and possibly well founded, but the generalizing manner in which he made it was unlikely to convince any court of law.

However, the most intensely contested issue of all between the expert and defense lawyer concerned the ethnic origins and classification of the Hema. In his expert report, Prunier had referred to the Hema as a sub-Saharan Bantu people, on the basis of the language they speak. Defense counsel Biju-Duval labored to refute this categorization and to supplant it with the view that the Hema are a Nilotic, Saharan people (originating from the Nile Valley), citing court expert witness Roberto Garretón's report in support of that view.[40] Garretón was a Chilean human rights lawyer during the military dictatorship of General Augusto Pinochet and a former UN Special Rapporteur on Human Rights in the Democratic Republic of the Congo between 1997 and 2001. Playing the African-insider card, Prunier rejected Garretón's conclusions outright: "I doubt very much this person . . . is from the region."[41] Prunier added that Garretón's reliance on ethnologists is proof that "he doesn't know anything about it himself."[42] Prunier cited as his sources not anthropologists but administrators and inhabitants from the region and his own ability to distinguish between Nilotic and Bantu languages, even though he conceded that does not speak the languages himself.[43]

---

[39] 26 March, 83/21–5.
[40] 26 March, 25–26.
[41] 26 March 28/24–5.
[42] 26 March, 29/5.
[43] 26 March 29/20–1.

The point to take away from this exchange is not the dispute between experts on a question of ethnic classification but the desire on the part of the defense to categorize Hemas as a Saharan people and to underscore the ethnic character of conflict. A sizable portion of the defense counsel's cross-examination consisted of listing massacres and violence toward the Hema civilian population and asking why those were not contained in the expert's report.[44] The defense drew attention to the ethnic animus in Ituri to a much greater degree than the prosecution, and it was the only party at trial to conjure up the image of "ethnic hatred" to describe the atmosphere at the time of the alleged crimes.[45] The judges picked up on this, and Judge Odio Benito of Costa Rica sought clarification as to whether the Ituri conflict was ethnic, economic, or a combination of the two. Prunier's response was instructive: "[A]t the beginning it was an economic conflict and that ethnicity was instrumentalised . . . and used as a tool to fuel the conflict. And this has to do with the nature of African societies, where ethnicity is something which plays a very major role."[46]

The defense drew attention to the ethnic dimensions of the conflict because it served its overall strategy in the trial. The defense went to great pains in its cross-examination of the expert witness to show not only that the Hemas were under constant attack but also that the UN Mission had failed to provide adequate security, and so understandably "reprisals were taken in this atmosphere of hatred."[47] Defense counsel Biju-Duval posed one notably plangent question to the witness: "So given the fact that violence spread and the Hema civilian population as well, and given there was this ideology, this extremist ideology that was evolving, could one say that the Hema population may have felt threatened, that they may have felt that their very existence was threatened?"[48] It was vital for the defense to establish that the Hemas were Nilotic to buttress their claim that they were related to Tutsis, the ethnic group subjected to genocide in Rwanda, and to claim that the very existence of associated ethnic groups like the Hema were similarly threatened by Bantu groups in the Democratic Republic of the Congo. Congolese Hemas, the defense narrative contended, like their benighted kin the Tutsis, were facing crimes against humanity, if not actual genocide itself. This sounds very much like the defense arguments heard at the ICTY and ICTR, as well as the *tu quoque* defense outlined in Chapter 6. Indeed, in this exchange, the defense's theory of the case was coming clearly into view. Presiding Judge Fulford was quick to interject at the end of this

---

[44] 26 March, 42–43; 27 March 8/19–21.
[45] 26 March, 43/24.
[46] 27 March, 38/13–14.
[47] 26 March, 43/22–3.
[48] 26 March, 46/14.

round of defense questioning, saying statements such as that the Hemas' "very existence was threatened" had two possible implications: one for exploring the background and context of the alleged crimes, which is entirely legitimate, and the other involving "notions [such] as either self-defense or necessity."[49] Judge Fulford inquired whether the defense was mounting a necessity defense and informed Biju-Duval that they had reached the stage in the trial where the court would benefit from knowing the defense's strategy, and then he called a break for lunch. On readjourning, Biju-Duval denied that he was mounting a necessity defense, repudiated the view that he was seeking exoneration of the accused from criminal liability, and instead claimed to have been merely asking about the expert's sources. Then he proceeded unabashedly to pursue the same necessity defense line of questioning, as if the judge had said nothing at all.[50]

As with the *tu quoque* defense, there is very little elucidation of the necessity defense in international criminal law textbooks and in the international law literature more widely. International law specialists seem much more interested in the court and the prosecution than the defense, and in the legal judgments, rules, and regulations rather than what actually transpires in the courtroom. Perhaps because of his extensive experience in the ICTY Trial Chamber, Antonio Cassese (2003:242–3) recognizes the prevalence of the necessity defense and defines it thus: "Necessity may be urged as a defense when a person, acting under a threat of severe and irreparable harm to his life or limb, or to life and limb of a third person, perpetrates an international crime."[51] The necessity defense has its own distinctive features, but it also shares some elements of the *tu quoque* defense that has been so prevalent at the ICTY. Whereas the *tu quoque* defense seeks to allow or mitigate the commission of a crime on the grounds that an adversary behaved in the same reprehensible manner, the necessity defense seeks to allow or mitigate the commission of a crime on the grounds that an adversary behaved in such a way that the defendant faced a real and imminent danger to his or her existence and therefore acted under duress. Both defenses share a real or perceived and imminent threat from a third party, but the necessity defense accentuates the element of duress in the commission of the prohibited act. What matters for our discussion is that here again, in an entirely new court setting, the defense's strategy of

---

[49] 26 March, 57/18–58/17, 59/15.
[50] 26 March, 59/7–12.
[51] See also Cryer et al. (2007:339–40) on necessity in international criminal law. *Black's Law Dictionary* (Garner 2006) defines necessity in domestic U.S. criminal law as a justification defense for a person who acts in an emergency that he or she did not create and who commits a harm less severe than the crime that would have occurred but for the person's actions.

mitigation became a driving force behind the historical questions debated in an international criminal trial.

8.4. STANDING BY YOUR SOURCES: THE UN SPECIAL RAPPORTEUR AS COURT-APPOINTED EXPERT

After the testimony of Gérard Prunier, the next expert witness to appear in the Lubanga trial was Roberto Garretón. Appointed by the judges rather than the parties, his courtroom appearance had an even less adversarial quality still. Judge Fulford took a central role in introducing the witness and guiding the testimony. He explicitly endorsed the court's decision to venture outside the time frame of the charges: "it is appropriate to explore matters of history in this way, solely to assist on the issues that are to be determined in this trial (i.e., the crimes charged) by placing them in their alleged factual context."[52] Fulford furnished advance verbal summaries of the submissions by the prosecution and victim's groups on issues they wished to examine the expert witness on, yet another instance of the ICC's unique level of judicial case management.

The Presiding Judge commenced the questioning of the expert witness, something not seen, to my knowledge, at the ICTY and ICTR. Garretón's lengthy opening statement began with the Berlin Conference of 1885, which carved Africa into colonies of Europe, and he identified the ignoring of natural boundaries as one of the "major causes of the tragic events" in African history.[53] Although Garretón agreed with Prunier that the origins of the Ituri conflict were fundamentally economic rather than ethnic, he diverged on the ethnic origins and classification of groups. He classified the Hemas with Nilotic groups of the North and the Tutsi of Rwanda, to the satisfaction of the defense team. In so doing, Garretón used an outmoded terminology based on early-twentieth-century racial classifications not in common usage in the social sciences for decades, rather than Prunier's contemporary definition based on language. As we saw at the ICTR in the previous chapter, judges seem to feel more comfortable with passé racial and ethnic terminology, given its customary usage and aura of scientific stability and precision, however spurious it might be.

Garretón's history of Ituri posited generally nonviolent relations between Hemas and other groups such as the Lendus. Although there were some conflicts, these were resolved by the traditional leaders, the tribal chiefs.[54]

---

[52] 17 June, 2009, 3/18–4/8, 8/10–13.
[53] 17 June, 18/17–18.
[54] A point also made in Garretón's (2009:5) expert report to the court.

Peaceable ethnic cohabitation prevailed before and during colonialism, but all this changed with the intervention of outsiders. At one point in his testimony, Garretón listed ten "internationalized armed conflicts" occurring on DRC soil, of relevance to the trial because half of the charges against Lubanga related to war crimes committed in an international armed conflict.[55] Garretón (2009:6) pinpointed 1994 as the crucial date when the war in Rwanda spilled over into what was then Zaire. Both Rwanda and Uganda lent support to a rebellion fronted by Laurent Kabila, who renamed the country the Democratic Republic of the Congo in 1997. Garretón referred to the displacement of Rwandans as "a major cause of the violence" in the DRC. The displacement of Rwandans led to the absorption of the Hema into the Rwandan Tutsi and the ethnicizing and internationalizing of the local conflict made it much more acute: "As for the conflict between Hema and Lendu, what really sparked the violence was the presence of Rwandans."[56] Added to the Rwandan presence were Ugandan troops, who crossed the border into the DRC while pursuing an insurgency and exacerbated the violence: "These ethnic groups had lived together perfectly well. There had been conflicts. . . . [T]here had been clashes. But these conflicts had always been resolved successfully by traditional chiefs. Now a foreign element came into play and that is the Ugandan army, which was absolutely biased in favor of the Hema ethnic group."[57]

Ituri fell under foreign domination, and decisions over the fate of the population were made in Kampala, Uganda, and Kigali, Rwanda, rather than the country's ostensible capital, Kinshasa.[58] The two main foreign powers had different aims, however. Uganda was engaging in a counterinsurgency war, whereas Rwanda harbored territorial and geopolitical objectives. Paul Kagame's government in Rwanda secretly wished to hold a new "Berlin II Conference," reprising the Berlin conference of European colonial powers, and to redraw the boundaries of African states. Garretón portrayed this as "an absolute taboo in Africa at the time" that could have potentially plunged the region into an all-out war of states.[59] Garretón's extensive probing into the international dimensions of the conflict was rather unusual for an international criminal trial, and the Trial Chambers at the ICTY and ICTR generally abjured such combustible discussions.

After the judges had completed their examination, Mr. Joseph Keta, the lawyer from Bunia in Ituri, DRC, representing victims' groups, examined the

[55] 17 June, 48/22.
[56] 17 June, 80/22–3.
[57] 17 June, 49/18–23.
[58] 17 June, 82/7.
[59] 17 June, 87/25.

witness. This had never happened at the *ad hoc* tribunals because victims had no standing in the court, so it is intriguing to see how the innovation of including victims' legal representatives changed the dynamic of the trial. Keta posed long-winded questions to the expert witness, more elaborate pronouncements on the region and conflict than anything, and Judge Fulford intervened on several occasions to stop Keta from speechifying. Overall, the victims' legal representative seemed to hold two objectives in his cross-examination: to determine the ethnic and racial classifications of Hema and Lendu as Nilotic and Sudanese groups, respectively, and to blame the Hema as a group for the conflict. The ethnic character of the conflict was of appreciably more interest to Keta than either the prosecutor or the expert witness, and Garretón resisted the lawyer's attempts to comprehend the conflict through an ethnic lens.[60]

In accordance with Rule 140(2) of the ICC Rules of Procedure and Evidence, the defense has the right to be the last party to examine a witness. Garretón was handled more gently during the defense cross-examination than was Prunier, with Biju-Duval adopting a more respectful and careful demeanor. In many ways, Garretón was the more vulnerable target because he had significantly less experience and knowledge of Africa and the DRC in particular. Still, as the court-appointed expert chosen by the judges, Garretón was more authorized by the court and by default considered more neutral and impartial. It would be a poor strategy for the parties to confront him in the way that Prunier was tested by the defense, as a confrontation with the witness could potentially antagonize the judges. Such considerations did not deflect the content or direction of Biju-Duval's cross-examination, however. The defense lawyer launched into the same line of questioning of Garretón as he had with the prosecution expert witness Prunier. Biju-Duval recounted a series of incidents in which Hemas were attacked by other ethnic groups and took flight and sought refuge with Ugandan forces.[61] That Biju-Duval was laying the foundations for a necessity defense was obvious from questions such as this one: "Did this situation in which the civilian population suffered massacres possibly lead certain communities – and I will focus my question on the Hema community specifically – did this situation potentially lead this community to a concern for its own protection?"[62] The defense counsel suggested that the Hema armed themselves and created militias not to pursue a policy of aggression but out of a purely defensive "security motive."[63]

---

[60] 18 June, 20/19–25, 21/1–4.
[61] 18 June 2009, 57–62.
[62] 18 June, 68/22–5.
[63] 18 June, 70/8.

At this point in the trial, Garretón appeared caught between two poles of pro-Hema and anti-Hema propaganda, with the defense counsel and victims' representatives replaying local ethnic animosities in the Ituri region on the stage of an international courtroom in The Hague. This restating of ethnic and national and religious animosities also occurred at the ICTY and ICTR, but in the conventional adversarial relationship between prosecution and defense. At the ICC, not only are the judges interposed between the two opposed parties – so are the victims, who may share the interests of the prosecution in many ways but who also have their own fixations and, indeed, axes to grind. This creates a much more complex courtroom scenario, where fact and expert witnesses are pulled in four directions at once instead of just the usual two. Whether this novel format results in a fuller account of the events leading up to a conflict remains to be seen.

Garretón dealt with all this with equanimity, accepting many of the rhetorical points put to him and showing little impatience or irritation. His overall approach and delivery were markedly plainer than the prosecution witness: he relied on documents. Garretón (2009:1) opened his expert report to the court with a list of the documents on which the report was based, primarily UN reports he had submitted to UN bodies such as the Security Council, the General Assembly, and the Commission on Human Rights. Unlike Prunier, Garretón had held an official UN position in Ituri, as the former UN Special Rapporteur on Human Rights, which granted him more authority and made him the official source of the very documents to which he referred. Garretón did not offer overly complicated answers to questions or engage in sweeping generalizations about Africa and analogous situations elsewhere on the continent or in the world. He adopted the disinterested and realist approach to facts that judges value. In contrast to Prunier's relativism and reliance on undocumented field interviews (also known as "hearsay" in a common law court), Garretón stood by the credibility of his sources. He defended the integrity of the investigations carried out by the UN Mission in the DRC and by the representatives of the UN High Commissioner for Human Rights stationed in Ituri. Garretón's presence on the stand was most forceful and emphatic when he resisted attempts by Biju-Duval to introduce a corrosive note of uncertainty into his findings. One incident that generated controversy concerned the murder of six staff of the International Committee of the Red Cross (ICRC) in 2001, shortly after Garretón released a report on human rights violations in the region. There was some speculation locally that the murders were an act of retaliation. Rebuffing Biju-Duval's expressions of disbelief, Garretón took the categorical view that the ICRC staff were "undoubtedly" killed by

Hema militia members.[64] No everything-is-elastic African-style truths were evident there.

These exchanges allow for further insights into the distinctiveness of scholarly and legal ways of knowing, and into the reception of two different types of expertise: that of an experienced African historian and that of a UN-appointed lawyer dedicated to documenting human rights violations. The latter figure was more able to provide the type of knowledge recognized and required by the courtroom, as that had been Garretón's engagement with Africa all along – producing facts that would stand up in a court of law. As a result, the redoubtable Garretón was almost certainly more effective as an expert witness, although we cannot know definitively until the Trial Chamber releases its judgment. What is undeniable is that by emphatically rejecting both the defense's attempt to sow doubt about the conflict and the defense's desire to comprehend the conflict through the lens of race and ethnicity, the court-appointed witness was of more value to the prosecution than was the prosecution's own expert witness.

8.5. HISTORY IN THE ABSENCE OF SPECIAL INTENT

The arrival of a new and permanent international criminal court promises a new relationship between international law and historical discussions of the origins and causes of international armed conflicts. Some aspects of the Lubanga trial are very familiar and reproduce many of the same strategies and arguments that we saw in the two *ad hoc* tribunals of the 1990s. In each setting, the defense aims to sow uncertainty about the alleged crimes and to represent any crimes as retaliatory responses that any rational person or group would carry out when faced with a mortal danger. Defense attempts at mitigation at the ICC can share the same structural imperative as at the ICTY, namely unified trials that combine trying the facts and sentencing. I have made clear my view that this mistakenly comingles two contradictory legal processes and incites the defense to distort the historical record in objectionable ways. However, the ICC Statute allows either party to request a bifurcated trial, and the Chamber may decide to hold a separate sentencing hearing.[65] In the meantime, Biju-Duval has not lost any opportunity to prefigure a necessity defense.

There are also many innovations at the ICC that make the feel of the trial quite different from trials at the ICTY and ICTR. Judicial case management,

[64] 17 June, 82/11–2.
[65] Article 76 of ICC Statute and Rule 143 of the Rules of Procedure and Evidence.

though increasingly a feature of the *ad hoc* tribunals, is already much more pronounced at the ICC. One of the main lessons that the architects of the ICC drew from the experiences of the ICTY and ICTR was the need to integrate more elements of the civil law system into the trial and to grant more powers to the judges to control both the procedural aspects and content of the trial. There are some benefits to this. Even though the overall Lubanga case has dragged on, the prosecution case itself took fewer than seven months, which is much shorter than comparable cases at the ICTY and ICTR. The courtroom also appears less polarized and adversarial, which seems to carry over into the treatment of witnesses, be they fact witnesses from the region or expert witnesses. Cross-examination may still be robust and testing, but thus far it seems that witnesses are more likely to be shielded by the bench, and up to this point (of course, this may change), they have received more respectful treatment at the ICC.[66] There are also drawbacks. In principle it may be desirable to give victims' legal representatives some role at the Court, but in practice, in the Lubanga trial they channeled local ethnic antipathies into the courtroom and did not especially enhance the quality of the proceedings. Further, the enhanced managerial judging model may grant too much authority to judges to shape the content of the defense and prosecution cases, thus undermining the parties' ability either to defend the accused or to pursue the charges with vigor.

One of the more remarkable things about the Lubanga trial compared with other trials included in this book is just how unimportant DRC and Ituri history was to the prosecution case. In reviewing the prosecution's questioning of both Prunier and Garretón, one gets a sense that very little is at stake in their testimony for the prosecution. This results in part from the nature of the charges against the accused. The charge of recruiting child soldiers in a localized region is most unlike genocide or crimes against humanity such as persecution. The charges against Lubanga do not require such extensive proof of widespread and systematic crimes or a connection to a policy or program of the state. Crucially, no additional element of intent is required to prove the crimes. Lubanga's criminal intention is self-evidently a key point of dispute in the trial, but the prosecution is not required to prove special intent, as in genocide cases. The charges do not demand proof of discriminatory intent, as is required to uphold charges of persecution at the ICTY or of charges of crimes against humanity at the ICTR. Because special intent and discriminatory intent are not central to proving the crimes, and there is general agreement that though the conflict took on ethnic dimensions, it did not originate in ethnic animosity, the prosecution can afford to focus more narrowly on the

---

[66] The ICC also has a specially dedicated Victims and Witnesses Unit (VWU).

immediate facts of the case. It need not, as some prosecutors felt they had to at the ICTY, delve back into history to demonstrate a long-standing animus between groups that had a causal effect on modern ideology and actions. This comparison of the place of historical arguments at the ICC, ICTY, and ICTR can help confirm one of the main deductions of this book. Where an additional threshold of intention (e.g., special intent, discriminatory intent) is central to the criminal charges, a trial is more likely to feature historical evidence, and that evidence is more likely to be intensely contested by the opposing parties.

9

Conclusion: New Directions in International Criminal Trials

9.1. THROUGH THE PAST, DARKLY

Criminal law's methods for determining the facts have been transformed by the rise of modern science since the seventeenth century, when the French court trying Jean Calas for murder held that joining many light pieces of evidence together created a grave one, and two grave ones added up to a violent one, at which point questioning the accused under torture was deemed warranted.[1] Yet modern law still constitutes a distinctive system of knowledge that is guided by its own principles for comprehending human behavior. The evidence allowed in a trial regarding the actions and intentions of accused persons is circumscribed with guidelines that steer jurists away from both specialist and nonspecialist (read "commonsense") forms of knowing into a domain that is uniquely legal. Upon reviewing numerous trials at three international justice institutions, it is apparent that the critiques of domestic law presented at the beginning of this book can also apply to international criminal tribunals. Legal ways of knowing at international tribunals are at times utterly distinctive, as seen in their predilection (especially in leadership cases) for documents over other forms of evidence and witnessing. Not only are documents preferred as sources, but also there exists a hierarchy of documents in which primary documents are accorded greater probative value than secondary documents, and official documents are given more weight than unofficial ones. When they construe documents as the solid basis for objective knowledge about a situation, international courts may overlook the degree to which documents are created by individuals and are therefore just as "subjective" and contingent as other forms of evidence.

---

[1] Furbank (2005:68).

At times, then, it seems as if the law operates in a hermetically sealed textual universe of tightly controlled documentary evidence. These observations substantiate recent research by law-and-society scholars such as Sarat et al. (2007) and anthropologists such as Latour (2004), who notes that even though the law may officially endorse the scientific method, its ways of knowing diverge widely from science and epistemological realism. In his study of the supreme French legal body the Conseil d'État, Latour describes how *conseillers* move from one text to another; from case files to legal case law books to memoranda, "always remaining in the world of texts" (75). Contrasting scientific and legal ways of knowing, Latour claims that there is no truth to law in a scientific sense, as law establishes truth only through its own legal rhetoric and textual exegesis: "The strange thing about legal objectivity is that it quite literally is *object-less*, and is sustained entirely by the production of a mental state, a bodily *hexis*, but is still quite unable to resign its faculty of judgment by appealing to incontrovertible facts" (107). Compared with science, legal epistemology is "a mode of unfettered arbitrariness" (109). Latour's comments accurately depict one aspect of fact-finding in international trials, even if they overstate law's reliance on documents and neglect other, nondocumentary forms of evidence (e.g., the oral testimonies of fact witnesses).

International criminal law's conceptions of causality and determination also diverge from those of science, social science, or history, which confirms studies in national court settings by legal anthropologists such as Anthony Good (2007:30–1). The causal connections between two acts or events is an intricately regulated area of law, in which various levels of causality are isolated and accorded distinct weight in judgment and sentencing. Criminal courts require linear connections that establish which acts caused which others, and they seek a particular kind of knowledge about the subjective intentions of actors committing said acts, with a view to assigning criminal responsibility. As Good (2007:30) remarks, "For lawyers . . . an event's cause is inseparable from allocation of responsibility for it." History and social science are less concerned with establishing causality and apportioning responsibility, and when they do perceive a link between events, their assertions often acknowledge a greater level of uncertainty. The greatest disparity of all, however, lies in the degree to which historical and social science research recognizes multiple layers of causality and apprehends connections between events in a systemic and holistic manner. Lawyers and judges are more likely to radically pare down the context so as to isolate the events and acts. Although this may be necessary to arrive at a clear-cut determination, legal decontextualization comes at a high price. The difference of opinion concerning causality explains why scholars often refused to change their entire understanding of a conflict while on the stand, after cross-examining attorneys presented them with an incontrovertible piece of evidence about a single event. Of course, some experts may have been simply evading unpalatable truths when they replied, "It is more complex than that" to a prosecutor or defense attorney, but many were defending an ingrained historical and sociological axiom; namely, any single human act is embedded in an intricate matrix of causal relations.

These reflections go some way toward explaining why expert-witness evidence regarding the underlying character of an armed conflict was often lost in translation in the international criminal courtroom. At the same time, an inordinate emphasis on the contrasts between legal and nonlegal ways of knowing can lead to an incomplete picture. International trials are not driven by two disconnected logics, one inside and the other outside the law, that clash with each other. Overstressing the divergence between legal and historical ways of knowing can forestall a more complete awareness of how they are effectively combined in some international criminal trials. One of the main findings of this book is that, like it or not, historical discussions are a permanent feature of international criminal justice, because historical evidence has become an integral part of prosecution and defense cases. History has legal relevance and is not merely a "chapeau" requirement emanating from the florid preamble of an international criminal tribunal statute.

The parties call expert witnesses to give historical and background testimony in pursuit of decidedly legal objectives that arise from the imperatives of international legal concepts. Despite their opposed goals, both the prosecution and defense employ history for analogous purposes, as when they review the origins of the armed conflict so as to frame the crimes contained in the indictment. Even as historical discussions that frame a set of crimes articulate only an indirect causality, the parties take advantage of their weak determinative force to cast the character of the accused in an oblique light (or shadow). Historical research has contributed significantly to the construction of prosecution and defense theories of the case. Historians introducing documents in the trial chamber have constructed the narrative scaffolding on which individual pieces of evidence (e.g., primary documents) might be hung. Certain lines of argumentation, however, are specific to the parties. As we saw in the monumental history of the Slobodan Milošević trial, some prosecution teams reinforced their case for special intent to commit genocide by reference to a long-standing animus nurtured in a nationalist mind-set. For their part, defense teams used history in the service of a capacity defense (the chaos defense) when they made historical references to a Bosnian culture of vengeance and to extensive popular participation in intercommunal violence.

Defense lawyers have sought to mitigate the sentence imposed on the accused by chronicling a lengthy history of mortal threats and provocations against the accused and his or her social group.

If we concentrate on the concrete and changing strategies of legal actors rather than the clash of two abstract logics, then we are obliged to make more cautious generalizations about international criminal law. Understanding the place of contextual evidence and expert witnesses requires close attention to the charges in each case, the statutory framework of each tribunal, and the internal organizational transformations occurring over time. Much of what happens in a trial depends on the kind of case it is and, more specifically, on the nature of the charges. In reviewing various international trials, it appears that the parties introduce more historical evidence when the charges require proof of special intent (e.g., genocide) or discriminatory intent (e.g., persecution). Next, each international criminal tribunal operates with a different mandate, statute, and rules of procedure and evidence. As we saw in Chapter 7, the ICTR Statute required proof of discriminatory intent for all crimes against humanity, whereas other tribunals do not, and this led to distortions in the ICTR's account of Rwandan history and society. Although the ICTY and ICTR were constituted as adversarial tribunals, the ICC began its work with a civil law model already in place, which gives its trials a unique flavor all of their own. Finally, the willingness to embrace or reject historical evidence seems to change over the life of an institution. All three tribunals included in this book were more receptive to background evidence in their first few trials, but this space closed down at the *ad hoc* tribunals as they adopted a managerial judging model.

Even as we recognize the distinctiveness of legal epistemology, the actual record of trials at the ICC, ICTR, and ICTY mitigates an overwhelmingly negative assessment of the relationship between law and history. In a number of trials, historical and background experts provided the kind of contextual knowledge necessary to make sense of an armed conflict and to see the conflict as a broader social and cultural phenomenon, not just as a procession of discrete violations of international humanitarian law. In the *Brđanin* trial, the prosecution called internal and external experts who presented complementary microhistories and elegantly weaved a web of context surrounding the crimes. Their expert testimony composed a narrative arc that gave order and unity to the disparate documents and items of evidence in the case. The prosecution does not hold a monopoly on historical truths, and it can at times succumb to strong legal imperatives to oversystematize the organizational dimensions of an armed conflict. In ICTY trials of Bosnian Serbs, there was a genuine need for the defense to test the prosecution's claims that a centrally coordinated and coherently orchestrated Serb policy existed throughout Bosnia and to bring contrary evidence showing a long-standing fragmentation of governance structures. In such cases, the truth of the historical matters in dispute often lay in the unresolved tension between the defense and prosecution accounts, which illustrates the value of courtroom historical discussion, regardless of whether either version is exactly correct in its entirety. Without such open debate about the past, the accounts of armed conflicts produced by international courts would be impoverished and, in a profound way, utterly incomprehensible.

Finally, we ought to recognize the ways in which the legal process, idiosyncratic as it is, can augment and enhance standard historical research methods. Although the capacity of the adversarial legal process to try mass crimes has been repeatedly called into question, this method has the advantage of testing the evidence thoroughly and repeatedly. Whereas a historian or social scientist writing an account of a war may make a point, add a few supplementary footnotes, and then move on, international criminal tribunals return again and again to scrutinize a major speech, military order, or a key programmatic statement such as Radovan Karadžić's "Six Strategic Goals." Ultimately, this can contribute to creating a firm baseline of understanding that serves as a bulwark against the historical revisionism, denial, and outright lies about the past that are prevalent in the public culture of postconflict countries.

9.2. LOOKING TO THE FUTURE

At the risk of hubris, this final section seeks to identify good practice that can be applied in the future, and it offers suggestions for improving the creation, presentation, and reception of historical evidence in international criminal trials. A variety of proposals are aired, and not all of them are complementary, as the aim is to encourage thought and discussion on the topic rather than to propose a single blueprint for change. The first set of proposals concerns the rules, regulations, and statutes of international tribunals.

A dominant thread in the discussion has been the hybrid system adopted by international criminal tribunals and the changing mixture of adversarial and civil law rules and procedures in each tribunal. I am persuaded that the ICC, with its more civil law and managerial system, has created a positive institutional setting for hearing historical and expert-witness evidence in the courtroom and that it represents a model for the future. Tribunals could follow the ICC's lead by maintaining a list of external expert witnesses nominated by the parties, whose expertise has been verified in advance, and whose presence in a trial all parties accept. If the parties can all reach agreement on the terms of their participation, court-appointed experts are preferable because the expert's first loyalty is to the court rather than to the legal or ideological cause of one of the parties. By calling more court-appointed experts who have been jointly instructed, there might be fewer partisan historical accounts and hostile cross-examination of experts. A move to employing pretrial conferences as seen at the ICC can be productive when the parties agree on joint instructions regarding, among other things, the documentary record to be reviewed by the expert and the themes and time period the expert should analyze. Pretrial conferences should create as long a list as possible of agreed-on facts, including historical facts, which potentially hastens the judge's process of codifying facts of common knowledge about a conflict. At the ICC, by the time a trial gets under way, the pretrial conferences have usually hammered out a consensus on a number of issues, a process that takes much longer in the more adversarial setting of the Trial Chamber. As a caveat, not all civil law modifications are to be embraced. Along with other observers, I sense that the ICC has gone too far down this road – judges have excessive authority, for instance, to "change the legal characterization of facts" (Regulation 55), to amend the charges against the accused at a confirmation hearing (as occurred in the Lubanga and Bemba trials), and to inordinately influence the content of the prosecution and defense cases.

International tribunals presently lack an explicit and detailed statement of the criteria to be used by judges when presented with historical and social science expert knowledge. International criminal law desperately needs an international equivalent of *Daubert*, the trilogy of U.S. Supreme Court cases that codified how U.S. courts should assess expert evidence. Whether or not one agrees with how *Daubert* endorsed Karl Popper's theory of knowledge, and whether individual states and judges actually grasp and follow *Daubert's* guidelines, at least a blueprint for evaluating expert evidence exists, and the rules of the game are explicitly revealed for all to see. Given the salience of the civil law approach to evidence in international criminal institutions, such a statement would likely look nothing like *Daubert* in terms of its content, but the effect would be the same: to clarify what tests are to be applied to expert-witness evidence so as to reduce the variation in tribunal judgments, some of which incorporate large amount of expert evidence and some of which utterly dismiss such evidence. Judicial guidelines for evaluating expert-witness evidence could be laid out in the judgment or decision of an appeals chamber of an international criminal tribunal. Alternatively, it could be formulated by a combined panel of judges drawn from several international tribunals, assisted by the UN International Law Commission, which has navigated a path through thorny problems in international law since 1949.

The statutes of all future international criminal tribunals should make provision for separate stages of judgment and sentencing. The sentencing component needs to be taken out of the body of the trial to create two distinct phases. First, the trial chamber would make findings of fact regarding the charges and then the same chamber would consider aggravating or mitigating factors affecting the charges that have already been proved. As seen in Chapter 6, the ICTY and ICTR statutes placed the defense in a disadvantaged and contradictory position, having to argue for both innocence and mitigation during a trial. This modification would have the added benefit of removing the need for *tu quoque* arguments in the body of the trial and inserting them where they might be more appropriate, in a discrete sentencing hearing. As argued in Chapter 4, the prosecution has led more historical evidence in trials where the charges include an added element of intent, either as special intent or discriminatory intent. An excessive concern with historical matters in an effort to fulfill a *mens rea* requirement can distort a court's perception of the past, as the prosecution bends history to display a long-standing intergroup animus. An added element of intent is an inherent part of the crimes of genocide and persecution, but conventionally it is not a requirement for proving other crimes against humanity. Therefore, future statutes of international criminal tribunals should not include a discriminatory intent requirement for all crimes against humanity, as in the ICTR Statute.

Now for the tricky part: to consider the actors in the legal process – jurists, prosecutors, defense attorneys, and expert witnesses – and to suggest ways to overcome the frustrating insularity of both legal actors and scholars, in order to facilitate meaningful dialogue between them.

Even the hint of a suggestion that international judges may not possess all the requisite knowledge needed to try the cases brought before them is usually met with profound resistance by judges and others. This is exacerbated in international tribunals because the majority of judges are from inquisitorial legal systems in which they are accustomed to assuming the roles of prosecution, defense, and jury, and in which they enjoy a status not normally accorded to common law judges. As we saw in Chapter 3, survey research on U.S. judges has demonstrated that they are no more scientifically literate than the broader population. Only a small minority could understand and apply the scientific criteria that have been formulated at the federal level for the purpose of evaluating expert evidence. Many are dismissive of historical and social science research, even that which is at the experimental hard-science end of the continuum. This has prompted some commentators to identify a pressing "need for more science based judicial education."[2] Unfortunately,

---

[2] Gatowski et al. (2001:455).

there is presently no comparable research on international criminal tribunal judges, but I speculate that they are in no better or worse a position than U.S. judges to apprehend and interrogate social science and historical research in an informed manner. From the scores of trial transcripts I have read, it is apparent that some judges can follow and digest expert evidence and ask probing questions of experts. Many others, however, seem ill at ease and unprepared to engage seriously with another system of knowledge.

There are tangible benefits to having judges who are familiar with the methods and theories of history and the social sciences, and especially with demography, statistics, and historical research on ideology and nationalism. International criminal trials will only be enhanced by judges who can discern a sophisticated research design from a flawed one can translate fluidly between legal and nonlegal ways of knowing. This could necessarily entail some kind of training program for judges that can provide a solid grounding in humanistic and scientific forms of inquiry. Ongoing support for judges would be necessary, which could be achieved by forming a team of research advisers in the chambers who could furnish a research capacity independent of the parties. During a trial, research officers in judges' chambers would assist judges, advising them on the process of evaluation of the expert reports submitted by the prosecution and defense. Judges would still make the final determination, but they would receive backup assistance in identifying any weaknesses in the research design and in selecting any court-appointed experts that they may wish to call to fill the gaps in the parties' accounts.

For some inexplicable reason, the positive experience of the Leadership Research Team (LRT) and the Military Analysis Team in the Office of the Prosecutor at the ICTY has not been reproduced in subsequent international criminal tribunals. A recent joint report of the ICTY and the UN Interregional Crime and Justice Research Institute (UNICRI) dedicated to preserving the legacy of the Tribunal (ICTY 2009:25) recommended as follows: "A prosecution team attached to a specialized tribunal or war crimes unit, that employs a multi-disciplinary approach to investigations, should develop a great deal of in-house expertise. . . . [T]he prosecution must take care to ensure that in-house experts retain the necessary degree of detachment if they are to give evidence." To reaffirm the findings and recommendations of this report, the Office of the Prosecutor at all international criminal tribunals should contain a research unit similar to the LRT. This kind of team operates best when there is a loose reporting relationship with prosecuting attorneys and enough independence and autonomy to justify being called to testify in a trial as an expert witness. Research teams ought to include regional experts not only at country-specific tribunals (e.g., Cambodia, Lebanon, Sierra Leone) but also at the ICC, given its initial concentration on a few locales such as Central Africa and Africa's Great Lakes region. Researchers would provide the knowledge necessary to understand the social, cultural, and historical milieus and would possess the methodological expertise to generate accurate statistical and demographic data. They would assist prosecutors in the development of the theory of the case. As at the LRT, they would process documentary material brought in by investigators and prosecutors, and they would share their archival expertise in reports and court testimony. They would liaise with external consultants, compile documents for them to analyze, and help explain to them their work and the scope of their mandate.

As for the training and education of prosecuting and defense attorneys, I am rather more skeptical. Each party uses research material to buttress its arguments for guilt or innocence, and to expect anything else is probably naive. Antagonism between two parties in the courtroom is a time-honored feature of Anglo-American criminal law, and there are many good reasons for it. Despite these comments, both prosecutors and defense attorneys could afford to translate more effectively between the languages of different disciplines in the courtroom. Concretely, this would involve handling expert witnesses rather differently and making more of an effort to explain to judges the experts' methods and theories, as well as the relevance of expert reports and testimony to the immediate task of legal fact-finding. As we have seen, defense attorneys remonstrate about the inequality of arms at international criminal tribunals, and in my view, their complaints do have a basis. Many human rights advocates of international justice overlook the fact that, over the long term, the credibility of international law requires skilled and well-resourced defense teams with a comparable research capacity to the prosecution. When the ICTY and ICTR were first founded, defense counsel did not even have an office on the tribunal premises, and although this situation has improved, defense teams could use significantly more assistance from the legal institutions they work in. Defense teams stand to gain a great deal from a semiautonomous research unit that can provide them with high-quality research and analysis and engage a variety of activities, from broad sociocultural study to combing documentary collections.

Expert witnesses for both the defense and prosecution require more guidance and training from international criminal justice institutions, to be provided by a neutral body such as the registry. Registry staff would familiarize the uninitiated with the place of experts in the overall criminal law process and explain how to serve as a credible and reliable expert witness. With a better understanding of what they are getting into, potential experts would be able to make a more informed decision about proceeding further. Experts need to be told in advance that the court requires a level of primary documentation above and beyond what is usually customary in their own discipline's publications.

The often-unstated scholarly assumptions about knowledge need to be made explicit in the criminal courtroom, from the highly circumscribed understandings of expertise to the level of doubt conveyed by different verbal expressions. Expert witnesses must be able to explain the degree of uncertainty to judges who may not fully understand measurement bias or a margin of error in a statistical survey, or how those concepts relate to the legal idea of "beyond reasonable doubt." Experts must outline their methods in a way that is comprehensible to nonspecialists and be willing to field questions regarding those methods.

Without prior experience, even experts who are highly esteemed in their profession seldom anticipate the unfamiliarity of the courtroom, and they often treat it as a wide-ranging seminar, which does not sit well with the judges. Learning to give economical answers without sacrificing the integrity of historical and social science research is truly an art. Other simple pieces of advice would go a long way toward forestalling the errors commonly committed by scholars in the Trial Chamber: avoid speculation and refrain from commenting on matters that exceed your expertise; do not allow yourself to be drawn into controversies not included in your expert report; take a balanced approach; show no animus toward the accused or his or her group; refrain from long and convoluted answers to questions; and perhaps most important, back up all your assertions with empirical evidence contained in documents that can be referenced.

There are also a number of radical structural alternatives to the present system that might also be considered, with the aim of taking court history out of the more or less exclusive control of the opposed parties. For instance, one might envisage an international criminal research unit that is independent not only of the defense and prosecution but also of an international criminal court. Here, independent researchers would have access to all the documentary and analytical material recovered by investigators of the Office of the Prosecutor and by the defense, and they would be called by judges and ideally jointly instructed by the parties. This idea is not my own; it first occurred to me when reading a survey response by a senior member of the ICTY's Office of the Prosecutor:

> I regard the work done by historians and social scientists, both staff and outsiders as invaluable. It must be borne in mind, however, (1) that a criminal trial is held primarily to determine guilt or innocence of individual accused, (2) that lawyers and judges are not trained historians, (3) that lawyers and judges will always seek and prefer simple explanations when reality is much more complex, and (4) under the adversarial system, trial lawyers prefer a version of history that supports their case (they are not looking for objective [?] truth). As someone with some background in and a great interest in history,

as well as a legal background, I do have some reservations about using a court room to flesh out [historical] issues. There is a tendency to produce "cooked history." . . . Perhaps, and I say this with a great deal of trepidation, it would have been better to use historians more as "objective, in so far as possible" friends of the court and not as experts for a given side.

There is no preexisting institutional model that could be followed, although some precursors might help inform our thinking, such as the Institut für Zeit-geschichte (IFZ, or Institute of Contemporary History), established in Munich in 1949 that has contributed greatly to the understanding of the rise of National Socialism and militarism in Germany before World War II. This is a national institution, but one could also imagine a new research institution established within the UN system, or perhaps associated with existing UN bodies such as the UNICRI. An independent research institute could serve a number of international criminal courts and tribunals around the world. The potential advantages of this arrangement are significant. Although it would perhaps not augur the end of the familiar sight of warring experts fighting to a stalemate, it might at least diminish the level of hostilities. Training of expert witness would be less of an issue, as experts would build up courtroom experience over time. Judges may worry less about credibility and reliability of expert reports and pay more attention to experts who know the kind of evidence that a criminal law courtroom is looking for. An independent research institution could resolve the inequality-of-arms problem, as the defense and prosecution would receive the same reports from the same researchers. Both the defense and prosecution would have access to vast government archives at more or less the same time, thereby reducing the number of incidents surrounding dis-closure of information that have beleaguered international prosecutors. The complex confidentiality arrangements entered into with governments would still be a limiting factor, but an institution separate from a tribunal might have more room for maneuver in this regard. Finally, an independent research body might also resolve a few pressing issues that face the ICTY and ICTR as they come to the end of their work: Where does all the trial evidence and documen-tation go when the tribunals close their doors? How might historians and other researchers gain greater access to the treasure trove of information amassed by the tribunals and begin the process of evaluating the information, outside of the legal process of attributing individual criminal responsibility? Ultimately, international criminal tribunals come and go, but historical research on the underlying factors of armed conflict, conducted for its own sake, carries on.

Appendix: Methodology and the Survey Instrument

The survey instrument was developed in early 2009 by Andrew Corin, Ahmad Wais Wardak, and Richard Ashby Wilson, and a preliminary version was reviewed by the assistant director of the Center for Survey Research and Analysis at the University of Connecticut. The modified version was tested on a focus group of six individuals who were former ICTY staff members and consultant expert witnesses who had not been included in the survey. Participants in the focus group encouraged us to better define some of the terms being used, especially "historian" and "historical evidence." We included a fuller definition in the survey preamble and on the Internet page linked to the survey, which explained the rationale for the research project.

The questions that constituted the final survey instrument were divided into two parts. Part 1 elicited information about the background of respondents, including the organ of the ICTY (including defense) with which the respondent was last associated, the form and length of the respondent's participation in the work of the ICTY, the nature of the respondent's professional activities at the time when he or she first became associated with the ICTY, and the respondent's familiarity with the former Yugoslavia and criminal justice systems before his or her association with the Tribunal. Part 2 elicited responses on the substantive issues addressed by the survey. The survey comprised twenty-two numbered questions, although some of these were multiple related questions, thus, the number of questions to which a respondent could reply was in fact thirty-six. The format of the questions in part 2 varied between multiple choice (or multivalue) and true or false. The final open-ended question invited respondents to provide any comments that they chose, of any length, in regard to the survey. This question was phrased to allow remarks either about the topics addressed in the survey or about the survey itself and the manner in which it was compiled and conducted.

One limitation to the accessibility of the survey for prospective participants, and thus potentially to its objectivity, concerns language. The survey instrument was composed solely in English. Although this may have limited access for some potential respondents, it eliminated any possibility of ambiguous interpretation of questions and responses due to issues of translation. Moreover, because potential respondents were inevitably highly educated individuals, we judged that the number of such persons lacking sufficient knowledge of English to complete the survey would be sufficiently limited so as not to overly skew the results. For the final open-ended question, which allowed respondents to enter their own prose comments, we invited respondents to answer in one of several languages, including those of the former Yugoslavia.

One of the most challenging aspects of our preparation was compiling the pool of potential participants and securing the participation of a sufficient number of respondents from that pool. Defining a pool of desired participants was not in itself difficult. We initially anticipated soliciting participation from three bodies of persons who had participated in the work of the ICTY. The first consisted of former staff members of any organ (Office of the Prosecutor, Chambers, and Registry) of the ICTY. The second consisted of members of defense teams, as they are not members of the ICTY staff. The third group of participants was to be drawn from among external expert consultants who had participated in the work of the ICTY through expert testimony, submission of expert reports, or informal consultation with one or another organ of the ICTY (to the extent, of course, that such consultation was public knowledge). We sought to appeal to external expert consultants for both the prosecution and defense, including the defense teams for accused persons from various national and ethnic groups.

Defining a desired pool of participants proved less challenging than securing the participation of a sufficient number of such persons. It was our initial hope that the ICTY would agree to assist through the minimal step of informing staff members by e-mail of the existence of the survey. This would have ensured access to the survey for participants from across the spectrum of roles and perspectives represented in the three main organs of the ICTY: Registry, Office of the Prosecutor, and Chambers. The ICTY, however, declined to assist. In the absence of any public-domain lists of ICTY staff, we attempted to identify the names of potential participants and contact information for them from personal recollections, published sources such as the public-domain ICTY weekly bulletins for the years 1996–2004, and focused searches of trial transcripts. In light of the ICTY's attitude, moreover, we chose to actively solicit the participation only of former Tribunal staff members, so as to avoid placing current staff members in a delicate position. So as to exclude any possibility of violating the confidentiality of UN information, we limited our pool of potential participants to former staff members whose participation in the work of the ICTY was known through published open sources, and for whom we could identify contact information from publicly available sources.

These restrictions severely limited the pool of potential participants from the ranks of persons who had served as ICTY staff members. We were ultimately able to secure the participation of a sufficient number of former staff members from the Office of the Prosecutor. We judged responses from former staff members of the Registry and Chambers, however, insufficient to allow for significant comparison, and we reluctantly excluded them from the analysis. Securing the participation of members of defense teams proved less difficult. The Association of Defense Counsel maintains a public Internet site containing a list of names and contact information of members. Although some of the contact information proved out of date, this list, together with information that we discovered through our own public-domain searching, allowed us to contact a sufficient number of defense team members to allow for significant results.

With regard to external expert consultants, there exists no master list of such persons, nor are there public-domain witness lists for most ICTY cases, and so we found ourselves in much the same situation encountered with ICTY staff members. We therefore applied the same methodology and rules to identify those individuals. Names were drawn in part from the public-domain ICTY weekly bulletins between 1996 and 2004, as well as from transcripts of those cases for which we were aware that historical evidence had been used in the case. As with former ICTY staff members, we approached such individuals only through contact information that we identified from public-domain Internet sources. Finally, we published a call for participation directed to former ICTY staff members, members of defense teams, and expert consultants on the survey Web site. In an attempt to achieve a sufficiently large and balanced set of responses, we received a joint endorsement from both Richard Goldstone, the first prosecutor of the ICTY, and Michael G. Karnavas, president of the Association of Defense Counsel practicing before the ICTY.

The survey was administered online between March and September 2009. Before making any contact, we established an Internet page for the survey on the site of the Human Rights Institute of the University of Connecticut. The page contained a brief summary, the call for participation (including the endorsement), a rationale and discussion of the themes, recommended readings on the topic, and short biographies of the investigators. In total, 351 e-mail invitations to participate in the survey were sent out. The largest group approached were members of defense teams (201). Another 116 survey invitations were sent to former ICTY staff from the Office of the Prosecutor, Registry, and Chambers. Finally, we invited thirty-four consultant experts for the prosecution and defense, most of them from academic institutions in North America and Europe, including universities and research institutions in the former Yugoslavia. All responses were anonymous and confidential, and results were presented only in aggregate, with no names or other identifying information attached.

The total number of responses collected was seventy-five, which indicates a response rate of 21 percent. There were six incomplete responses, which were excluded from the analysis, leaving sixty-nine responses. That final figure was used to calculate a margin of error of 12 percent.[1] Disaggregating the overall numbers, we found that there was an approximate parity in responses between members of defense teams (twenty-five) and staff from the Office of the Prosecutor (thirty-one). Responses from staff of the Chambers and Registry were not at the same level, and as a result, we did not include those categories in our analysis of the results. Responses from external expert consultants (thirteen), though representing a smaller population, were judged sufficient for inclusion in the analysis. Although we recognize that these numbers are relatively small, we hope that they still might be sufficient to initiate a scholarly discussion on the uses of historical evidence at the ICTY and other international criminal tribunals and to serve as a pilot study for future large-sample surveys.

---

[1] Margin of error (MOE) is the probability of how different the true population is from the sample collected. How well a survey represents a population depends on margin of error and confidence level. In this survey, we calculated the MOE on the basis of the confidence level of 95 percent ($\alpha = 0.05$). The confidence level is the amount of uncertainty that can be tolerated. On the basis of our estimate, we expect that the total population of our participants would not be more than eight thousand. However, to be conservative, we used the total population of twenty thousand for our estimates. Further, we assumed the response distribution to be normal for the data we have collected for this study. On the basis of our analysis, we found the MOE to be 11.5 percent. To be conservative in our inferences about the study, we used a MOE of 12 percent.

Bibliography

NATIONAL LEGAL CASES

Brown v. Board of Education, 347 U.S. 483 (1954).
Brown v. Board of Education, 349 U.S. 294 (1955).
Daubert v. Merrell Dow Pharmaceuticals, Inc., 509 U.S. 579 (1993).
District of Columbia v. Heller, 128 S. Ct. 2783 (2008).
Folkes v. Chadd, 3 Dougl. 157, 99 Eng. Rep. 589 (K.B. 1782).
Frye v. United States, 293 F. 1013 (D.C. Cir. 1923).
Guardians Assn. v. Civil Svc. Comm'n, 463 U.S. 582 (1983).
Kumho Tire Co. v. Carmichael, 526 U.S. 137 (1999).
R. v. Moloney 1 A.C. 905 (1985).

INTERNATIONAL LAW

International Court of Justice (ICJ)

Application of the Convention on the Prevention and Punishment of the Crime of Genocide (*Bosnia and Herzegovina v. Serbia and Montenegro*). Judgment of 26 February 2007.

International Criminal Tribunal for Rwanda (ICTR)

Prosecutor v Jean Paul Akayesu (Case No. ICTR-96-4).
Trial Chamber Judgment, ICTR-96-4-T, 2 September, 1998 (*Akayesu* Trial Judgment).
Prosecutor v. Casimir Bizimungu (Case No. ICTR-99-45).
Decision on Casimir Bizimungu's Requests for Disclosure of the Bruguière Report and the Cooperation of France, ICTR Trial Chamber II, Case No. ICTR-99-45-T, 25 September 2006.
Prosecutor v. Jean Kambanda (Case No. ICTR-97-23).
Trial Chamber Judgment, ICTR-97-23-S, 4 September 1998 (*Kambanda* Trial Judgment).
Prosecutor v. Édouard Karemera, Mathieu Ngirumpatse, Joseph Nzirorera (Case No. ICTR-98-44).

Decision on the Prosecution Motion for Judicial Notice, ICTR-98–44-AR73(C), 9 November 2005.
Decision on Prosecutor's Interlocutory Appeal of Decision on Judicial Notice, ICTR-98–44-AR73(C), 16 June 2006.
Prosecutor v. Clément Kayishema and Obed Ruzindana (Case No. ICTR-95–1).
Trial Chamber Judgment, ICTR-95–1-T, 21 May 1999 (*Kayishema* Trial Judgment).
Prosecutor v. Alfred Musema (Case No. ICTR-96–13).
Trial Chamber Judgment, ICTR-96–13-T, 27 January 2000 (*Musema* Trial Judgment).
Prosecutor v. Ferdinand Nahimana, Jean-Bosco Barayagwisa, Hassan Ngeze (Case No. ICTR-99–52).
Trial Chamber Judgment, ICTR-99–52-T, 3 December 2003 (*Nahimana* Trial Judgment).
Prosecutor v. Georges Anderson Rutuganda (Case No. ICTR-96–3).
Trial Chamber Judgment, ICTR-96–3-T, 6 December 1999 (*Rutuganda* Trial Judgment).
Prosecutor v. Omar Serushago (Case No. ICTR-98–39).
Trial Chamber Judgment, ICTR-98–39-S, 5 February 1999 (*Serushago* Trial Judgment).

International Criminal Tribunal for the Former Yugoslavia (ICTY)

Prosecutor v. Vidoje Blagojević and Dragan Jokić (Case No. IT-02–60).
Trial Chamber Judgment, IT-02–60-T, 17 January 2005 (*Blagojević and Jokić* Trial Judgment).
Appeals Chamber Judgment, IT-02–60-A, 9 May 2007 (*Blagojević and Jokić* Appeals Judgment).
Prosecutor v. Tihomir Blaskić (Case No. IT-95–14).
Decision on the Standing Objection of the Defense to the Admission of Hearsay with No Inquiry as to Its Reliability, IT-95–14-T, 21 January 1998.
Trial Chamber Judgment, IT-95–14-T, 3 March 2000 (*Blaskić* Trial Judgment).
Appeals Chamber Judgment, IT-95–14-A, 29 July 2004 (*Blaskić* Appeals Judgment).
Prosecutor v. Radoslav Brđanin (Case No. IT-99–36).
Trial Chamber Judgment, IT-99–36-T, 1 September 2004 (*Brđanin* Trial Judgment).
Prosecutor v. Stanislav Galić (Case No. IT-98–29).
Trial Chamber Judgment, IT-98–29-T, 5 December 2003 (*Galić* Trial Judgment).
Prosecutor v. Sefer Halilović (Case No. IT-01–48).
Trial Chamber Judgment, IT-01–48-T, 6 November 2005 (*Halilović* Trial Judgment).
Prosecutor v. Goran Jelisić (Case No. IT-95–10).
Trial Chamber Judgment, IT-95–10-T, 14 December 1999 (*Jelisić* Trial Judgment).
Appeals Chamber Judgment, IT-95–10-A.5, July 2001 (*Jelisić* Appeals Judgment).
Prosecutor v. Dario Kordić and Mario Čerkez (Case No. IT-95–14/2).
Trial Chamber Judgment, IT-95–14/2-T, 26 February 2001 (*Kordić and Čerkez* Trial Judgment).
Prosecutor v. Momčilo Krajišnik (Case No. IT-00–39).
Trial Chamber Judgment, IT-00–39-T, 27 September 2006 (*Krajišnik* Trial Judgment).
Prosecutor v. Radislav Krstić (Case No. IT-98–33).
Trial Chamber Judgment, IT-98–33-T, 2 August 2001 (*Krstić* Trial Judgment).

Appeals Chamber Judgment, IT-98–33-A, 19 April 2004 (*Krstić* Appeals Judgment).
Prosecutor v. Zoran Kupreskić et al. (Case No. IT-95–16).
Decision on Evidence of the Good Character of the Accused and the Defence of *Tu Quoque*, IT-95–16-T, 17 February 1999.
Trial Chamber Judgment, IT-95–16-T, 14 January 2000 (*Kupreskić* et al. Trial Judgment).
Prosecutor v. Kvocka et al. (Case No. IT-98–30/1).
Appeals Chamber Judgment, IT-98–30/1-A, 28 February 2005 (*Kvocka* Appeals Judgment).
Prosecutor v. Slobodan Milošević (Case Nos. IT-99–37, IT-01–50, IT-01–51, IT-02–54).
Decision on Motion for Judgment of Acquittal. IT-02–54-T, 16 June 2004.
Prosecutor v. Momčilo Perišić (Case IT-04–81).
Decision on the Defense Motion to Exclude the Expert Reports of Robert Donia, IT-04–81-T, 27 October 2008.
Decision on the Defense Motion to Exclude the Expert Reports of Patrick Treanor, IT-04–81-T, 27 October 2008.
Decision on Admissibility of Expert Report of Patrick Treanor, Separate Opinion of Judge Moloto, IT-04–81-T, 27 November 2008.
Prosecutor v. Vujadin Popović et al. (Case IT-05–88).
Trial Chamber Judgment, IT-05–88-T, 10 June 2010 (*Popović* et al. Trial Judgment).
Prosecutor v. Jadranko Prlić et al. (Case IT-04–74).
Decision on Adoption of New Measures to Bring the Trial to an End within a Reasonable Time, IT-04–74-T, 13 November 2006.
Prosecutor v. Duško Sikirica and Others (Case No. IT-95–8).
Judgment on Defense Motions to Acquit, IT-95–8-T, 3 September 2001.
Prosecutor v. Blagoje Simić, Miroslav Tadić, and Simo Zarić (Case No. IT-95–9).
Trial Chamber Judgment, IT-95–9-T, 17 October 2003 (*Blagoje Simić* et al. Trial Judgment).
Prosecutor v. Milomir Stakić (Case No. IT-97–24).
Trial Chamber Judgment, IT-97–24-T, 31 July 2003 (*Stakić* Trial Judgment).
Prosecutor v. Duško Tadić (Case No. IT-94–1-T).
Decision on the Defence Motion for Interlocutory Appeal on Jurisdiction, IT-94–1-AR72, 2 October 1995.
Decision on the Defense Motion on Hearsay, IT-94–1-T, 5 August 1996.
Trial Chamber Judgment, IT-94–1-T, 7 May 1997 (*Tadić* Trial Judgment).
Appeals Chamber Judgment, IT-94–1-A, 15 July 1999 (*Tadić* Appeals Judgment).

BOOKS AND ARTICLES

Akhavan, Payam. 1998. "Justice in the Hague, Peace in the Former Yugoslavia?" *Human Rights Quarterly.* Vol. 20, No. 4, pp. 737–816.
Amman, Diane Marie. 1999. "Prosecutor v. Akayesu. Case ICTR-96–4-T." *American Journal of International Law.* Vol. 93, No. 1, pp. 195–199.
Anderson, Jill C. 2008. "Just Semantics: The Lost Readings of the Americans with Disabilities Act." *Yale Law Journal.* Vol. 117, pp. 992–1069.
Anderson, Terence, David Schum, and William Twining. 2005. *Analysis of Evidence.* 2nd ed. Cambridge: Cambridge University Press.

Anzulović, Branimir. 1999. *Heavenly Serbia: From Myth to Genocide*. New York: NYU Press.

Arendt, Hannah. 1965. *Eichmann in Jerusalem: A Report on the Banality of Evil*. Revised edition. New York: Viking Press.

Badar, Mohamed Elewa. 2005. "Mens Rea – Mistake of Law and Mistake of Fact in German Criminal Law: A Survey for International Criminal Tribunals." *International Criminal Law Review*. Vol. 5, No. 2, pp. 203–246.

Banać, Ivo. 1992. "The Fearful Asymmetry of War: The Causes and Consequences of Yugoslavia's Demise." *Daedalus*. Vol. 121, No. 2, pp. 141–174.

Barahona de Brito, Alexandra, C. Gonzaléz-Enríquez and P. Aguilar, eds. 2001. *The Politics of Memory: Transitional Justice in Democratizing Societies*. Oxford: Oxford University Press.

Bass, Gary Jonathan. 2000. *Stay the Hand of Vengeance: The Politics of War Crimes Tribunals*. Princeton, NJ: Princeton University Press.

Berger, John. 1972. *Ways of Seeing*. London: Penguin.

Berlin, Isaiah. 2001. *The Roots of Romanticism*. Princeton, NJ: Princeton University Press.

Blattmann, René, and Kirsten Bowman. 2008. "Achievements and Problems of the International Criminal Court." *Journal of International Criminal Justice*. Vol. 6, No. 4, pp. 711–730.

Bloxham, Donald. 2001. *Genocide on Trial: War Crimes Trials and the Formation of Holocaust History and Memory*. Oxford: Oxford University Press.

Boas, Gideon. 2001. "Developments in the Law of Procedure and Evidence at the International Criminal Tribunal for the Former Yugoslavia and the International Criminal Court." *Criminal Law Forum*. Vol. 12, pp. 167–183.

———. 2007. *The Milosevic Trial: Lessons for the Conduct of Complex International Criminal Proceedings*. Cambridge: Cambridge University Press.

Boraine, Alex. 2001. *A Country Unmasked*. Oxford: Oxford University Press.

Borneman, John. 1997. *Settling Accounts: Violence, Justice and Accountability in Post-socialist Europe*. Princeton, NJ: Princeton University Press.

Brace, Loring. 2005. *Race Is a Four Letter Word: The Genesis of the Concept*. New York: Oxford University Press.

Braman, Donald, and Dan M. Kahan. 2007. "Legal Realism as Psychological and Cultural (Not Political) Realism." In Austin Sarat, Lawrence Douglas, and Martha Merrill Umphrey (eds.), *How Law Knows*. Stanford, CA: Stanford University Press, pp. 93–125.

Brandwein, Pamela. 2007. "A Judicial Abandonment of Blacks? Rethinking the 'State Action' Cases of the Waite Court." *Law and Society Review*. Vol. 41, No. 2, pp. 343–386.

Bringa, Tone. 2002. "Averted Gaze: Genocide in Bosnia-Herzegovina, 1992–1995." In A. L. Hinton (ed.), *Annihilating Difference: The Anthropology of Genocide*. Berkeley: University of California Press, pp. 194–225.

Brooks, Peter, and Paul Gewirtz, eds. 1996. *Law's Stories: Narrative and Rhetoric in the Law*. New Haven, CT: Yale University Press.

Budding, Audrey Helfant. 2003. "Serbian Nationalism in the Twentieth Century: Historical Background and Context." Prosecution Exhibit 508. *Prosecutor v. Slobodan Milošević* (Case Nos. IT-99-37, IT-01-50, IT-01-51, IT-02-54).

Bundy, Colin. 1999. "South Africa: Truth...or Reconciliation." *Southern Africa Report*. Vol. 14, No. 4, p. 8.

Buur, Lars. 2001. "The South African Truth and Reconciliation Commission: A Technique of Nation-State Formation." In T. B. Hansen and F. Stepputat (eds.), *States of Imagination: Ethnographic Explorations of the Postcolonial State*. Durham, NC: Duke University Press, pp. 149–181.

Cassese, Antonio. 2003. *International Criminal Law*. Oxford: Oxford University Press.

Choi, Eun Young. 2007. "Veritas, Not Vengeance: An Examination of the Evidentiary Rules for Military Commissions in the War against Terrorism." *Harvard Civil Rights and Civil Liberties Law Review*. Vol. 42, No. 1, pp. 139–189.

Clarke, Kamari. 2009. *Fictions of Justice: The International Criminal Court and the Challenge of Legal Pluralism in Sub-Saharan Africa*. New York: Cambridge University Press.

Conley, J. M., and W. O'Barr. 1998. *Just Words: Law, Language and Power*. Chicago: University of Chicago Press.

Cover, Robert M. 1983. "The Supreme Court, 1982 Term: Foreword: *Nomos* and Narrative." *Harvard Law Review*. Vol. 97, No. 1, pp. 4–68.

Cowan, Jane, Marie-Bénédicte Dembour, and Richard A. Wilson. 2001. *Culture and Rights: Anthropological Perspectives*. Cambridge: Cambridge University Press.

Cryer, Robert, Hakan Friman, Darryl Robinson, and Elizabeth Wilmshurst. 2007. *An Introduction to International Criminal Law and Procedure*. Cambridge: Cambridge University Press.

Cushman, Thomas. 2009. "Genocidal Rupture and Performative Repair in Global Civil Society: Reconsidering the Discourse of Apology in the Face of Mass Atrocity." In Thomas Brudholm and Thomas Cushman (eds.), *The Religious in Responses to Mass Atrocity: Interdisciplinary Perspectives*. Cambridge: Cambridge University Press, pp. 213–241.

Danet, B. 1980. "Language in the Legal Process." *Law and Society Review*. Vol. 14, pp. 445–564.

DeLeire, Thomas. 2000. "The Unintended Consequences of the Americans with Disabilities Act." *Regulation*. Vol. 23, No. 1, pp. 21–24.

Del Ponte, Carla. 2008. *Madam Prosecutor: Confrontations with Humanity's Worst Criminals and the Culture of Impunity: A Memoir* (with Chuck Sudetic). New York: Other Press.

Dembour, Marie-Bénédicte, and E. Haslam. 2004. "Silencing Hearings? Victim-Witnesses at War Crimes Trials." *European Journal of International Law*. Vol. 15, No. 1, pp. 151–177.

Dembour, Marie-Bénédicte, and Tobias Kelly, eds. 2007. *Paths to International Justice: Social and Legal Perspectives*. Cambridge: Cambridge University Press.

Des Forges, Alison. 1999. *Leave None to Tell the Story: Genocide in Rwanda*. New York: Human Rights Watch.

Dickens, Charles. 1970. *Oliver Twist*. London: J. M. Dent and Sons. (First published serially 1837–1839.)

Dickinson, Laura. 2003. "Notes and Comments: The Promise of Hybrid Courts" *American Journal of International Law*. Vol. 97, No. 2, pp. 295–310.

Dixon, Rosalind. 2002. "Rape as a Crime in International Humanitarian Law: Where to from here?" *European Journal of International Law*. Vol. 13, No. 3, pp. 697–719.

Donia, Robert. 2001. "Bosanski Šamac and the History of Bosnia and Herzegovina." Prosecution Exhibit.P1. *Prosecutor v. Blagoje Simić, Miroslav Tadić, and Simo Zarić* (Case No. IT-95-9).

———. 2002. "Bosnian Krajina in the History of Bosnia and Herzegovina" Exhibit P53. *Prosecutor v. Radoslav Brđanin* (Case No. IT-99-36).

———. 2004. "Encountering the Past: History at the Yugoslav War Crimes Tribunal." *Journal of the International Institute: University of Michigan.* Winter–Spring/Summer, pp. 1–2, 15.

Dörmann, Knut. 2003. *Elements of War Crimes under the Rome Statute of the International Criminal Court: Sources and Commentary.* Cambridge: Cambridge University Press.

Douglas, Lawrence. 1995. "Film As Witness: Screening *Nazi Concentration Camps* Before the Nuremberg Tribunal." *Yale Law Journal.* Vol. 105, No. 2, pp. 449–481.

———. 2001. *The Memory of Judgment: Making Law and History in the Trials of the Holocaust.* New Haven, CT: Yale University Press.

Drumbl, Mark A. 2007. *Atrocity, Punishment, and International Law.* Cambridge: Cambridge University Press.

Dworkin, Ronald. 1977. "No Right Answer?" In P. M. S. Hacker and J. Raz (eds.), *Law, Morality and Society.* Oxford, UK: Clarendon Press, pp. 58–84.

———. 1986. *Law's Empire.* London: Fontana.

Eltringham, Nigel. 2004. *Accounting for Horror: Post-Genocide Debates in Rwanda.* London: Pluto Press.

———. 2006. "'Invaders Who Have Stolen the Country': The Hamitic Hypothesis, Race and the Rwandan Genocide." *Social Identities.* Vol. 12, No. 4, pp. 425–446.

Eriksen, Thomas. 1993. *Ethnicity and Nationalism: Anthropological Perspectives.* London: Pluto Press.

Evans, Richard J. 2002. "History, Memory and the Law: The Historian and Expert Witness." *History and Theory.* Vol. 41, No. 3, pp. 326–345.

Ewick, Patricia, and Susan Silbey. 1995. "Subversive Stories and Hegemonic Tales: Towards a Sociology of Narrative." *Law and Society Review.* Vol. 29, pp. 197–226.

Flint, Julie, and Alex de Waal. 2009. "Case Closed: A Prosecutor without Borders." *World Affairs.* Spring. http://www.worldaffairsjournal.org/articles/2009-Spring/full-DeWaalFlint.html.

Fleury-Steiner, Benjamin. 2002. "Narratives of the Death Sentence: Towards a Theory of Legal Narrativity." *Law and Society Review.* Vol. 36, No. 3, pp. 549–576.

Focardi, Filippo, and Lutz Klinkhammer. 2004. "The Question of Fascist Italy's War Crimes: The Construction of a Self-Acquitting Myth (1943–1948)." *Journal of Modern Italian Studies.* Vol. 9, No. 3, pp. 330–348.

Freeman, Michael. 1991. "The Theory and Prevention of Genocide." *Holocaust and Genocide Studies.* Vol. 6, No. 2, pp. 185–199.

Friedlander, Saul, ed., 1992. *Probing the Limits of Representation.* Cambridge, MA: Harvard University Press.

Friedman, Lawrence M. 2006. *A History of American Law.* 3rd ed. Norwalk, CT: Easton Press.

Furbank, P. N. 2005. "Cultivating Voltaire's Garden." *New York Review of Books.* 15 December 2005, pp. 68–70.

Galanter, Marc. 1974. "Why the 'Haves' Come Out Ahead: Speculations on the Limits of Legal Change." *Law and Society Review*. Vol. 9, pp. 95–160.

Garner, Bryan A., ed. 2006. *Black's Law Dictionary*. 3rd ed. St. Paul, MN: Thomson West.

Garretón, Roberto. 2009. "Report for the International Criminal Court." International Criminal Court: EVD-CHM-0005.

Gatowski, S. I., S. A. Dobbin, J. T. Richardson, G. P. Ginsburg, M. L. Merlino, and V. Dahir. 2001. "Asking the Gatekeepers: A National Survey of Judges and Judging Expert Evidence in a Post-*Daubert* World." *Law and Human Behavior*. Vol. 25, No. 5, pp. 433–458.

Geertz, Clifford. 1983. "Fact and Law in Comparative Perspective." In *Local Knowledge: Further Essays in Interpretative Anthropology*. New York: Basic Books, pp. 167–234.

Glenny, Misha. 1992. *The Fall of Yugoslavia*. London: Penguin.

———. 2001. *The Balkans: Nationalism, War & the Great Powers, 1804–1999*. London: Penguin.

Golsan, Richard J., ed. 2000a. *The Papon Affair: Memory and Justice on Trial*. New York: Routledge.

———. ed. 2000b. "History and the 'Duty to Memory' in Postwar France: The Pitfalls of an Ethic of Remembrance." In Howard Marchitello (ed.), *What Happens to History: The Renewal of Ethics in Contemporary Thought*. New York: Routledge, pp. 23–39.

Good, Anthony. 2007. *Anthropology and Expertise in the Asylum Courts*. London: Routledge.

———. 2008. "Cultural Evidence in Courts of Law." *Journal of the Royal Anthropological Institute*. Special Issue, pp. S47–S60.

Goodale Mark, and Sally Engle Merry. 2007. *The Practice of Human Rights: Tracking Law between the Global and the Local*. New York: Cambridge University Press.

Greenwalt, Alexander. 1999. "Rethinking Genocidal Intent: The Case for a Knowledge-Based Interpretation." *Columbia Law Review*. Vol. 99, No. 8, pp. 2259–2294.

Hagan, John. 2003. *Justice in the Balkans: Prosecuting War Crimes in the Hague Tribunal*. Chicago: University of Chicago Press.

Harris, Phil. 1993. *An Introduction to Law*. 4th ed. London: Butterworths.

Hartmann, Florence. 2007. *Paix et chatiment: Les guerres secrètes et la politique et de la justice internationales*. Paris: Flammarion.

———. 2008. "Vital Genocide Documents Concealed." Bosnian Institute. 21 January 2008. http://www.bosnia.org.uk/news/news_body.cfm?newsid=2341

Hazan, Pierre. 2004. *Justice in a Time of War: The True Story behind the International Criminal Tribunal for the Former Yugoslavia*. Translated by James Thomas Snyder. College Station: Texas A&M Press.

Helsinki Watch. 1993. *War Crimes in Bosnia-Hercegovina*. Vol. 2. New York: Human Rights Watch.

Hillgruber, Christian. 1998. "The Admission of New States to the International Community." *European Journal of International Law*. Vol. 9, pp. 491–509.

Hoare, Marko Attila. 2008. "Genocide in Bosnia and the Failure of International Justice." Working Paper Series No. 8, Helen Bamber Centre for the Study of Rights and Conflict at Kingston University, UK, April 2008.

International Criminal Court Rules of Procedure and Evidence. Adopted by the Assembly of States Parties. First session. New York, 3–10 September 2002. Official Records ICC-ASP/1/3. Legal citation: ICC-ASP/1/3, at 10, and Corr. 1 (2002), U.N. Doc. PCNICC/2000/1/Add.1 (2000).

International Criminal Tribunal for the Former Yugoslavia. 2006. *Rules of Procedure and Evidence.* IT/32/Rev.39. 22 September 2006. The Hague: ICTY.

———. 2009. *ICTY Manual on Developed Practices.* Turin: ICTY-UNICRI.

Jackson, Bernard S. 1994. "Narrative Theories and Legal Discourse." In Cristopher Nash (ed.), *Narrative in Culture: The Uses of Storytelling in the Sciences, Philosophy, and Literature.* London: Routledge, pp. 23–50.

Jackson, Jean. 2007. "Rights to Indigenous Culture in Colombia." In Mark Goodale and Sally Engle Merry (eds.), *The Practice of Human Rights: Tracking Law between the Global and the Local.* Cambridge: Cambridge University Press, pp. 204–241.

January, Sativa. 2009. "Tribunal Verité: Documenting Transitional Justice in Sierra Leone." *International Journal of Transitional Justice.* Vol. 3, No. 2, pp. 207–228.

Johansen, Robert. 2006. "The Impact of U.S. Policy toward the International Criminal Court." *Human Rights Quarterly.* Vol. 28, pp. 301–331.

Kecmanović, Nenad. 2002. "Report of the Expert Witness for the Defense in the Case of Blagoje Simić. Bosnia and Herzegovina in the Period from 1990–1995." Defense Exhibit D53/1. *Prosecutor v. Blagoje Simić, Miroslav Tadić, and Simo Zarić.* Case No. IT-95-9-T.

Kittichaisaree, K. 2001. *International Criminal Law.* Oxford: Oxford University Press.

Klarin, Mirko. 2009. "The Impact of the ICTY Trials on Public Opinion in the Former Yugoslavia." *Journal of International Criminal Justice.* Vol. 7, No. 1, pp. 89–96.

Kluger, Richard. 1976. *Simple Justice: The History of* Brown v. Board of Education *and Black America's Struggle for Equality.* New York: Knopf.

Kovera, Margaret Bull, and Bradley D. McAuliffe. 2000. The Effects of Peer Review and Evidence Quality on Judge Evaluations of Psychological Science: Are Judges Effective Gatekeepers? *Journal of Applied Psychology.* Vol. 85, pp. 574–586.

Lacey, Nicola. 1993. "A Clear Concept of Intention: Elusive or Illusory?" *Modern Law Review.* Vol. 56, No. 5, pp. 621–642.

———. 2007. "Space, Time and Function: Intersecting Principles of Responsibility across the Terrain of Criminal Justice." *Criminal Law and Philosophy.* Vol. 1, 233–250.

Langer, Máximo. 2005. "The Rise of Managerial Judging in International Criminal Law." *American Journal of Comparative Law,* Vol. 53, No. 4, pp. 835–909.

Latour, Bruno. 2004. "Scientific Objects and Legal Objectivity." In Alain Pottage and Martha Mundy (eds.), *Law, Anthropology and the Constitution of the Social: Making Persons and Things.* Cambridge: Cambridge University Press, pp. 73–114.

Lemkin, Raphael. 1944. *Axis Rule in Occupied Europe, Analysis of Government, Proposals for Redress.* Washington: Carnegie Endowment for International Peace.

Magnarella, Paul. 2000. *Justice in Africa: Rwanda's Genocide, its Courts, and the UN Criminal Tribunal.* Aldershot, UK: Ashgate.

Mamdani, Mahmood. 2001. *When Victims Become Killers: Colonialism, Nativism and the Genocide in Rwanda.* Oxford: James Currey.

Marrus, Michael. 1987. *The Holocaust in History.* Hanover, NH: University Press of New England.

————. 1997. *Nuremberg War Crimes Trial of 1945–6*. Boston, MA: Bedford Press.

Marrus, Michael, and Robert Paxton. 1995. *Vichy France and the Jews*. Stanford, CA: Stanford University Press.

Marsil, Dorothy F., Jean Montoya, David Ross, and Louise Graham. 2002. "Child Witness Policy: Law Interfacing with Social Science." *Law and Contemporary Problems*. Vol. 65, No. 1, pp. 209–241.

Meierhenrich, Jens. 2008. Book review of *The International Criminal Tribunals* by William A. Schabas. *The American Journal of International Law*. Vol. 102, No. 3, pp. 696–703.

McDonald, Gabrielle Kirk, and Olivia Swaak-Goldman, eds. 2000. *Substantive and Procedural Aspects of International Criminal Law: The Experience of International and National Courts*. Leiden: Martinus Nijhoff.

Merry, Sally Engle. 1997. "Legal Vernacularization and Transnational Culture: the Ka Ho'okolokolonui Kanaka Maoli, Hawai'i 1993." In Richard A. Wilson (ed.), *Human Rights, Culture and Context: Anthropological Perspectives*. London: Pluto Press, pp. 28–49.

————. 2006. *Human Rights and Gender Violence: Translating International Law into Local Justice*. Chicago: University of Chicago Press.

Mertus, J. 2000. "Truth in a Box: The Limits of Justice through Judicial Mechanisms." In Ifi Amadiume and Abdullahi A An-Na'im (eds.), *The Politics of Memory: Truth, Healing and Social Justice*. London: Zed Books, pp. 142–161.

Minow, Martha. 1998. *Between Vengeance and Forgiveness: Facing History after Genocide and Mass Violence*. Boston, MA: Beacon Press.

Moghalu, Kingsley Chiedu. 2008. *Global Justice: The Politics of War Crimes Tribunals*. Stanford, CA: Stanford University Press.

Montagu, Ashley. 1997. *Man's Most Dangerous Myth: Fallacy of Race*. 5th ed. Lanham, MD: Altamira Press.

Mundis, Daryl. 2001. "From 'Common Law' towards 'Civil Law': The Evolution of the ICTY Rules of Procedure and Evidence." *Leiden Journal of International Law*. Vol. 14, pp. 367–382.

Nettelfield, Lara. 2010. *Courting Democracy in Bosnia and Herzegovina: The Hague Tribunal's Impact in a Postwar State*. Cambridge: Cambridge University Press.

Nielsen, Laura Beth. 2000. "Situating Legal Consciousness: Experiences and Attitudes of Ordinary Citizens about Law and Sexual Harassment." *Law and Society Review*. Vol. 34, pp. 1055–1090.

Nietzsche, Friedrich. 1997. "On the Uses and Disadvantages of History for Life." In Daniel Breazeale (ed.), *Untimely Meditations*. Cambridge: Cambridge University Press, pp. pp. 57–124.

Nuijten, Monique, and Gerhard Anders, eds. 2009. *Corruption and the Secret of Law: A Legal Anthropological Perspective*. Farnham, MA: Ashgate.

Osiel, Mark. 2000. *Mass Atrocity, Collective Memory and the Law*. New Brunswick, NJ: Transaction.

Osiel, Mark. 2009a. *The End of Reciprocity: terror, torture and the law of war*. Cambridge: Cambridge University Press.

————. 2009b. *Making Sense of Mass Atrocity*. Cambridge: Cambridge University Press.

Panizza, Francisco. 1995. "Human Rights in the Processes of Transition and Consolidation of Democracy in Latin America." *Political Studies*. Vol. 43, pp. 168–188.

Papke, David R., ed. 1991. *Narrative and the Legal Discourse*. Liverpool, UK: Deborah Charles.

Parekh, Serena. 2004. "A Meaningful Place in the World: Hannah Arendt on the Nature of Human Rights." *Journal of Human Rights*. Vol. 3, No. 1, pp. 41–54.

Patterson, James T. 2001. *Brown v. Board of Education: A Civil Rights Milestone and Its Troubled Legacy*. Oxford: Oxford University Press.

Peel, Quentin. 2006. "Lessons for Prosecutors of War Crimes Trials." *Financial Times*. 13 March.

Peskin, Victor. 2008. *International Justice in Rwanda and the Balkans: Virtual Trials and the Struggle for State Cooperation*. Cambridge: Cambridge University Press.

―――. 2009. "Caution and Confrontation in the International Criminal Court's Pursuit of Accountability in Uganda and Sudan." *Human Rights Quarterly*. Vol. 31, pp. 655–691.

Phillips, Scott, and Ryken Grattet. 2000. "Judicial Rhetoric, Meaning-Making, and the Institutionalization of Hate Crime Law." *Law and Society Review*. Vol. 34, pp. 567–606.

Power, Samantha. 2002. *A Problem from Hell: America and the Age of Genocide*. New York: Basic Books.

Prunier, Gerald. 1995. *The Rwandan Crisis: History of a Genocide, 1959–1995*. New York: Columbia University Press.

―――. 2009. "The Ituri Conflict, a Background Study." Expert Report Submitted by the Prosecution in the Case of Thomas Lubanga Dyilo. EVD: OTP-0043.

Raab, Dominic. 2005 "Evaluating the ICTY and its Completion Strategy: Efforts to Achieve Accountability for War Crimes and their Tribunals." *Journal of International Criminal Justice*, Vol. 3, Issue 1, pp. 82–102.

Riles, Annelise. 2000. *The Network Inside Out*. Ann Arbor: University of Michigan Press.

Robertson, Geoffrey. 2002. *Crimes against Humanity: The Struggle for Global Justice*. London: Penguin.

―――. 2005. "Fair Trials for Terrorists?" In Richard A. Wilson (ed.), *Human Rights in the War on Terror*. Cambridge: Cambridge University Press, pp. 169–183.

Romkens, Renee. 2000. "Ambiguous Responsibilities: Law and Conflicting Expert Testimony on the Abused Woman Who Shot Her Sleeping Husband." *Law and Social Inquiry*. Vol. 25, No. 2, pp. 355–391.

Ross, Alex. 1995. "Watching for a Judgment of Real Evil." *New York Times*. 12 November 1995, p. 37.

Ross, Fiona C. 2002. *Bearing Witness: Women and the Truth and Reconciliation Commission in South Africa*. London: Pluto Press.

Rousso, Henry. 1996. "What historians will retain from the last trial of the purge." In Richard J. Golsan (ed.), *Memory, the Holocaust, and French Justice: The Bousquet and Touvier Affairs*. Hanover, NH and London: University Press of New England.

―――. 2000. "Letter to the President of the Bordeaux Assizes Court." 6 October 1997. In Richard J. Golsan (ed.), *The Papon Affair: Memory and Justice on Trial*. New York: Routledge, pp. 193–194.

Sadkovich, James J. 2002. "Argument, Persuasion and Anecdote: The Usefulness of History to Understanding Conflict." *Polemos*. Vols. 1–2, pp. 33–49.

Saks, Michael J., and David L. Faigman. 2005. "Expert Evidence after *Daubert*." *Annual Review of Law and Social Science*. Vol. 1, pp. 105–130.

Samaha, Joel. 1999. *Criminal Law*. 6th Edition. Belmont, CA: Wadsworth.

Sarat, Austin, Lawrence Douglas, and Martha Merrill Umphrey, eds, 2007. *How Law Knows*. Stanford, CA: Stanford University Press.

Saxon, Dan. 2005. "Exporting Justice: Perceptions of the ICTY among the Serbian, Croatian, and Muslim Communities in the Former Yugoslavia." *Journal of Human Rights*. Vol. 4, pp. 559–572.

Schabas, William A. 2001. *An Introduction to the International Criminal Court*. Cambridge: Cambridge University Press.

———. 2009. *Genocide in International Law: The Crime of Crimes*. 2nd ed. Cambridge: Cambridge University Press.

Scharf, Michael. 1999. "The Amnesty Exception to the Jurisdiction of the International Criminal Court." *Cornell International Law Journal*. Vol. 32, No. 3, pp. 507–527.

Scharf, Michael, and William Schabas. 2002. *Slobodan Milosevic on Trial: A Companion*. New York: Continuum Publishers.

Schiff, Benjamin N. 2008. *Building the International Criminal Court*. Cambridge: Cambridge University Press.

Schrag, Minna. 2003. *Lessons Learned from the ICTY Experience: Notes for the ICC Prosecutor*. (Contribution to an expert consultation process on general issues relevant to the ICC Office of the Prosecutor). 20 March, 2003. ICC: OTP.

Schuller, Regina A., and Patricia A. Hastings. 1996. "Trials of Battered Women Who Kill: The Impact of Alternative Forms of Expert Evidence." *Law and Human Behavior*. Vol. 20, No. 2, pp. 167–187.

Shapiro, Barbara. 2007. "'Fact' and the Proof of Fact in Anglo-American Law (c.1500–1850)." In Austin Sarat, Lawrence Douglas, and Martha Merrill Umphrey (eds.) *How Law Knows*. Stanford, CA: Stanford University Press, pp. 25–71.

Shaw, Martin. 2003. *War and Genocide: Organized Killing in Modern Society*. Cambridge, UK: Polity Press.

———. 2007. *What Is Genocide?* Cambridge, UK: Polity Press.

Shoup, Paul. 2004. "Report of the Expert Witness for the Defense in the Case of Radoslav Brdjanin." *Prosecutor v. Radoslav Brđanin*, Case No. IT-99-36-T. Defense Exhibit DB376.

Sieder, Rachel. 1999. *Guatemala after the Peace Accords*. London: Institute of Latin American Studies (ILAS).

———. 2001. "War, Peace and Memory Politics in Central America." In A. Barahona de Brito, C. Gonzaléz-Enríquez, and P. Aguilar (eds.), *The Politics of Memory*. Oxford: Oxford University Press, pp. 161–189.

Simpson, Gerry J. 1997. "Didactic and Dissident Histories in War Crimes Trials." *Albany Law Review*. Vol. 60, No. 3, pp. 801–839.

Staub, Ervin. 1994. *The Roots of Evil: The Origins of Genocide and Other Group Violence*. Cambridge: Cambridge University Press.

Stavenhagen, Rodolfo. 2008. "Cultural Rights and Human Rights: A Social Science Perspective." In Pedro Pitarch, Shannon Speed, and Xochitl Leyva Solano (eds.),

Human Rights in the Maya Region: Global Politics, Cultural Contentions, and Moral Engagements. Durham, NC: Duke University Press, pp. 27–50.

Stover, Eric. 2005. *The Witnesses: War Crimes and the Promise of Justice in The Hague*. Philadelphia: University of Pennsylvania Press.

Stover, Eric, and Harvey Weinstein. 2004. *My Neighbor, My Enemy: Justice and Community in the Aftermath of Mass Atrocity*. Cambridge: Cambridge University Press.

Tabeau, Ewa, and Jakub Bijak. 2005. "War-Related Deaths in the 1992–1995 Armed Conflicts in Bosnia and Herzegovina: A Critique of Previous Estimates and Recent Results." *European Journal of Population*. Vol. 21, pp. 187–215.

Tamanaha, Brian. 2004. *On the Rule of Law: History, Politics, Theory*. Cambridge: Cambridge University Press.

Taylor, Christopher. 1999. *Sacrifice as Terror: The Rwandan Genocide of 1994*. Oxford, UK: Berg Press.

Taylor, Telford. 1992. *The Anatomy of the Nuremberg Trials: A Personal Memoir*. Boston: Little, Brown.

Todorov, Tzvetan. 1996. "The Touvier Affair." In R. J. Golsan (ed.), *Memory, the Holocaust and French Justice: The Bousquet and Touvier Affairs*. Hanover, NH: University Press of New England, pp. 114–121.

Tolbert, David. 2009. Book review of *International Justice in Rwanda and the Balkans*. *International Journal of Transitional Justice*. Vol. 3, No. 2, pp. 284–286.

Tošić, Jelena. 2007. "Transparent Broadcast? The Reception of Milošević's Trial in Serbia." In Marie-Bénédicte Dembour and Tobias Kelly, eds. 2007. *Paths to International Justice: Social and Legal Perspectives*. Cambridge: Cambridge University Press, pp. 83–110.

Treanor, Patrick. 2003. "The Bosnian Serb Leadership 1990–1992 – Addendum: Governing Structures in the Autonomous Region of the Krajina 1991–2." Exhibits P2351, P2352. *Prosecutor v. Radoslav Brđanin* (Case No. IT-99-36).

Tromp-Vrkić, Nena. 2009. "Understanding the *Milosevic* Case: Legacy of an Unfinished Trial." Paper presented at the International Studies Association Annual Conference, New York City, 16 February 2009.

Truth and Reconciliation Commission South Africa, Report. Vols. 1–5. 1998. Cape Town: Juta.

Turković, Ksenija. 2003. "Historians in Search for Truth about Conflicts in the Territory of Former Yugoslavia as Expert Witnesses in Front of the ICTY." *Journal of Contemporary History (Zagreb)*. Vol. 36, No. 1, pp. 41–67.

United Nations. 1998. Rome Statute of the International Criminal Court. Adopted by the UN Diplomatic Conference of Plenipotentiaries in the Establishment of the International Criminal Court on 17 July 1998. U.N. Doc. A/CONF. 183/9; 37 ILM 1002 (1998); 2187 U.N.T.S. 90.

UN General Assembly. 1948. "Convention on the Prevention and Punishment of the Crime of Genocide." 78 U.N.T.S 277. Approved and proposed for signature and ratification or accession by General Assembly resolution 260 A (III) of 9 December 1948. Entry into force 12 January 1951.

UN General Assembly. 1965. "International Convention on the Elimination of All Forms of Racial Discrimination." Adopted and opened for signature and ratification by General Assembly resolution 2106 (XX) Annex, 20 U.N. GAOR Supp. (No. 14) at 47, U.N. Doc. A/6014 (1966), 660 U.N.T.S. 195, of 21 December 1965. Entry into force 4 January 1969.

UN Office of the High Commissioner for Human Rights. 2010. "Democratic Republic of the Congo, 1993–2003. Report of the Mapping Exercise documenting the most serious violations of human rights and international humanitarian law committed within the territory of the Democratic Republic of the Congo between March 1993 and June 2003." Released August 2010.

UN Security Council. Statute of the International Criminal Tribunal for the Former Yugoslavia. 1993. S.C. Res. 827, U.N. SCOR, 3217th mtg., adopted 25 May 1993, U.N. Doc. S/RES/827 (1993). http://www.icty.org/x/file/Legal%20Library/Statute/statute_sep09_en.pdf.

UN Security Council. Statute of the International Criminal Tribunal for Rwanda. 1994. S.C. Res. 955, U.N. SCOR, 3453d mtg., Annex, art. 6, U.N. Doc. S/RES/955 (1994), http://www.un.org/ictr/statute.html

Verdirame, Guglielmo. 2000. "The Genocide Definition in the Jurisprudence of the Ad Hoc Tribunals." *International and Comparative Law Quarterly*. Vol. 49, No. 3, pp. 578–598.

Verwimp, Philip. 2004. "Death and Survival during the 1994 Genocide in Rwanda." *Population Studies*. Vol. 58, No. 2, pp. 233–245.

Wald, Patricia. 2001a. "The International Criminal Tribunal Comes of Age: Some Observations on Day-to-Day Dilemmas of an International Court." *Washington University Journal of Law and Policy*. Vol. 5, pp. 87–118.

_____. 2001b. "To 'Establish Incredible Events by Credible Evidence': The Use of Affidavit Testimony in Yugoslav War Crimes Tribunal Proceedings." *Harvard International Law Journal*. Vol. 42, No. 2, pp. 535–553.

_____. 2004. "ICTY Judicial Proceedings – An Appraisal from Within." *Journal of International Criminal Justice*. Vol. 2, No. 2, pp. 466–473.

War Crimes Research Office. 2009. *Defining the Case against an Accused before the International Criminal Court: Whose Responsibility Is It?* Washington, DC: American University College of Law.

Wedgewood, Ruth. 2002. "Al Qaeda, Terrorism and Military Commissions." *American Journal of International Law*. Vol. 96, No. 2, pp. 328–337.

Weitz, Eric D. 2003. *A Century of Genocide: Utopias of Race and Nation*. Princeton, NJ: Princeton University Press.

Wieviorka, Annette. 2002. "France and Trials for Crimes against Humanity." In A. Sarat, Lawrence Douglas, and Martha Umphrey (eds.), *Lives in the Law*. Ann Arbor: University of Michigan Press, pp. 215–231.

Wilkinson, Harvie J. 2009. "Of Guns, Abortions and the Unraveling Rule of Law." *Virginia Law Review*. Vol. 95, No. 2, pp. 253–323.

Wilson, Richard Ashby. 1997. "Violent Truths: The Commission of Historical Clarification and the Politics of Memory in Guatemala." In R. Sieder and R. Wilson (eds.), *Negotiating Rights: The Guatemalan Peace Process. Accord: An International Review of Peace Initiatives*. London: Conciliation Resources, pp. 18–27.

_____. 2001. *The Politics of Truth and Reconciliation in South Africa: Legitimizing the Post-Apartheid State*. Cambridge: Cambridge University Press.

Wood, Nancy. 1999. *Vectors of Memory: Legacies of Trauma in Postwar Europe*. Oxford, UK: Berg.

Zacklin, Ralph. 2004. "The Failings of Ad Hoc International Tribunals." *Journal of International Criminal Justice*. Vol. 2, pp. 541–545.

Zwaan, Ton. 2003. "On the Aetiology and Genesis of Genocides and Other Mass Crimes Targeting Specific Groups." Prosecution Exhibit 639. *Prosecutor v. Slobodan Milošević* (Case Nos. IT-99–37, IT-01–50, IT-01–51, IT-02–54).

Index

Abreu Merelles, Fernando, 45
Accounting for Horror (Eltringham), 178
Ackerman, John, 12, 125–126, 127, 153, 157
Actus reus (guilty act), 90, 93
Admissibility of evidence
  complexity of trials, effect of, 62–63
  crimes against humanity, in, 68
  defense attorneys, attitudes of, 64–66
  documentary evidence (*See* Documentary
    evidence)
  expert witnesses (*See* Expert witnesses)
  generally, 49
  genocide, in, 68
  hearsay (*See* Hearsay)
  ICC, before, 196–197
  ICTR/ICTY, before, 56
  judges, attitudes of, 66–68
  Nuremberg Tribunal, before, 56
  prosecuting attorneys, attitudes of, 63
African Union, opposition to ICC, 195–196
Aggression, ICC jurisdiction, 31, 192
Agius, Carmel, 126
Akayesu, Jean-Paul, 30, 72, 97, 171–176, 181
Aleksovski, Zlatko, 123
Amman, Diane, 189–190
Amnesty International, 44
"Ancient hatreds" view, 22, 124
Anderson, Jill C., 52, 185–186
Annan, Kofi, 44
Anzulović, Branimir, 85
Arbour, Louis, 38, 92
Arendt, Hannah, 3–4, 20, 33, 69–70
Arusha Peace Agreement, 27, 28
Aspegren, Lennart, 182
Attorneys

defense attorneys (*See* Defense attorneys)
prosecuting attorneys (*See* Prosecuting
  attorneys)
Austro-Hungarian Empire, 74
Autonomy of international tribunals,
  36–39
*Axis Rule in Occupied Europe, Analysis of
  Government, Proposals for Redress*
  (Lemkin), 177, 186

Background witnesses, 15–16. *See also* Expert
  witnesses
Badinter Advisory Commission, 76
Bagosora, Théoneste, 30
Balkan region. *See specific nation*
Barbie, Klaus, 5, 8, 11–12, 34–35
al-Bashir, Omar, 195–196, 199
"Battered woman syndrome," 163
Battle of Kosovo (1389), 75, 108
Beara, Ljubisa, 27, 88
Ben-Gurion, David, 3
Benito, Odio, 207
Berger, John, 77, 78
Berlin Conference of 1885, 209
Bianchini, Stefano, 123
Biju-Duval, Jean-Marie, 202, 204–205, 206,
  207, 208, 211, 212–213
Blackmun, Harry, 51, 52
Blagojević, Vidoje, 88, 93, 94
Blaskić, Tihomir, 71, 124
Blewitt, Graham, 81
Bloxham, Donald, 9
Boas, Gideon, 5, 37, 60, 68, 102
Boban, Mate, 149
Bonomy, Iain, 136–137

Ethnic or racial groups (*cont.*)
    Karemera case, in, 183–184
    objective theory of, 181–182
    reification of, 184–187
    subjective nature of, 178–181, 187–188
European Union, support for ICTY, 37, 40
Evans, Joanna, 65
Evans, Richard, 6, 7, 79
Evans, Tony, 35
Evidence
    admissibility (*See* Admissibility of
        evidence)
    documentary evidence (*See* Documentary
        evidence)
    expert witnesses (*See* Expert witnesses)
    hearsay (*See* Hearsay)
Expert witnesses. *See also specific individual*
    background witnesses, 15–16
    Brđanin trial, in, 117, 125–126, 145–146
    "chaos defense," 152–154
    civil law model and, 221
    civil *versus* criminal trials, 52–53
    common law, in, 54–55
    context, establishing, 121–128
    Daubert test
        advent of, 51
        generally, 221
        practical effects of, 52
        problems in applying, 53
        reaction to, 51–52
    documentary evidence, re, 121–122, 123
    education and training, recommendation
        of, 224–225
    fact-finding function, 144–148
    Frye test, 50–51
    "gatekeeping" concept, 51
    ICC, before, 197–198
    ICTR, before
        generally, 55–56
        problems with, 57–58
        reforms re, 58–59
    ICTY, before
        generally, 55–56
        problems with, 57–58
        reforms re, 58–59
    internal expert reports, 129–134
    international tribunals, before, 55–59
    judges' receptiveness to, 80, 142
    judicial efficiency, 134–139
    Karadžić trial, in, 124
    legal facts and, 144–148

"linkage evidence," 130
managerial judging model
    generally, 59–61
    ICC, in, 213–214
    judicial efficiency, 134–139
    mass crimes, in, 53–54
    Milošević trial, in, 103–106
    Nuremberg Tribunal, before, 56
    preparation of, 113–115, 143
    problems with, 113–119
    Tadić trial, in, 73, 145
    tu quoque defense and, 156–157
    "war of experts," 146
    "web of context," 121–128
Extraordinary Chambers of the Courts of
    Cambodia, 31–32, 192

Fact-finding, 144–148
Faigman, David L., 52
Fichte, Johann Gottlieb, 105
"Field of Blackbirds" (1389), 75, 108
Flint, Julie, 199
Focardi, Filippo, 34
Folkes v. Chadd (1782), 50
Foreseeability, 154–155
Framing of crimes, 77–80
Friedlander, Saul, 9
Frustration with historical evidence, 112–113
Frye v. United States (1923), 50–51, 53
Fulford, Adrian, 201–202, 207–208, 209

Galanter, Marc, 132
Galić, Stanislav, 122–123, 160
Garašanin, Ilija, 101, 105
Garretón, Roberto, 199, 206, 209–213, 214
"Gatekeeping" concept of expert witnesses,
    51
Gatowski, S.I., 53
Geertz, Clifford, 9
Gellner, Ernest, 103
Geneva Conventions of 1949, 73, 119, 156–157
Genocide
    actus reus and, 90, 93
    admissibility of evidence in, 68
    Brđanin trial, in, 119, 120
    Convention on the Prevention and
        Punishment of the Crime of
        Genocide (*See* Genocide
        Convention)
    crimes against humanity distinguished, 91
    defined, 89–90